YOU MIGHT BE AN ARTIST IF...

BY LAUREN PURJE

You Might Be An Artist If... © 2017 Lauren Purje.

Published by Top Shelf Productions, PO Box 1282, Marietta, GA 30061-1282, USA. Top Shelf Productions is an imprint of IDW Publishing, a division of Idea and Design Works, LLC. Offices: 2765 Truxtun Road, San Diego, CA 92106. Top Shelf Productions®, the Top Shelf logo, Idea and Design Works®, and the IDW logo are registered trademarks of Idea and Design Works, LLC. All Rights Reserved. With the exception of small excerpts of artwork used for review purposes, none of the contents of this publication may be reprinted without the permission of IDW Publishing. IDW Publishing does not read or accept unsolicited submissions of ideas, stories, or artwork.

Editor-in-Chief: Chris Staros.
Designed by Lauren Purje with Chris Ross.

Visit our online catalog at www.topshelfcomix.com.

Printed in Korea.

ISBN 978-1-60309-406-1

21 20 19 18 17   5 4 3 2 1

DEDICATED TO THE
ARTSY-FARTSY FOLK.

Lauren Purje Drawing Herself Drawing Lauren Purje Drawing
Hrag Vartanian

I can't remember how I first encountered Lauren's art, but it was certainly online, and I felt an instant kinship. Her characters feel sincere, vulnerable, clumsy, confused, and self-aware, but they still manage to navigate the world and reveal its truths through struggle, success, failure, and accident.

After publishing a half dozen of her comics in *Hyperallergic*, I had the idea of formalizing her contribution into a weekly thing—thankfully, she agreed.

The world Lauren has since created gives us a little window into the artist's studio and helps to demystify the alchemy of art. We watch her struggle with melancholy, ennui, insecurity, imposter's syndrome, and we enjoy and relish her far-too-infrequent victories. She reflects, refracts, and distills the world around her into lines. Their sparseness is part of her message, like a story told by a friend at a weekly coffee date. She transforms everything she puts her pen to with a charm and humor that make it immediately endearing.

There's a hammer in our office that hangs on the wall. Lauren gave it to us when she came in one day; she'd collaged a series of uppercase letters from various printed media onto the hammer in a manner that resembles a ransom note. One side reads "Hyperallergic" and the other challenges you to: "Smash Boring Art Yeah Yeah." I haven't used it yet, and maybe I never will, but I love the message because it represents the core of what she does with her best work: she gives us permission to be ourselves, no matter how strange, anti-social, quirky, scared, bored, or fabulous we may be.

Hrag Vartanian
Editor-in-chief and Co-founder
Hyperallergic

THE ARTIST'S REAL INTENTIONS

BY LAUREN PURJE.

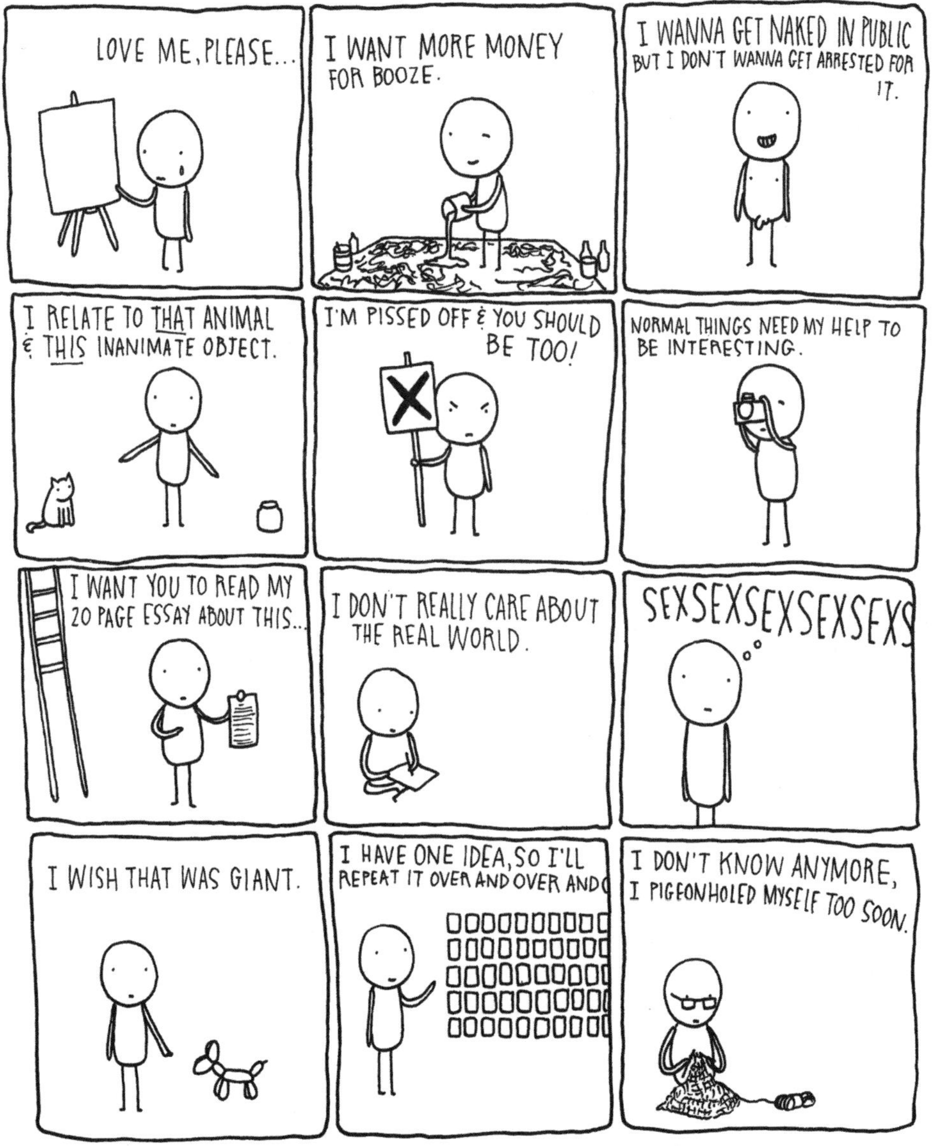

LOVE ME, PLEASE...
I WANT MORE MONEY FOR BOOZE.
I WANNA GET NAKED IN PUBLIC BUT I DON'T WANNA GET ARRESTED FOR IT.
I RELATE TO THAT ANIMAL & THIS INANIMATE OBJECT.
I'M PISSED OFF & YOU SHOULD BE TOO!
NORMAL THINGS NEED MY HELP TO BE INTERESTING.
I WANT YOU TO READ MY 20 PAGE ESSAY ABOUT THIS...
I DON'T REALLY CARE ABOUT THE REAL WORLD.
SEXSEXSEXSEXSEXS
I WISH THAT WAS GIANT.
I HAVE ONE IDEA, SO I'LL REPEAT IT OVER AND OVER AND O
I DON'T KNOW ANYMORE, I PIGEONHOLED MYSELF TOO SOON.

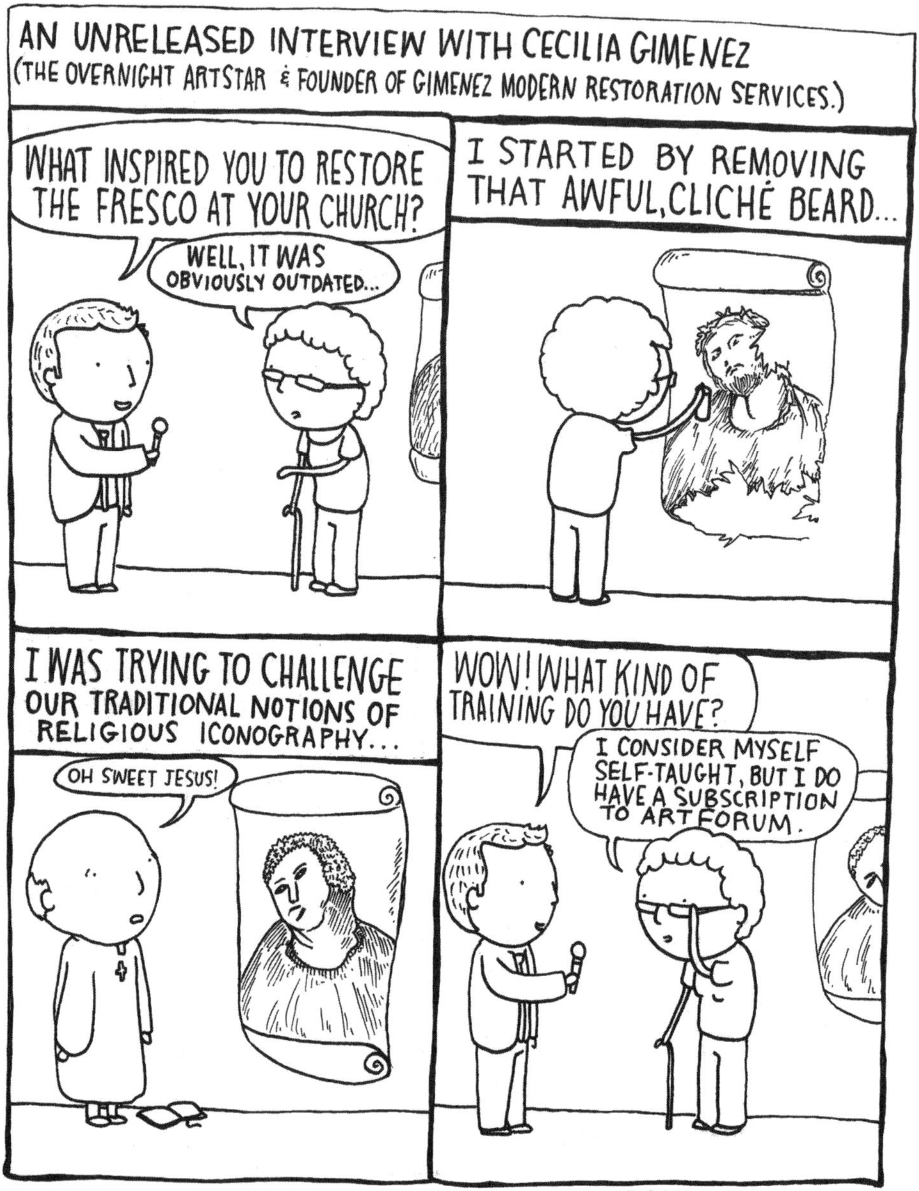
AN UNRELEASED INTERVIEW WITH CECILIA GIMENEZ
(THE OVERNIGHT ARTSTAR & FOUNDER OF GIMENEZ MODERN RESTORATION SERVICES.)
WHAT INSPIRED YOU TO RESTORE THE FRESCO AT YOUR CHURCH?
WELL, IT WAS OBVIOUSLY OUTDATED...
I STARTED BY REMOVING THAT AWFUL, CLICHÉ BEARD...
I WAS TRYING TO CHALLENGE OUR TRADITIONAL NOTIONS OF RELIGIOUS ICONOGRAPHY...
OH SWEET JESUS!
WOW! WHAT KIND OF TRAINING DO YOU HAVE?
I CONSIDER MYSELF SELF-TAUGHT, BUT I DO HAVE A SUBSCRIPTION TO ARTFORUM.

BY LAUREN PURJE.

ART CRUSH BY LAUREN PURJE.

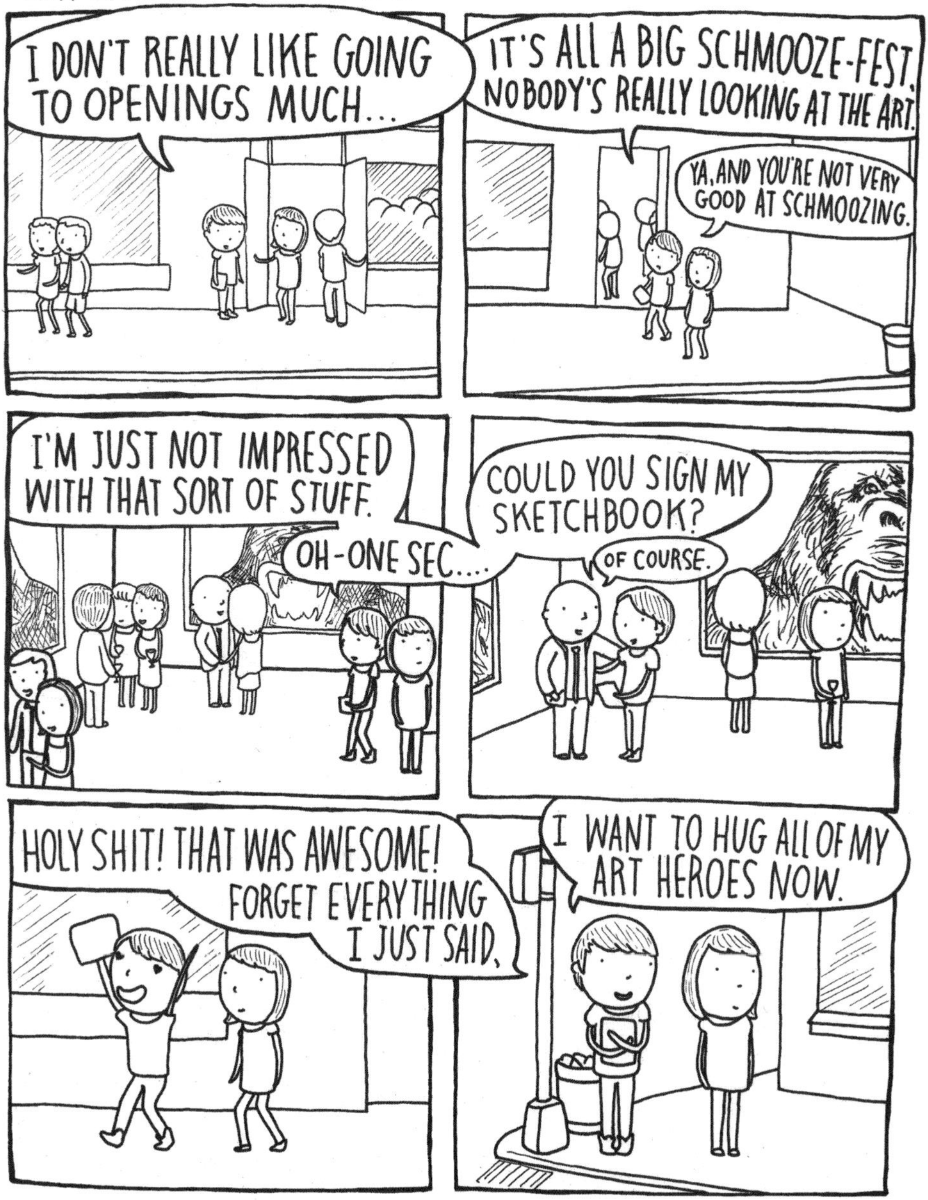
I DON'T REALLY LIKE GOING TO OPENINGS MUCH...
IT'S ALL A BIG SCHMOOZE-FEST. NOBODY'S REALLY LOOKING AT THE ART.
YA, AND YOU'RE NOT VERY GOOD AT SCHMOOZING.
I'M JUST NOT IMPRESSED WITH THAT SORT OF STUFF.
OH-ONE SEC....
COULD YOU SIGN MY SKETCHBOOK?
OF COURSE.
HOLY SHIT! THAT WAS AWESOME! FORGET EVERYTHING I JUST SAID.
I WANT TO HUG ALL OF MY ART HEROES NOW.

A DRAWING A DAY KEEPS THE DOCTOR AWAY

BY LAUREN PURJE.

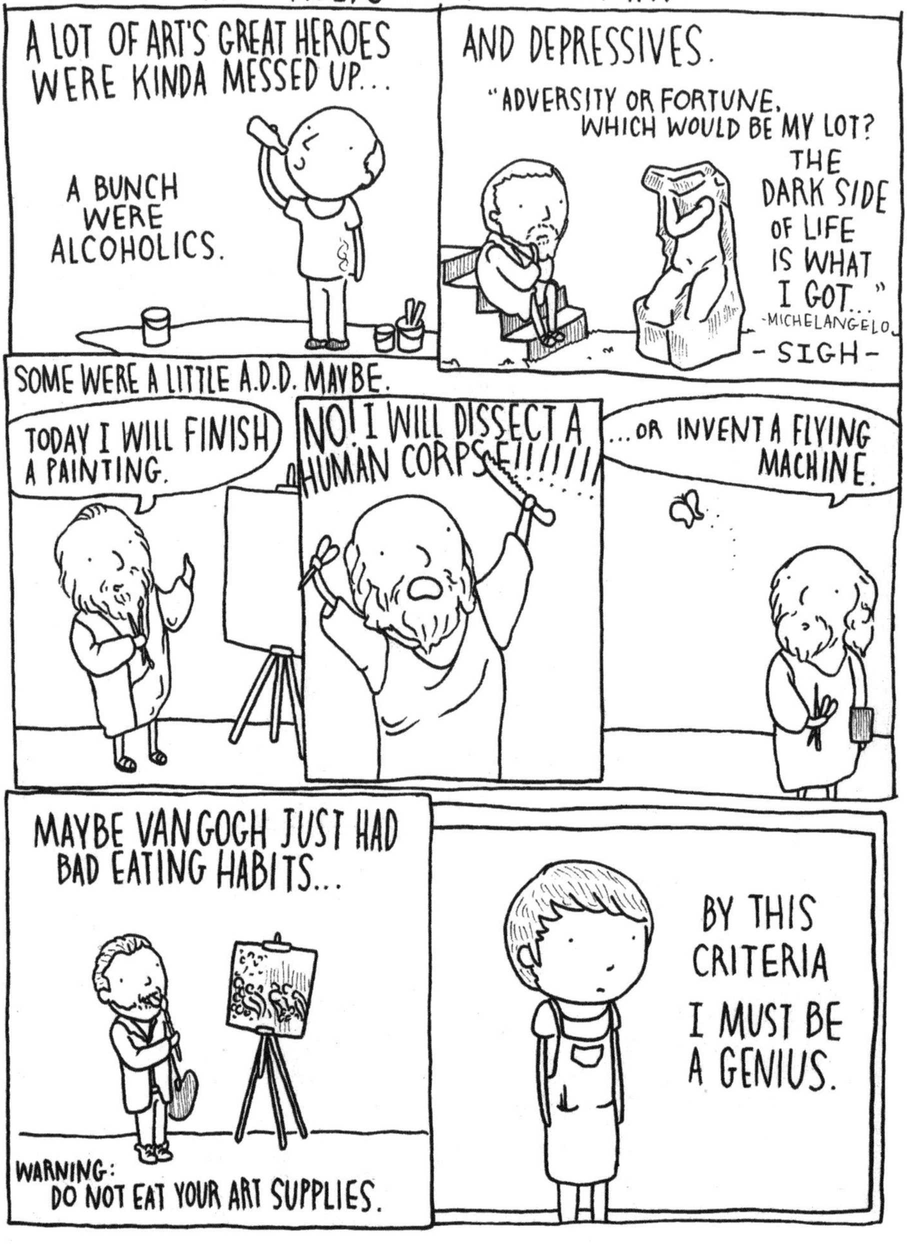

A LOT OF ART'S GREAT HEROES WERE KINDA MESSED UP...
A BUNCH WERE ALCOHOLICS.
AND DEPRESSIVES.
"ADVERSITY OR FORTUNE, WHICH WOULD BE MY LOT?
THE DARK SIDE OF LIFE IS WHAT I GOT..."
-MICHELANGELO.
-SIGH-
SOME WERE A LITTLE A.D.D. MAYBE.
TODAY I WILL FINISH A PAINTING.
NO! I WILL DISSECT A HUMAN CORPSE!!!!!!!
...OR INVENT A FLYING MACHINE.
MAYBE VAN GOGH JUST HAD BAD EATING HABITS...
WARNING: DO NOT EAT YOUR ART SUPPLIES.
BY THIS CRITERIA I MUST BE A GENIUS.

THE EVOLUTION OF THE ARTIST BY LAUREN PURJE.

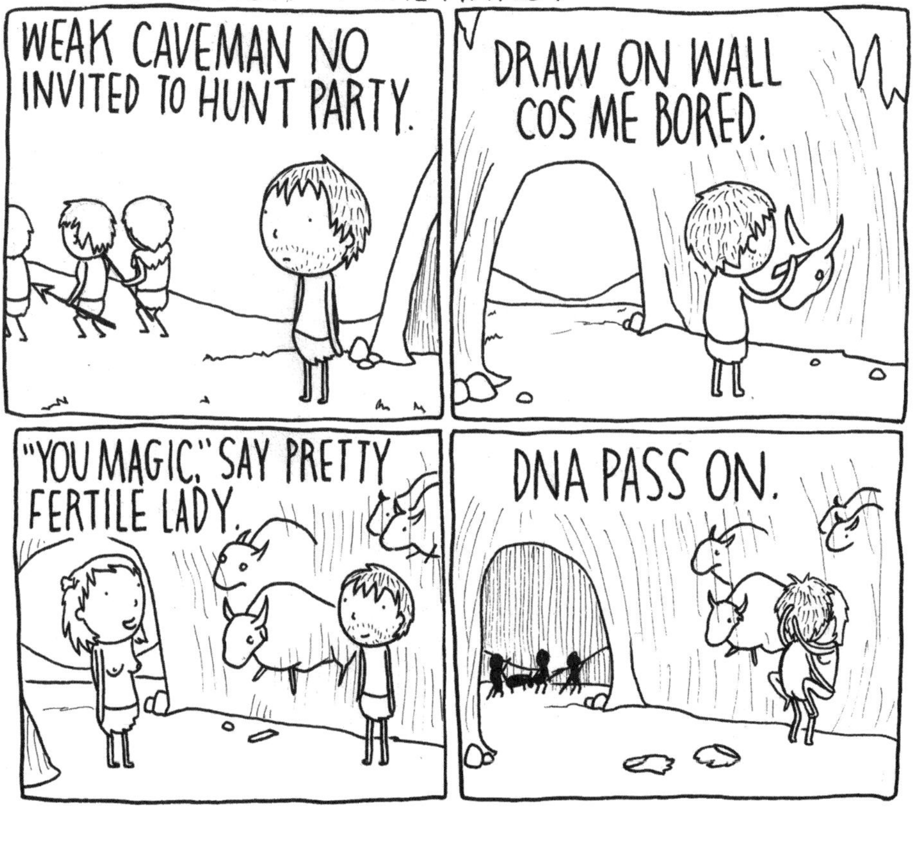
WEAK CAVEMAN NO INVITED TO HUNT PARTY.
DRAW ON WALL COS ME BORED.
"YOU MAGIC," SAY PRETTY FERTILE LADY.
DNA PASS ON.

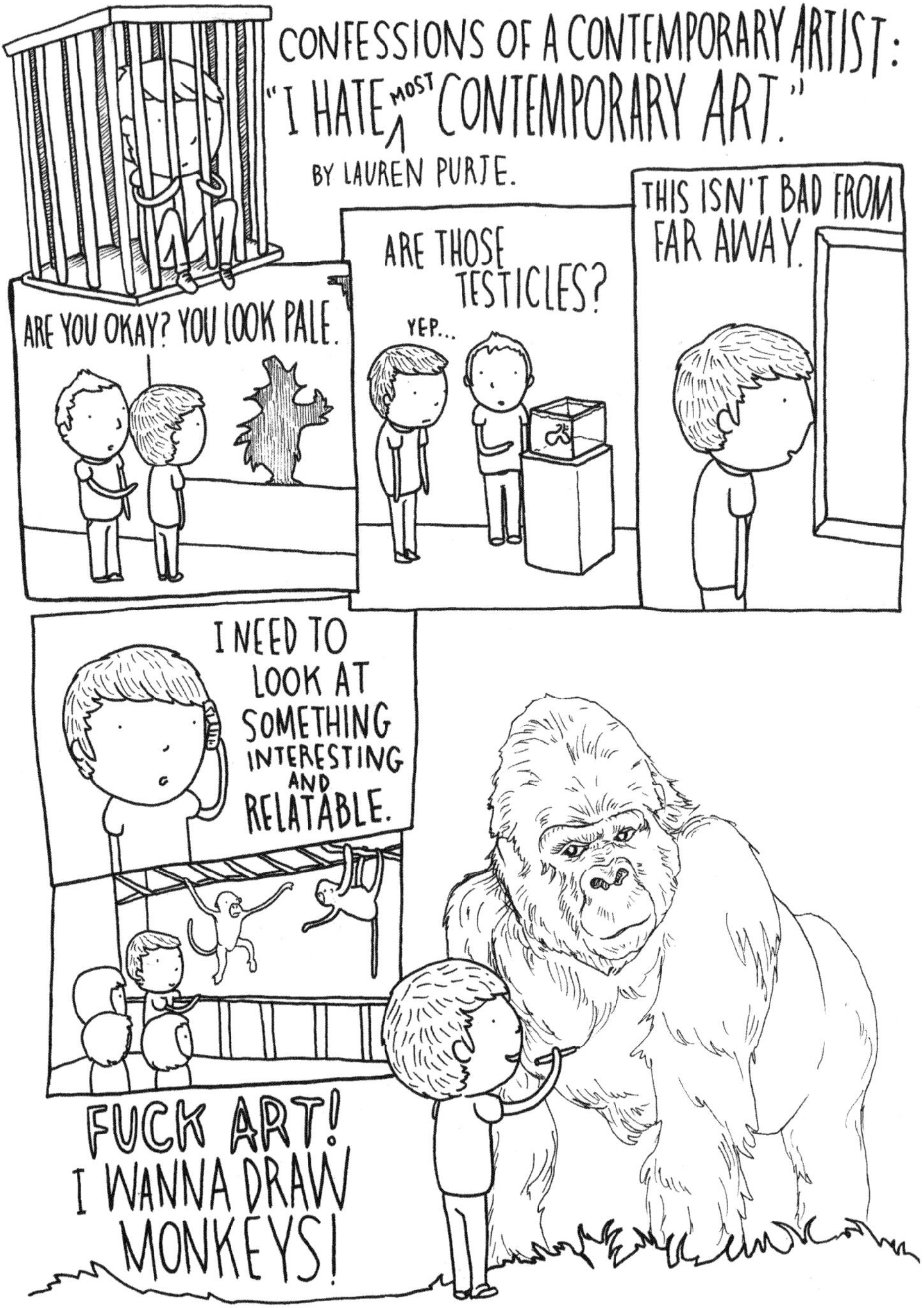

CONFESSIONS OF A CONTEMPORARY ARTIST:
"I HATE MOST "CONTEMPORARY ART."
BY LAUREN PURJE.
ARE YOU OKAY? YOU LOOK PALE.
ARE THOSE TESTICLES?
YEP...
THIS ISN'T BAD FROM FAR AWAY.
I NEED TO LOOK AT SOMETHING INTERESTING AND RELATABLE.
FUCK ART! I WANNA DRAW MONKEYS!

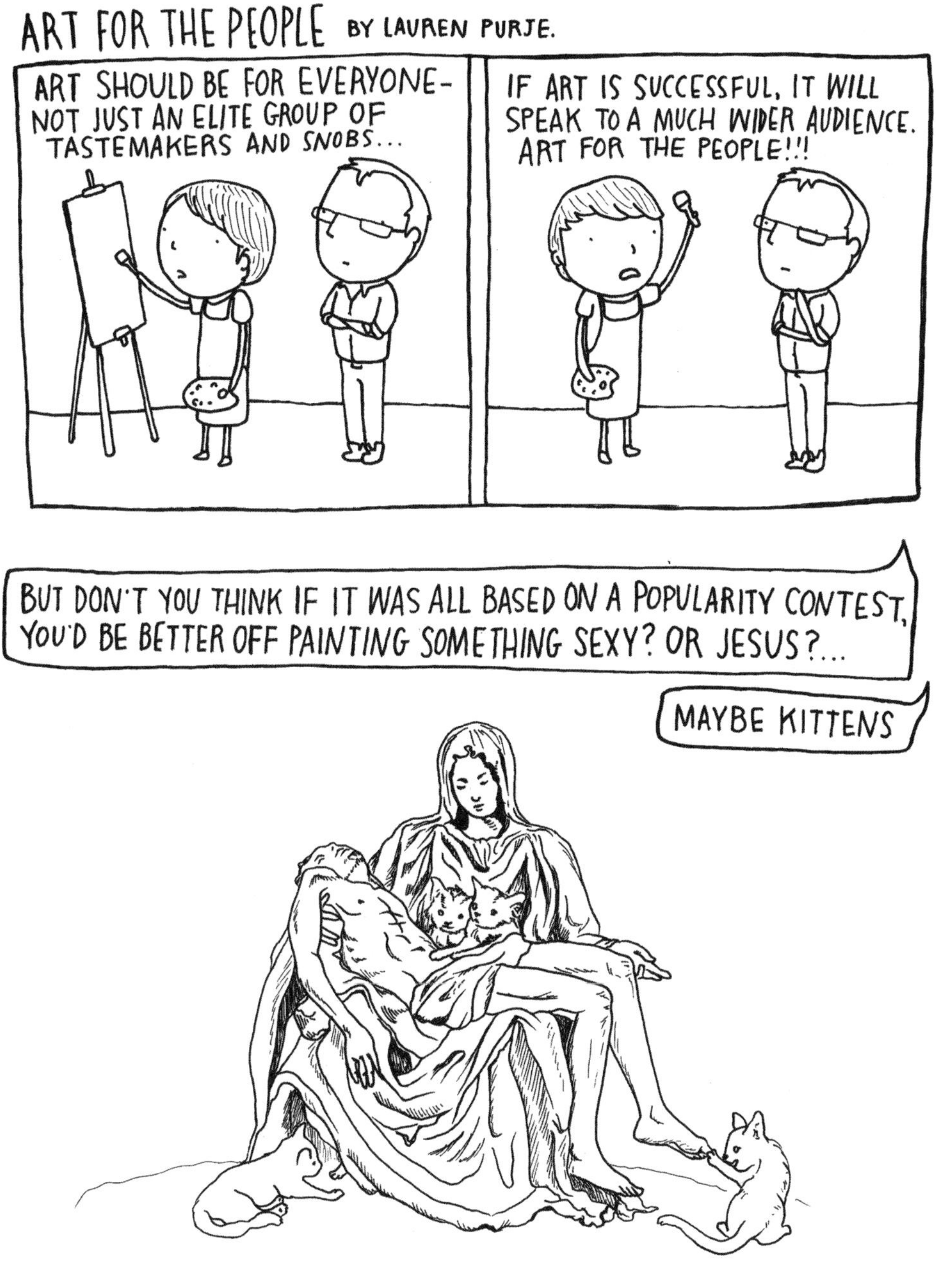
ART FOR THE PEOPLE BY LAUREN PURJE.
ART SHOULD BE FOR EVERYONE- NOT JUST AN ELITE GROUP OF TASTEMAKERS AND SNOBS...
IF ART IS SUCCESSFUL, IT WILL SPEAK TO A MUCH WIDER AUDIENCE. ART FOR THE PEOPLE!!!
BUT DON'T YOU THINK IF IT WAS ALL BASED ON A POPULARITY CONTEST, YOU'D BE BETTER OFF PAINTING SOMETHING SEXY? OR JESUS?...
MAYBE KITTENS

A POTENTIAL PIECE OF YELLOWISM

LAUREN PURJE.

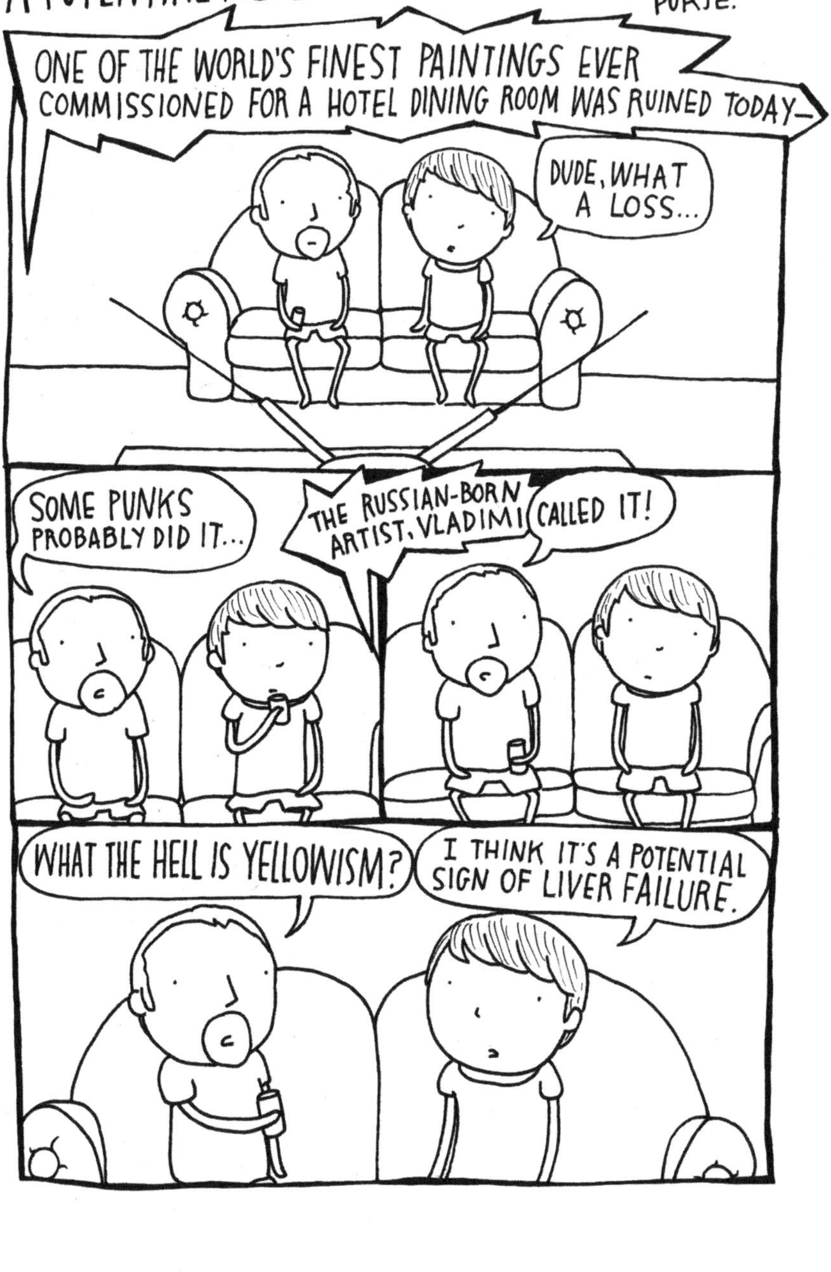

ONE OF THE WORLD'S FINEST PAINTINGS EVER COMMISSIONED FOR A HOTEL DINING ROOM WAS RUINED TODAY—
DUDE, WHAT A LOSS...
SOME PUNKS PROBABLY DID IT...
THE RUSSIAN-BORN ARTIST, VLADIMI
CALLED IT!
WHAT THE HELL IS YELLOWISM?
I THINK IT'S A POTENTIAL SIGN OF LIVER FAILURE.

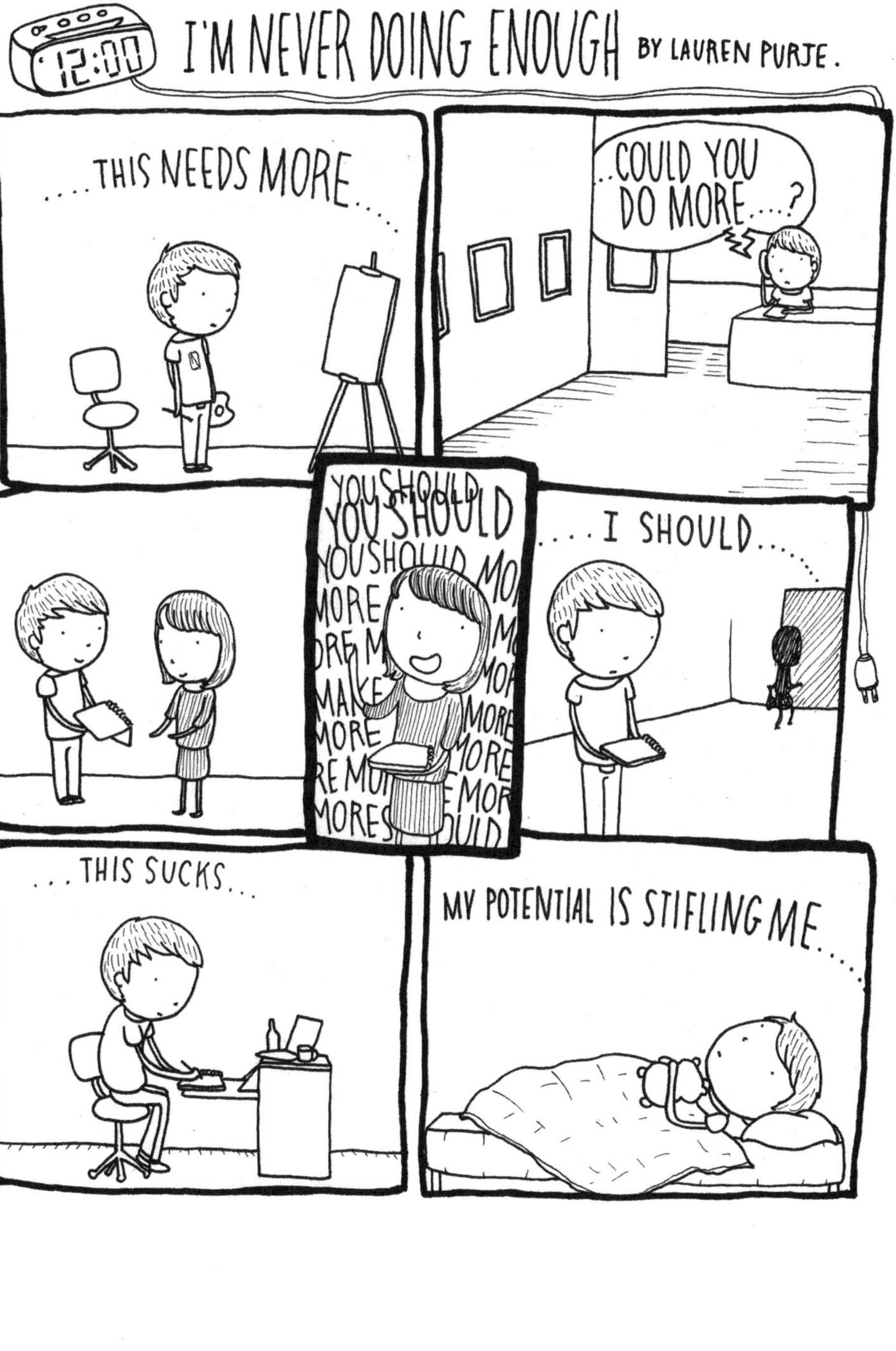
12:00
I'M NEVER DOING ENOUGH
BY LAUREN PURJE.
.....THIS NEEDS MORE.......
..COULD YOU DO MORE....?
YOU SHOULD
YOU SHOULD
MORE
....I SHOULD.....
...THIS SUCKS...
MY POTENTIAL IS STIFLING ME......

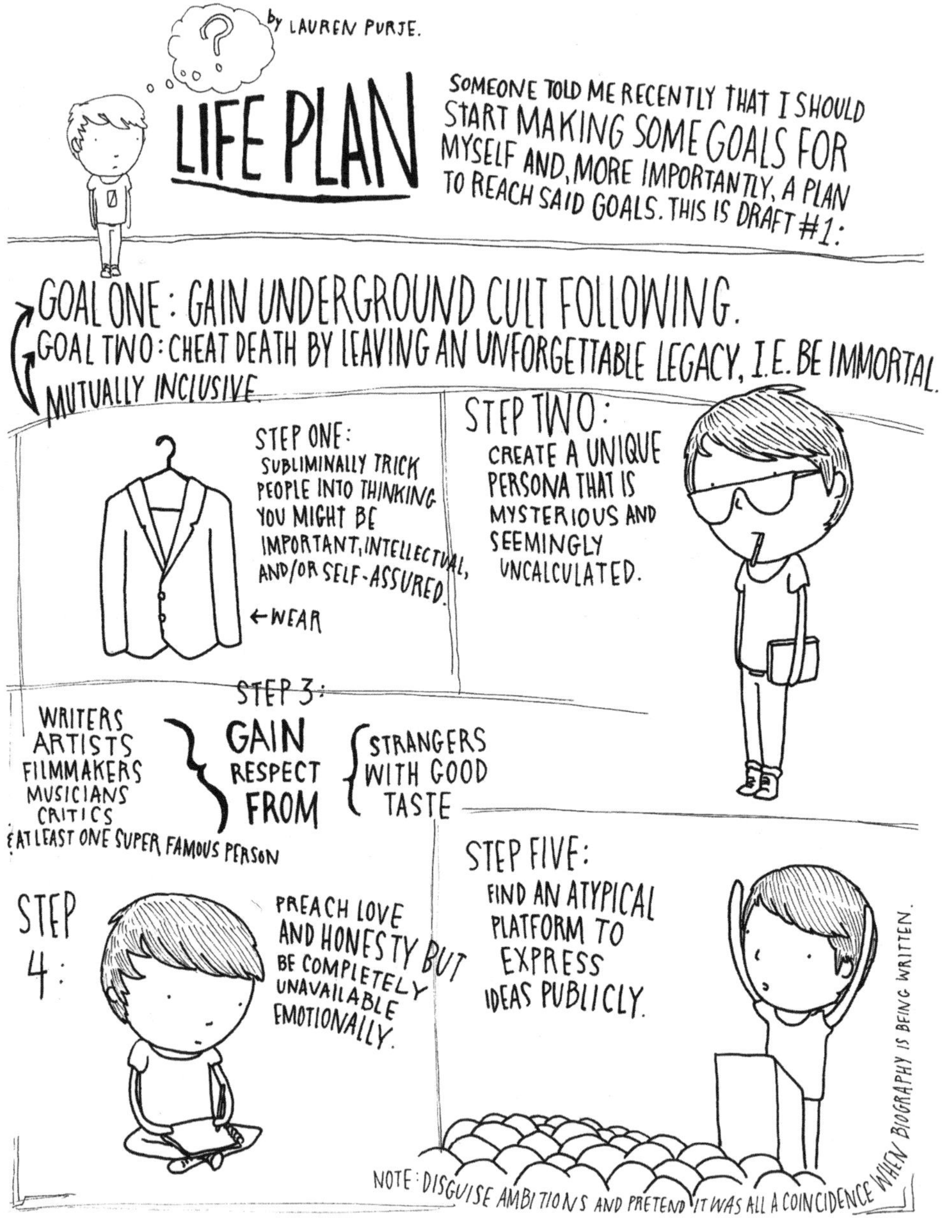
by LAUREN PURJE.
LIFE PLAN
SOMEONE TOLD ME RECENTLY THAT I SHOULD START MAKING SOME GOALS FOR MYSELF AND, MORE IMPORTANTLY, A PLAN TO REACH SAID GOALS. THIS IS DRAFT #1:
GOAL ONE: GAIN UNDERGROUND CULT FOLLOWING.
GOAL TWO: CHEAT DEATH BY LEAVING AN UNFORGETTABLE LEGACY, I.E. BE IMMORTAL.
MUTUALLY INCLUSIVE
STEP ONE: SUBLIMINALLY TRICK PEOPLE INTO THINKING YOU MIGHT BE IMPORTANT, INTELLECTUAL, AND/OR SELF-ASSURED.
←WEAR
STEP TWO: CREATE A UNIQUE PERSONA THAT IS MYSTERIOUS AND SEEMINGLY UNCALCULATED.
STEP 3:
WRITERS
ARTISTS
FILMMAKERS
MUSICIANS
CRITICS
& AT LEAST ONE SUPER FAMOUS PERSON
GAIN RESPECT FROM
STRANGERS WITH GOOD TASTE
STEP 4:
PREACH LOVE AND HONESTY BUT BE COMPLETELY UNAVAILABLE EMOTIONALLY.
STEP FIVE: FIND AN ATYPICAL PLATFORM TO EXPRESS IDEAS PUBLICLY.
NOTE: DISGUISE AMBITIONS AND PRETEND IT WAS ALL A COINCIDENCE WHEN BIOGRAPHY IS BEING WRITTEN.

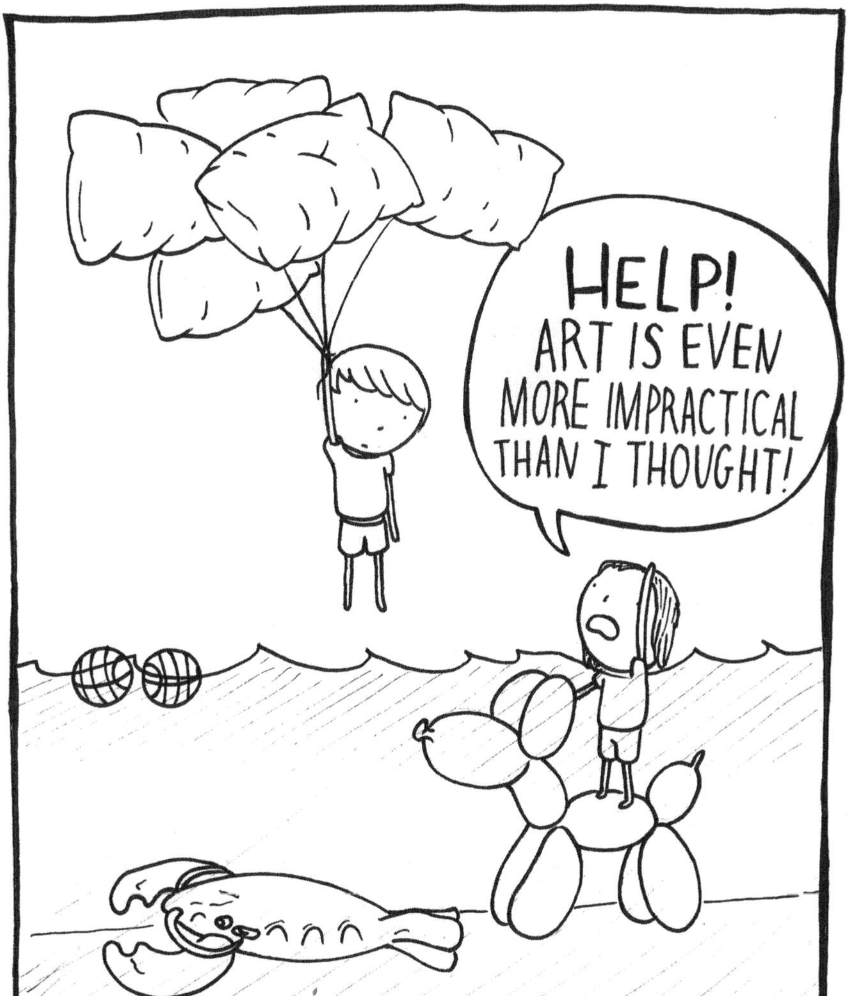
HELP!
ART IS EVEN
MORE IMPRACTICAL
THAN I THOUGHT!
LAUREN PURJE.

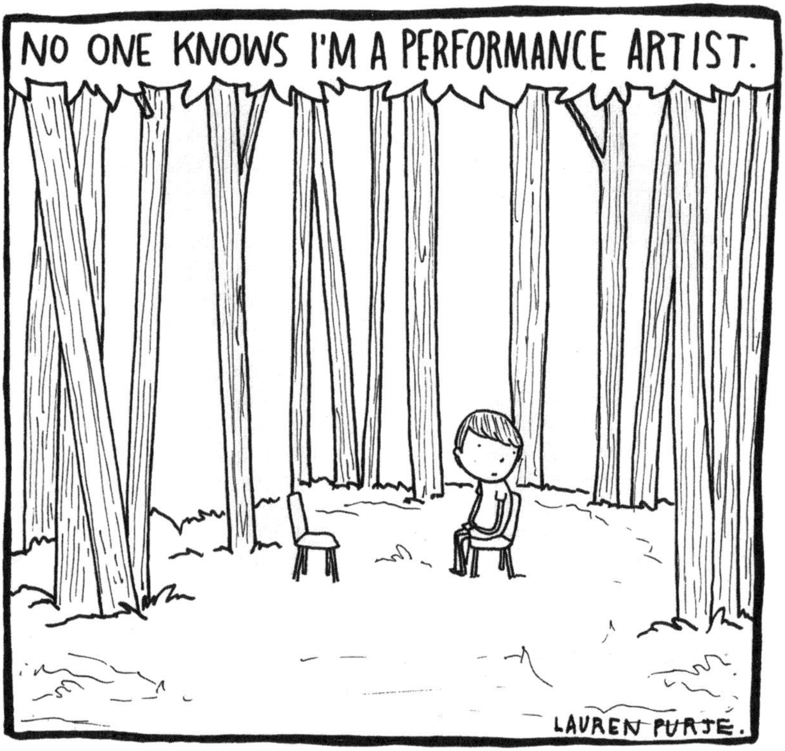
NO ONE KNOWS I'M A PERFORMANCE ARTIST.
LAUREN PURJE.

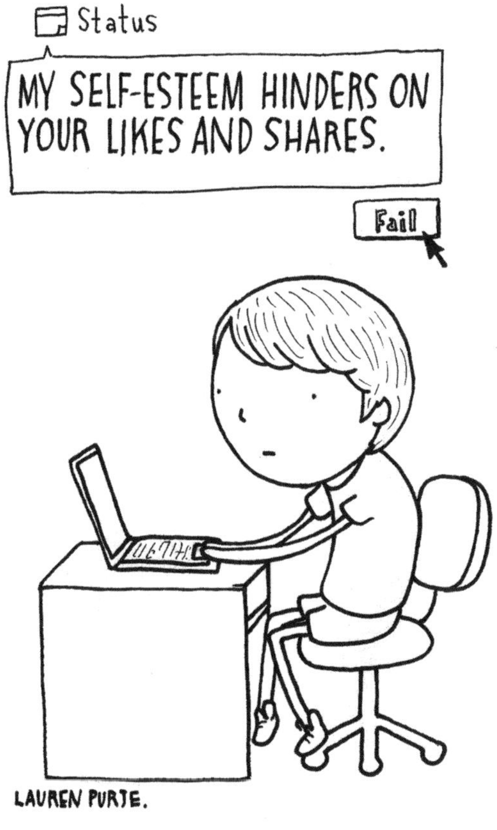
Status
MY SELF-ESTEEM HINDERS ON YOUR LIKES AND SHARES.
Fail
LAUREN PURJE.

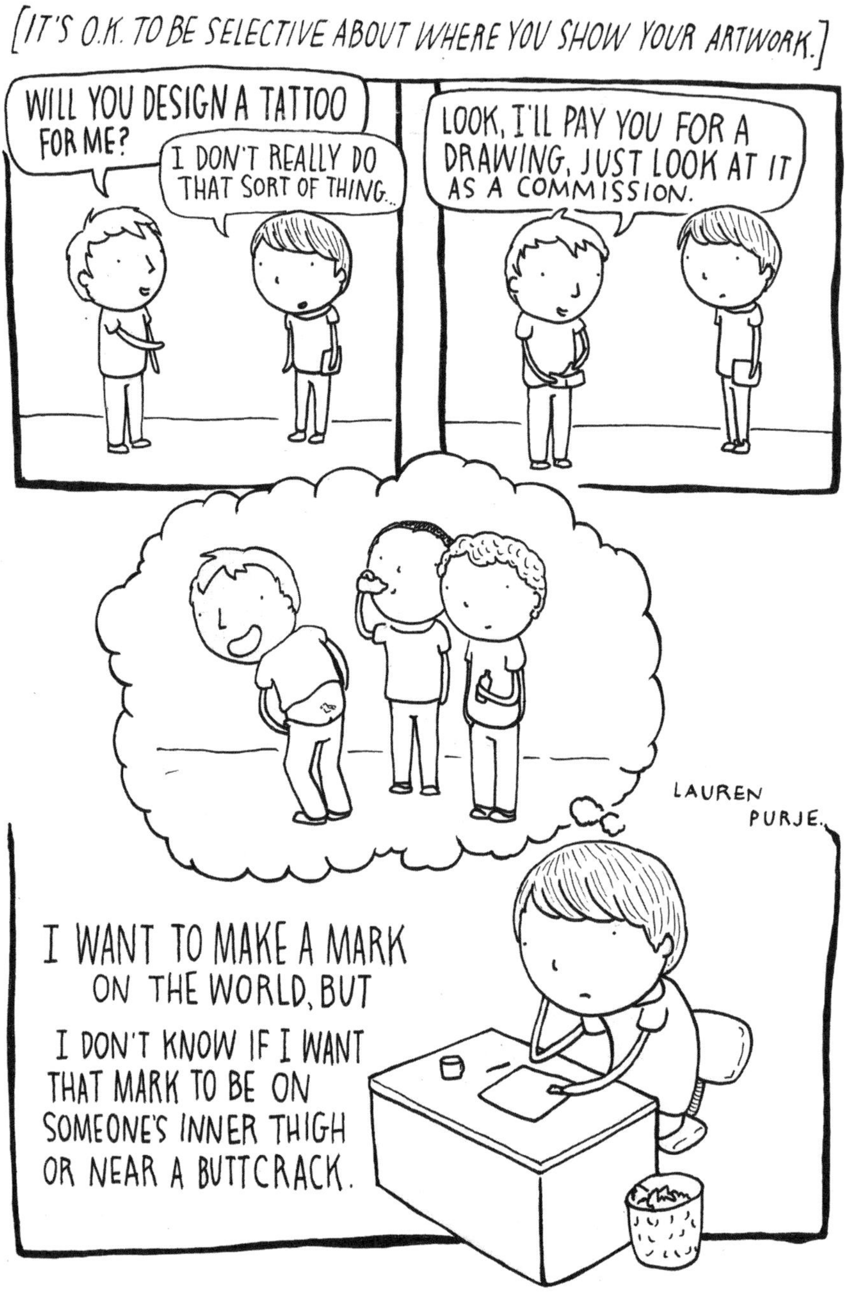
[IT'S O.K. TO BE SELECTIVE ABOUT WHERE YOU SHOW YOUR ARTWORK.]
WILL YOU DESIGN A TATTOO FOR ME?
I DON'T REALLY DO THAT SORT OF THING...
LOOK, I'LL PAY YOU FOR A DRAWING, JUST LOOK AT IT AS A COMMISSION.
LAUREN PURJE.
I WANT TO MAKE A MARK ON THE WORLD, BUT
I DON'T KNOW IF I WANT THAT MARK TO BE ON SOMEONE'S INNER THIGH OR NEAR A BUTTCRACK.

I AM NOT MY DAYJOB I AM NOT MY DAYJOB / BY LAUREN PURJE.

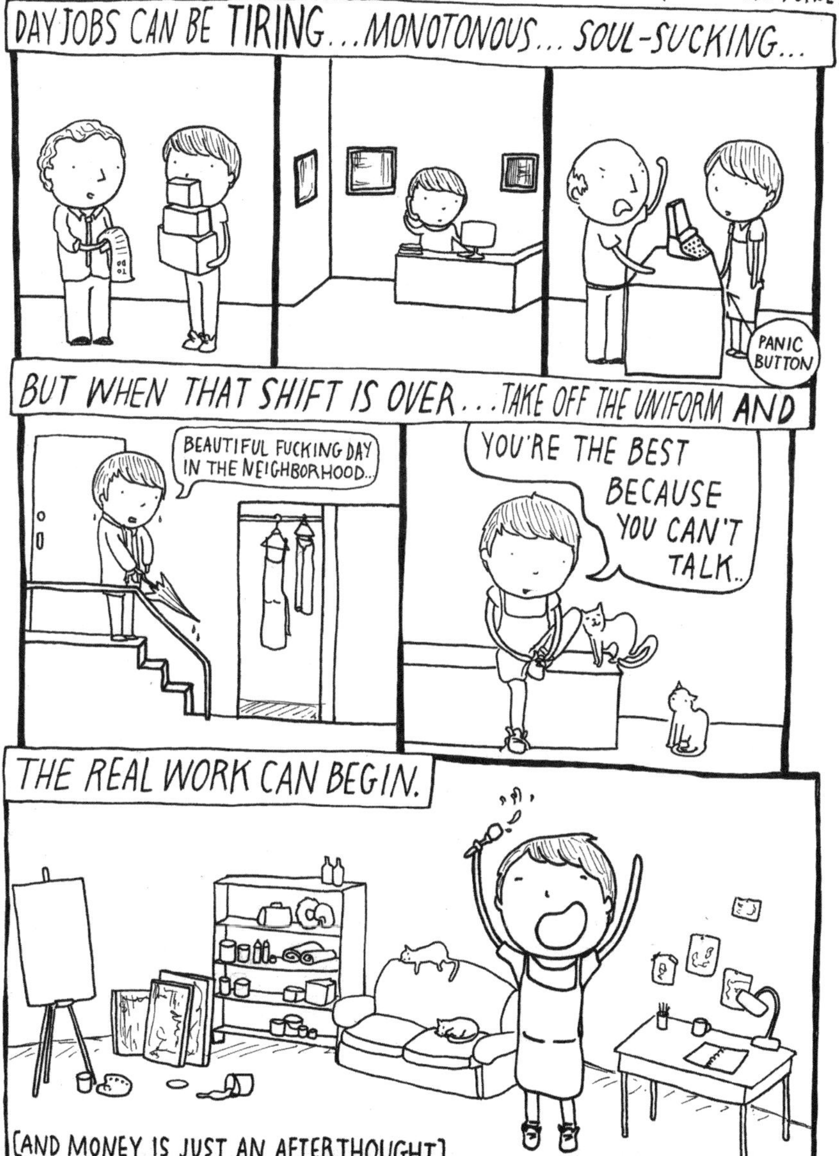
DAY JOBS CAN BE TIRING... MONOTONOUS... SOUL-SUCKING...
PANIC BUTTON
BUT WHEN THAT SHIFT IS OVER... TAKE OFF THE UNIFORM AND
BEAUTIFUL FUCKING DAY IN THE NEIGHBORHOOD..
YOU'RE THE BEST BECAUSE YOU CAN'T TALK..
THE REAL WORK CAN BEGIN.
[AND MONEY IS JUST AN AFTERTHOUGHT]

I JUST FOUND ABOUT 300 BETTER THINGS TO DO WITH ARTFORUM!

☆LAUREN PURJE.

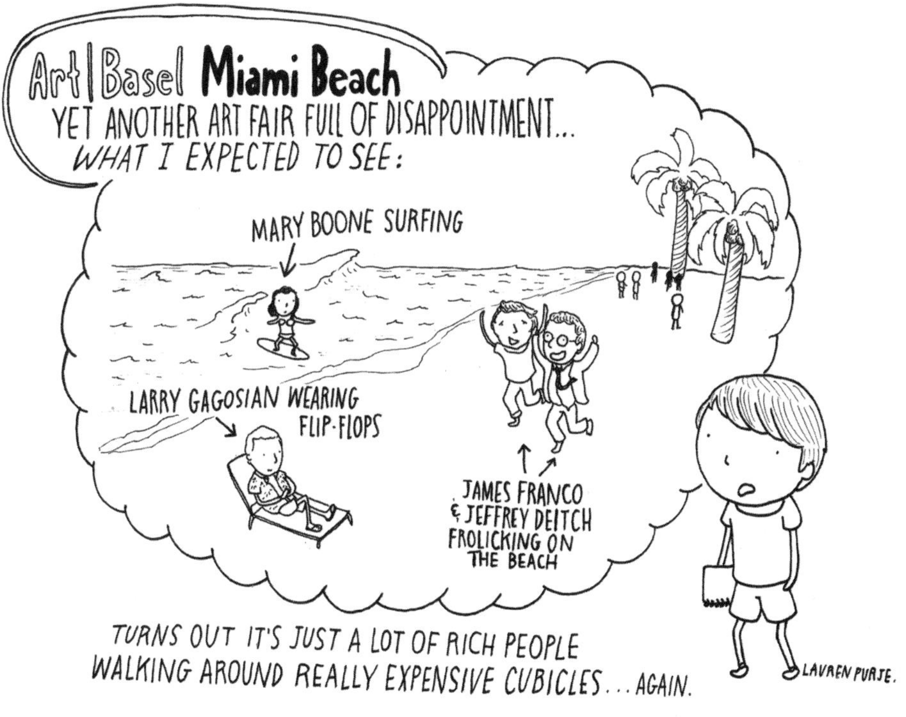
Art|Basel Miami Beach
YET ANOTHER ART FAIR FULL OF DISAPPOINTMENT...
WHAT I EXPECTED TO SEE:
MARY BOONE SURFING
LARRY GAGOSIAN WEARING FLIP-FLOPS
JAMES FRANCO & JEFFREY DEITCH FROLICKING ON THE BEACH
TURNS OUT IT'S JUST A LOT OF RICH PEOPLE WALKING AROUND REALLY EXPENSIVE CUBICLES... AGAIN.
LAUREN PURJE.

HOW A STAR IS BORN? BY LAUREN PURJE.

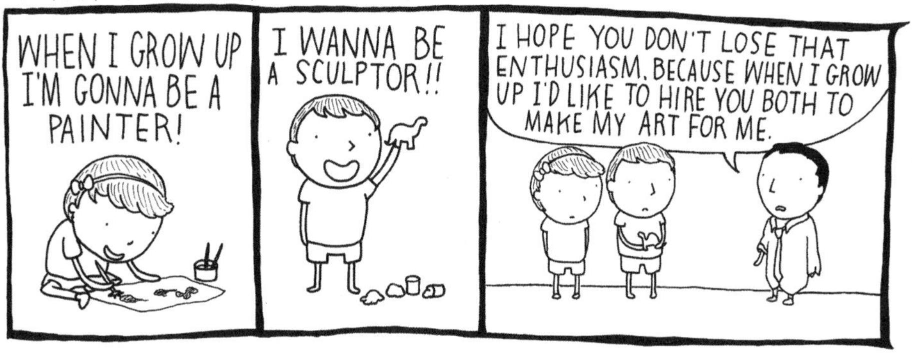
WHEN I GROW UP I'M GONNA BE A PAINTER!
I WANNA BE A SCULPTOR!!
I HOPE YOU DON'T LOSE THAT ENTHUSIASM, BECAUSE WHEN I GROW UP I'D LIKE TO HIRE YOU BOTH TO MAKE MY ART FOR ME.

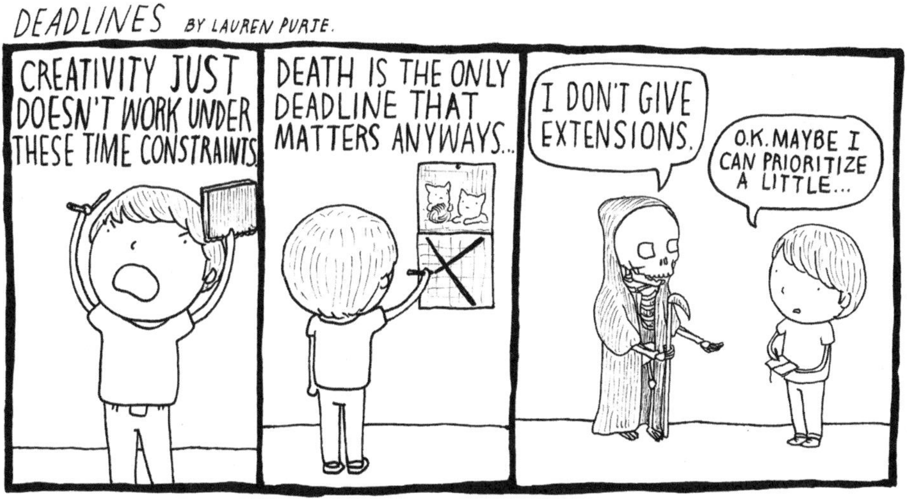
DEADLINES BY LAUREN PURJE.
CREATIVITY JUST DOESN'T WORK UNDER THESE TIME CONSTRAINTS
DEATH IS THE ONLY DEADLINE THAT MATTERS ANYWAYS...
I DON'T GIVE EXTENSIONS.
O.K. MAYBE I CAN PRIORITIZE A LITTLE...

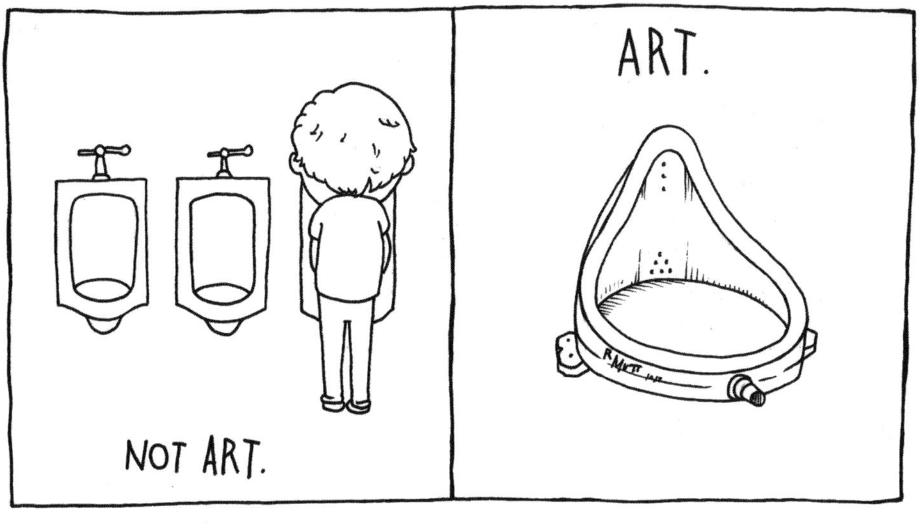
NOT ART.
ART.

HAPPY NEW YEARS - LAUREN PURJE.

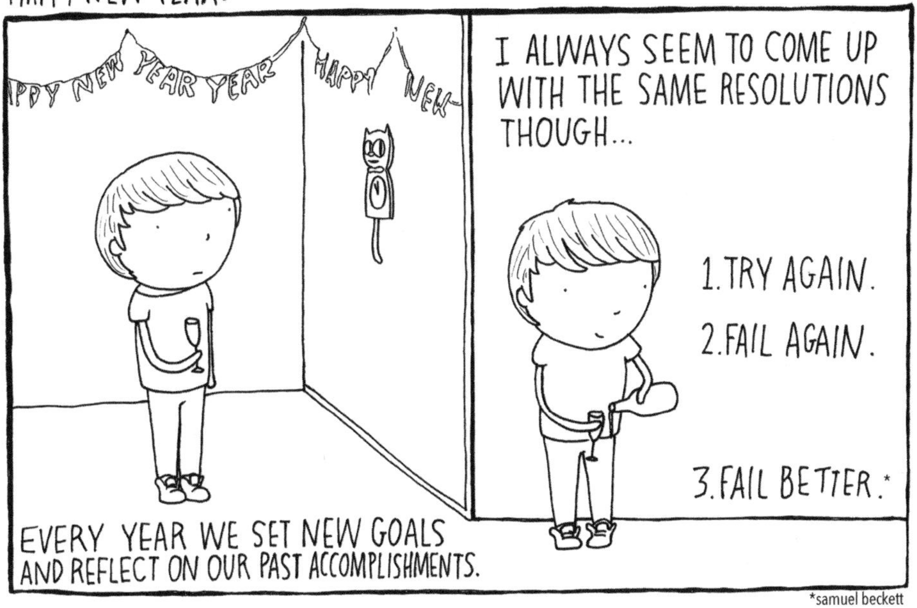
EVERY YEAR WE SET NEW GOALS AND REFLECT ON OUR PAST ACCOMPLISHMENTS.
I ALWAYS SEEM TO COME UP WITH THE SAME RESOLUTIONS THOUGH...
1. TRY AGAIN.
2. FAIL AGAIN.
3. FAIL BETTER.*

*samuel beckett

THE ART MEMENTO COLLECTOR

BY LAUREN PURJE.

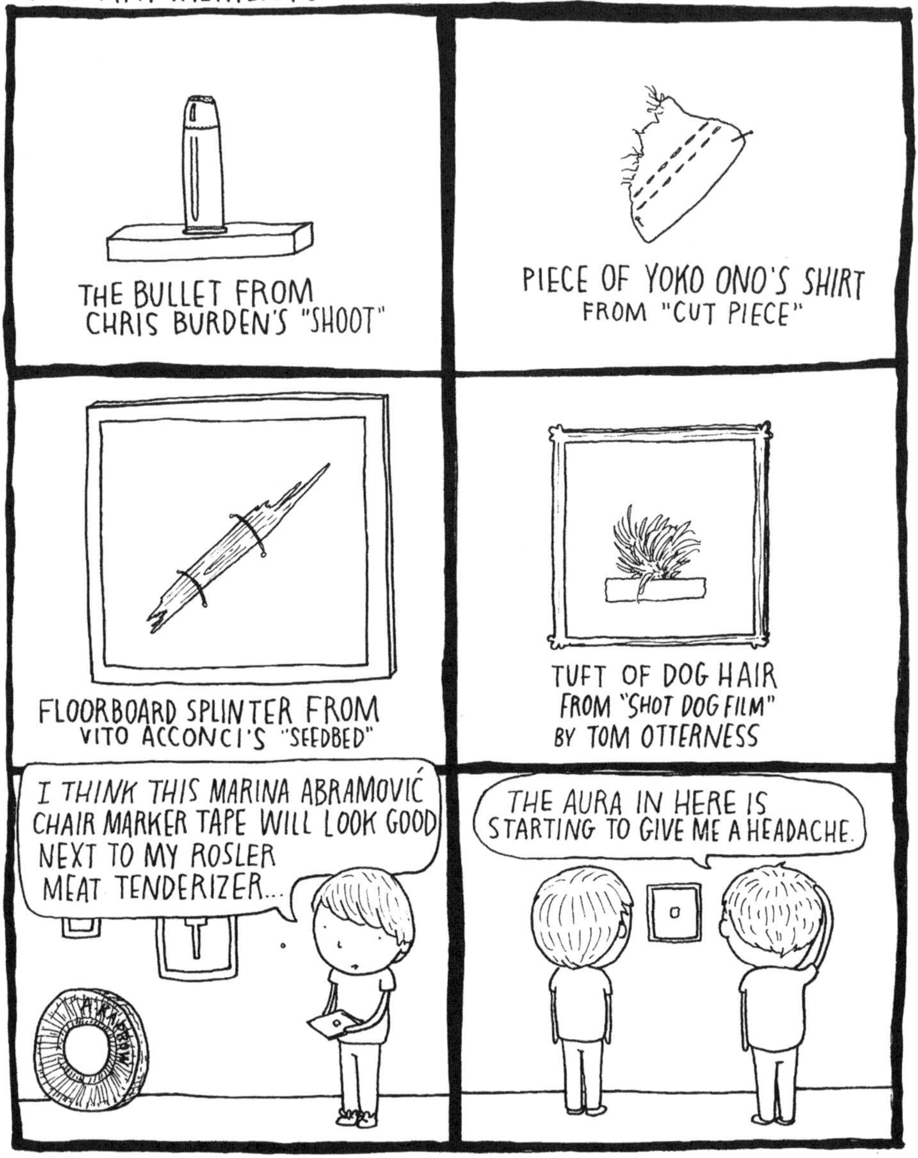

THE BULLET FROM CHRIS BURDEN'S "SHOOT"
PIECE OF YOKO ONO'S SHIRT FROM "CUT PIECE"
FLOORBOARD SPLINTER FROM VITO ACCONCI'S "SEEDBED"
TUFT OF DOG HAIR FROM "SHOT DOG FILM" BY TOM OTTERNESS
I THINK THIS MARINA ABRAMOVIĆ CHAIR MARKER TAPE WILL LOOK GOOD NEXT TO MY ROSLER MEAT TENDERIZER...
THE AURA IN HERE IS STARTING TO GIVE ME A HEADACHE.

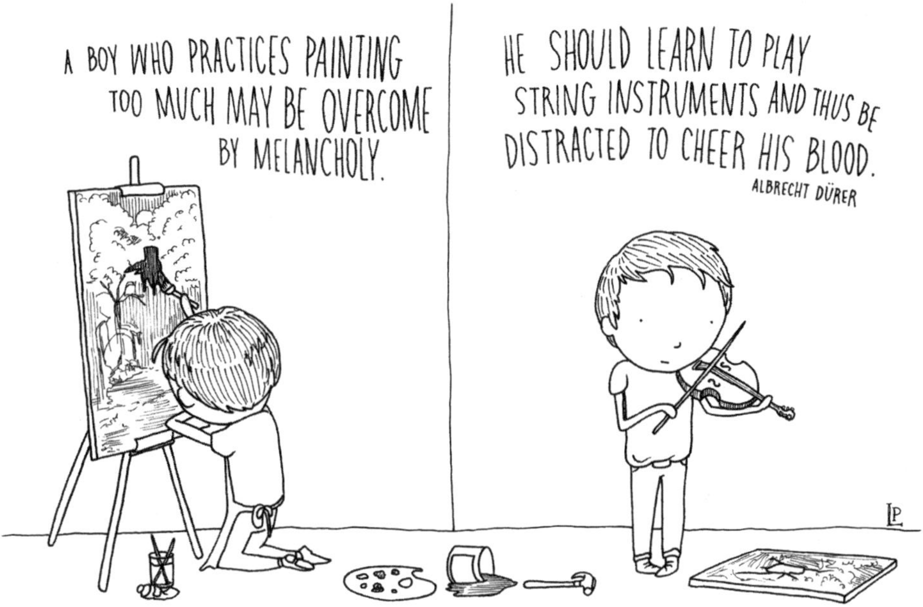
A BOY WHO PRACTICES PAINTING TOO MUCH MAY BE OVERCOME BY MELANCHOLY.
HE SHOULD LEARN TO PLAY STRING INSTRUMENTS AND THUS BE DISTRACTED TO CHEER HIS BLOOD.
ALBRECHT DÜRER
LP

YOU MIGHT BE AN ARTIST IF...

BY LAUREN PURJE.

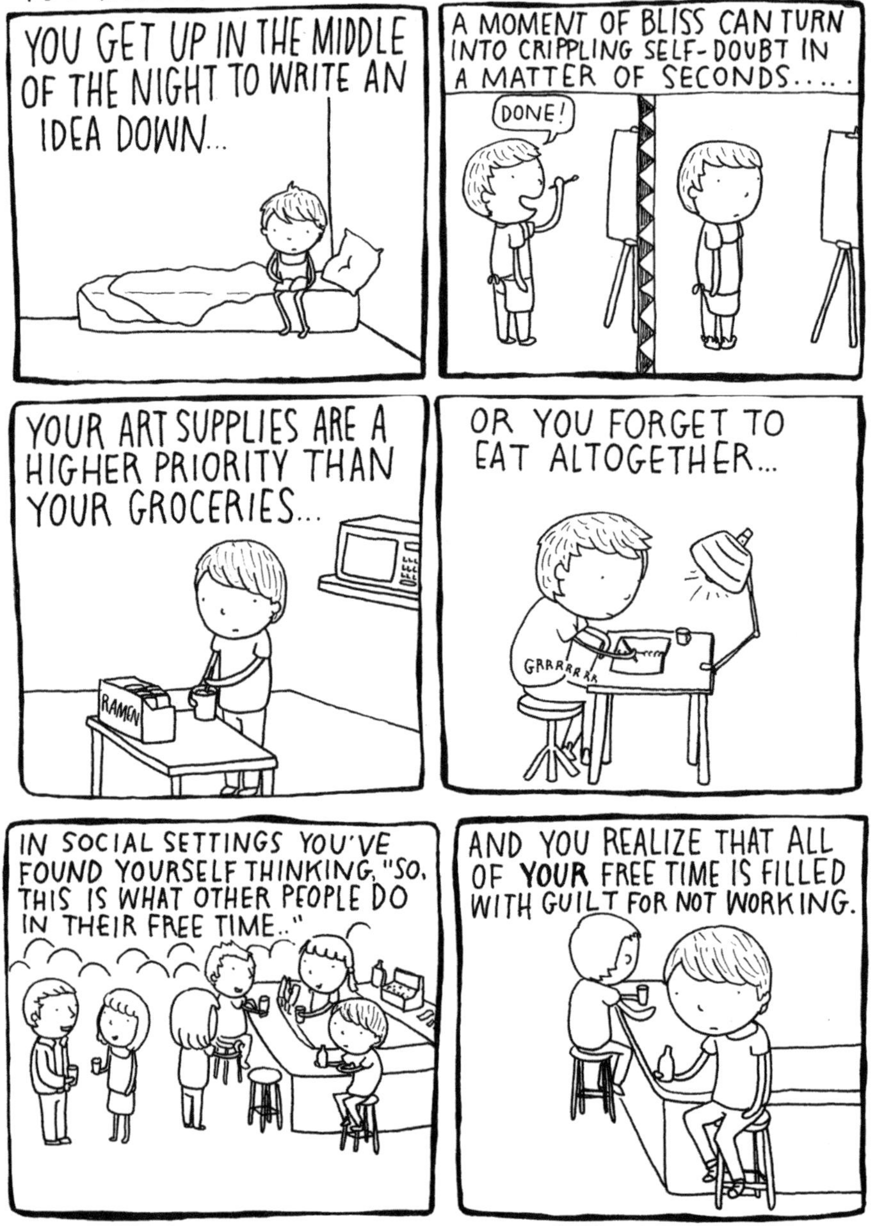
YOU GET UP IN THE MIDDLE OF THE NIGHT TO WRITE AN IDEA DOWN...
A MOMENT OF BLISS CAN TURN INTO CRIPPLING SELF-DOUBT IN A MATTER OF SECONDS.....
DONE!
YOUR ART SUPPLIES ARE A HIGHER PRIORITY THAN YOUR GROCERIES...
RAMEN
OR YOU FORGET TO EAT ALTOGETHER...
GRRRRRRRR
IN SOCIAL SETTINGS YOU'VE FOUND YOURSELF THINKING, "SO, THIS IS WHAT OTHER PEOPLE DO IN THEIR FREE TIME.."
AND YOU REALIZE THAT ALL OF **YOUR** FREE TIME IS FILLED WITH GUILT FOR NOT WORKING.

EXPOSURE BY LAUREN PURJE.

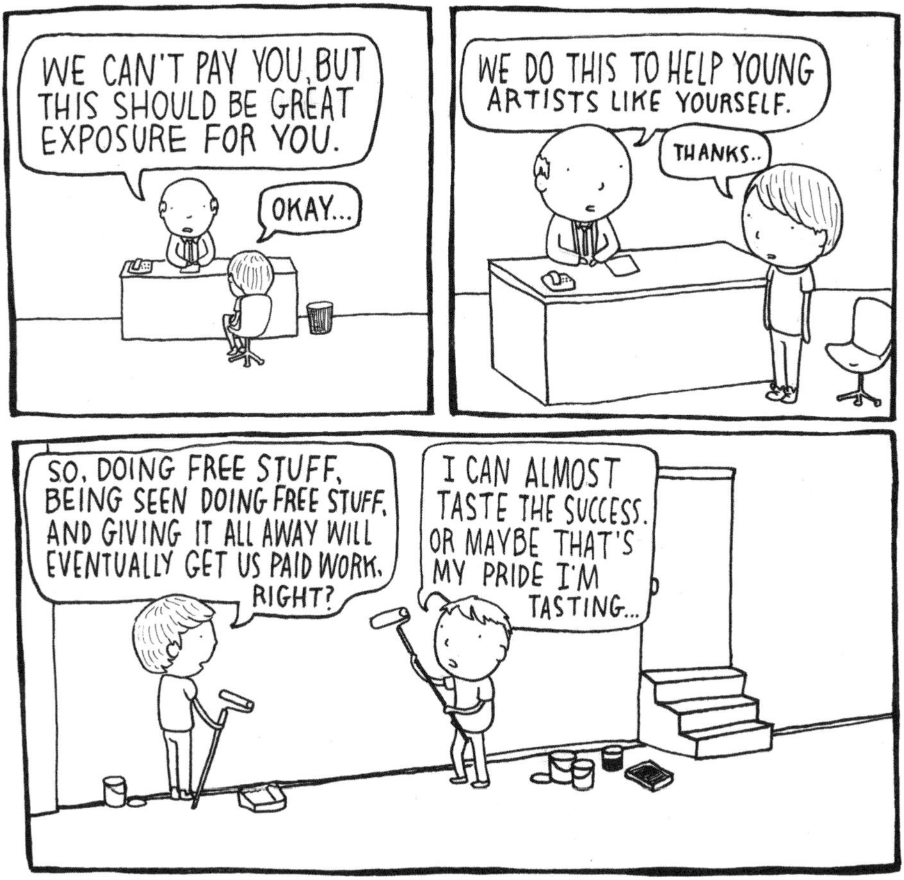
WE CAN'T PAY YOU, BUT THIS SHOULD BE GREAT EXPOSURE FOR YOU.
OKAY...
WE DO THIS TO HELP YOUNG ARTISTS LIKE YOURSELF.
THANKS..
SO, DOING FREE STUFF, BEING SEEN DOING FREE STUFF, AND GIVING IT ALL AWAY WILL EVENTUALLY GET US PAID WORK, RIGHT?
I CAN ALMOST TASTE THE SUCCESS. OR MAYBE THAT'S MY PRIDE I'M TASTING...

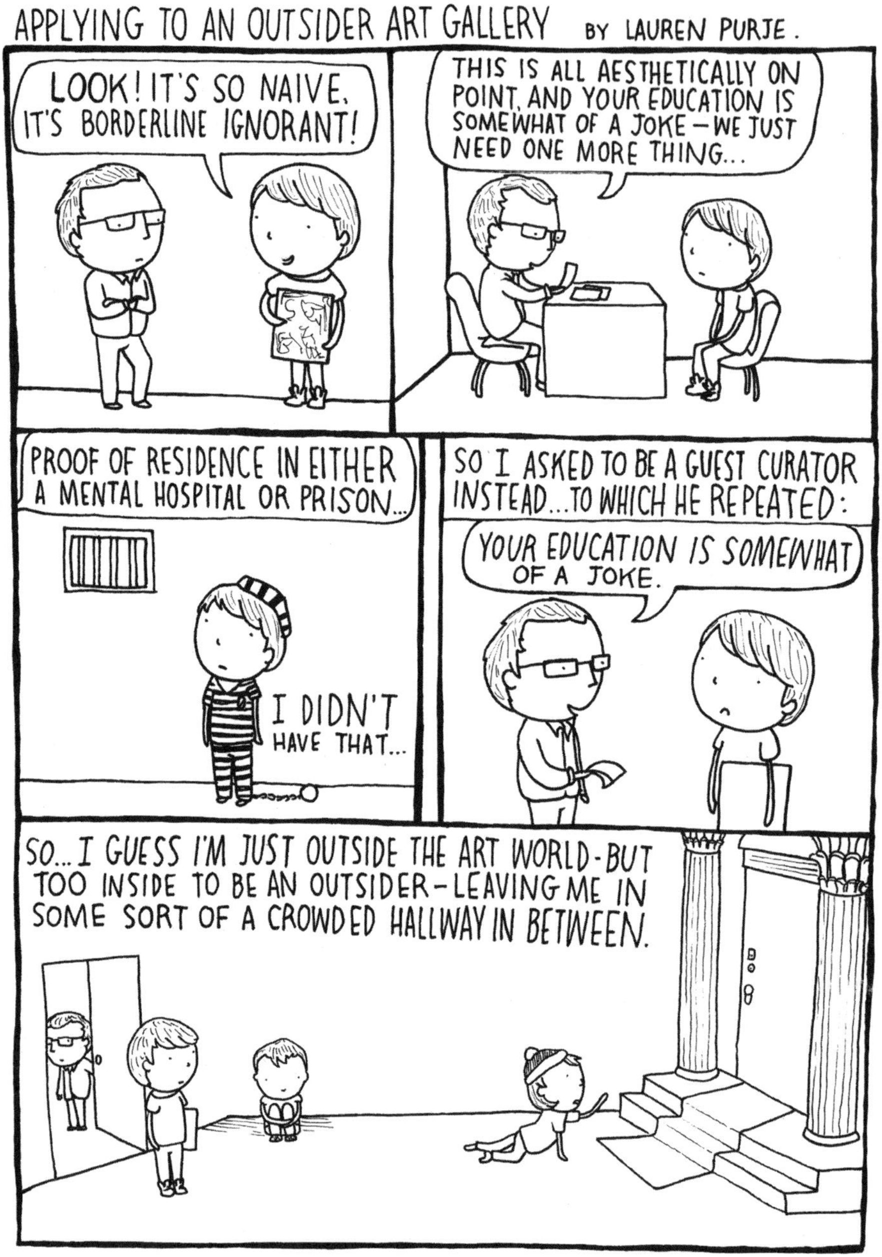
APPLYING TO AN OUTSIDER ART GALLERY BY LAUREN PURJE.
LOOK! IT'S SO NAIVE, IT'S BORDERLINE IGNORANT!
THIS IS ALL AESTHETICALLY ON POINT, AND YOUR EDUCATION IS SOMEWHAT OF A JOKE—WE JUST NEED ONE MORE THING...
PROOF OF RESIDENCE IN EITHER A MENTAL HOSPITAL OR PRISON...
I DIDN'T HAVE THAT...
SO I ASKED TO BE A GUEST CURATOR INSTEAD...TO WHICH HE REPEATED:
YOUR EDUCATION IS SOMEWHAT OF A JOKE.
SO...I GUESS I'M JUST OUTSIDE THE ART WORLD-BUT TOO INSIDE TO BE AN OUTSIDER-LEAVING ME IN SOME SORT OF A CROWDED HALLWAY IN BETWEEN.

WHAT HAPPENED?

LAUREN PURJE.

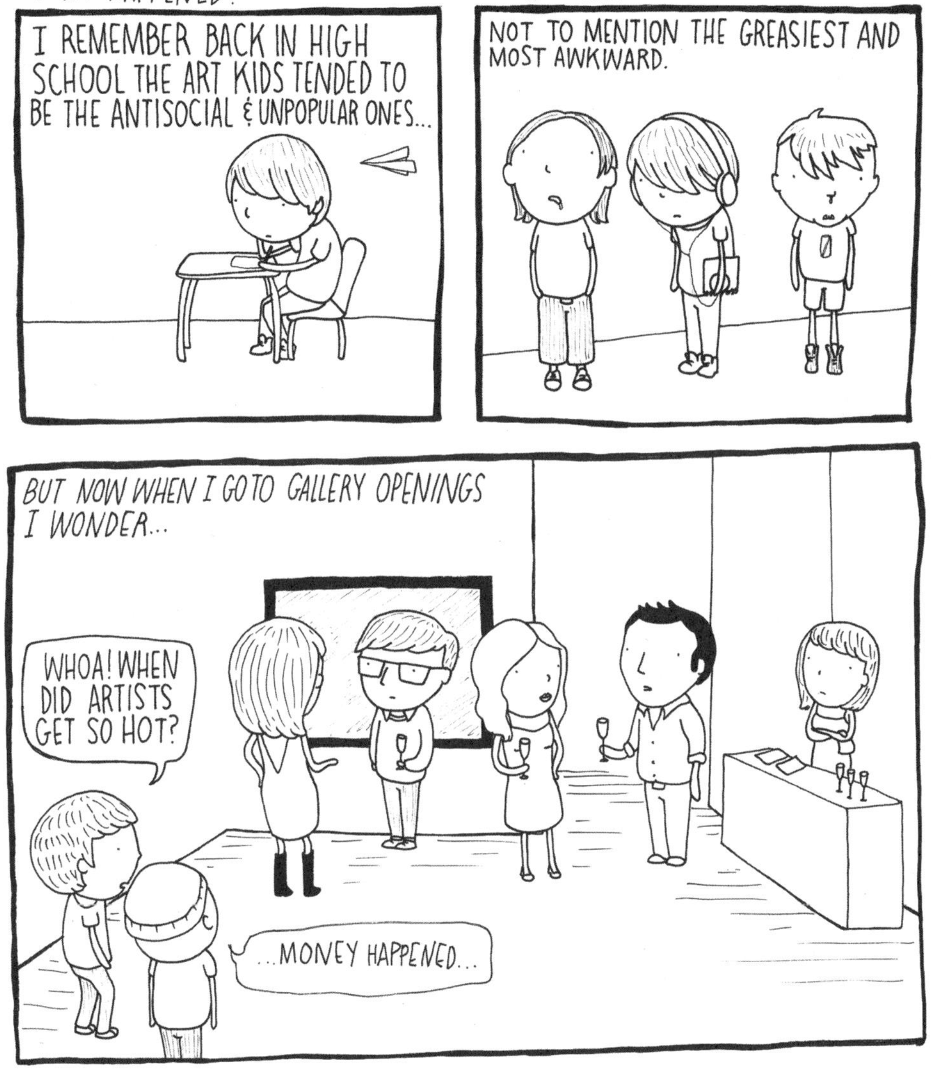

I REMEMBER BACK IN HIGH SCHOOL THE ART KIDS TENDED TO BE THE ANTISOCIAL & UNPOPULAR ONES...
NOT TO MENTION THE GREASIEST AND MOST AWKWARD.
BUT NOW WHEN I GO TO GALLERY OPENINGS I WONDER...
WHOA! WHEN DID ARTISTS GET SO HOT?
...MONEY HAPPENED...

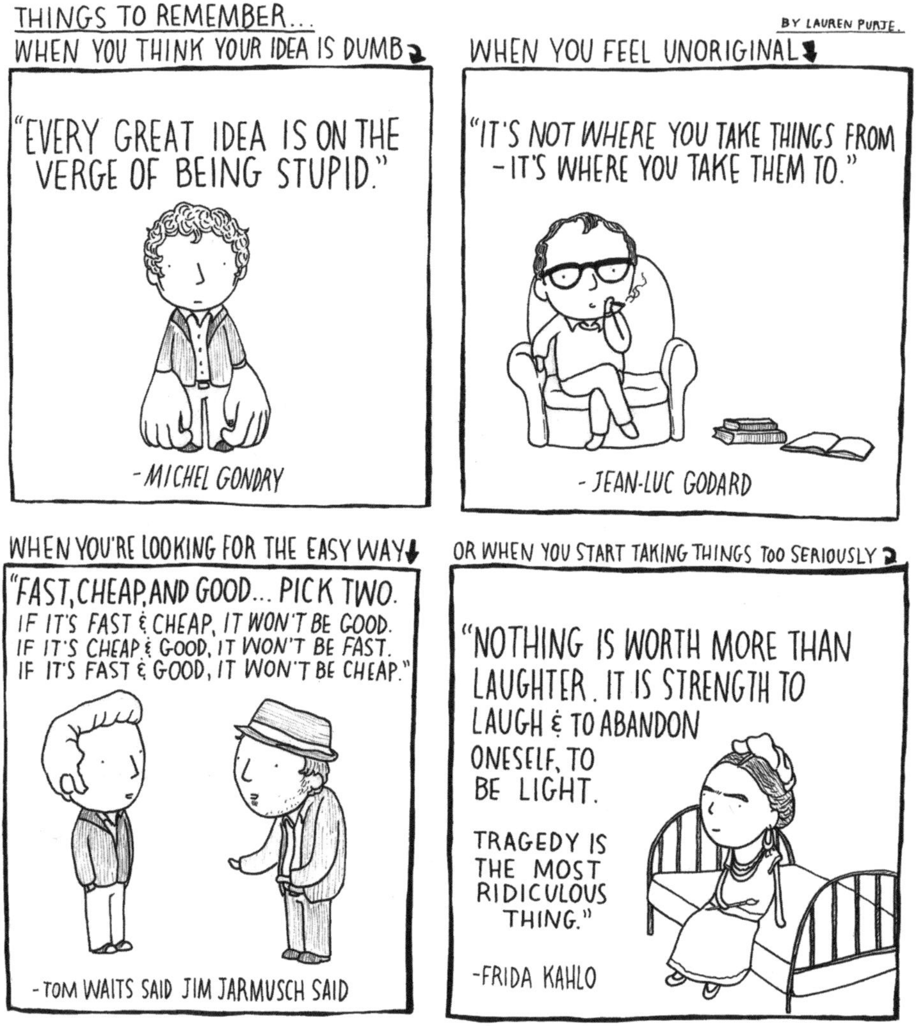
THINGS TO REMEMBER...
BY LAUREN PURJE.
WHEN YOU THINK YOUR IDEA IS DUMB
"EVERY GREAT IDEA IS ON THE VERGE OF BEING STUPID."
-MICHEL GONDRY
WHEN YOU FEEL UNORIGINAL
"IT'S NOT WHERE YOU TAKE THINGS FROM -IT'S WHERE YOU TAKE THEM TO."
-JEAN-LUC GODARD
WHEN YOU'RE LOOKING FOR THE EASY WAY
"FAST, CHEAP, AND GOOD... PICK TWO.
IF IT'S FAST & CHEAP, IT WON'T BE GOOD.
IF IT'S CHEAP & GOOD, IT WON'T BE FAST.
IF IT'S FAST & GOOD, IT WON'T BE CHEAP."
-TOM WAITS SAID JIM JARMUSCH SAID
OR WHEN YOU START TAKING THINGS TOO SERIOUSLY
"NOTHING IS WORTH MORE THAN LAUGHTER. IT IS STRENGTH TO LAUGH & TO ABANDON ONESELF, TO BE LIGHT.
TRAGEDY IS THE MOST RIDICULOUS THING."
-FRIDA KAHLO

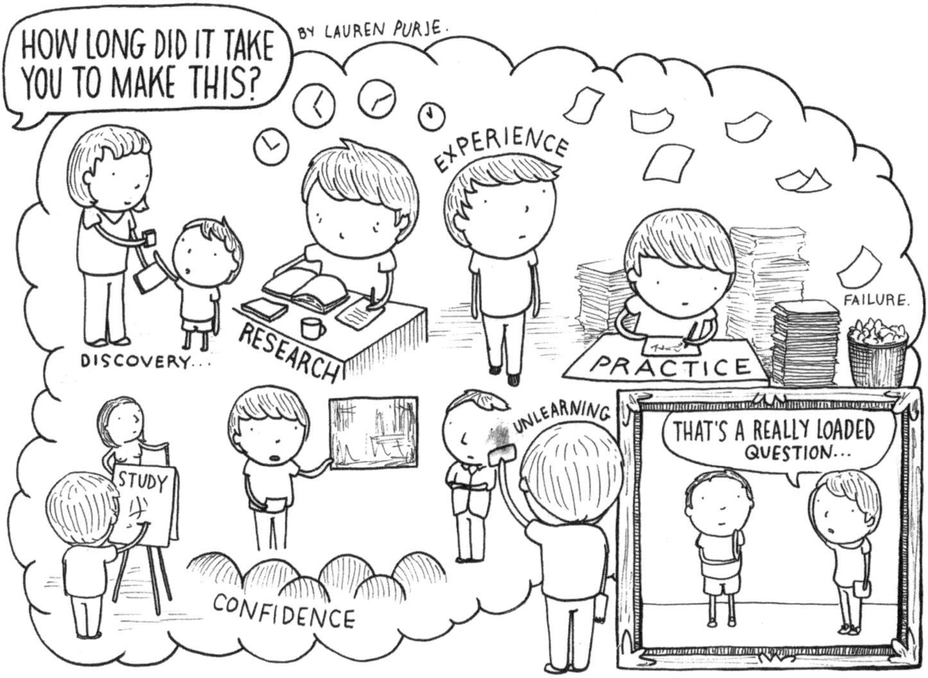
HOW LONG DID IT TAKE YOU TO MAKE THIS?
BY LAUREN PURJE.
DISCOVERY...
RESEARCH
EXPERIENCE
PRACTICE
FAILURE.
STUDY
CONFIDENCE
UNLEARNING
THAT'S A REALLY LOADED QUESTION...

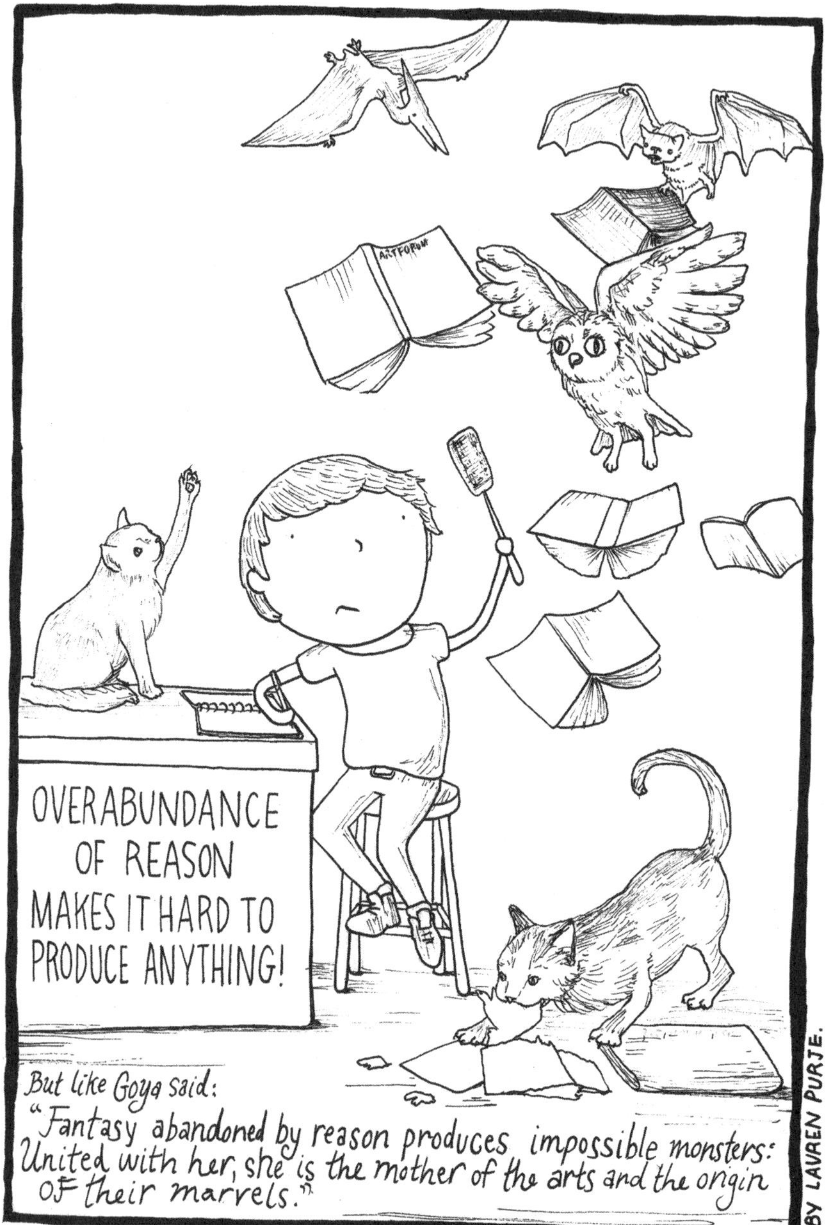
ARTFORUM
OVERABUNDANCE OF REASON MAKES IT HARD TO PRODUCE ANYTHING!
But like Goya said:
"Fantasy abandoned by reason produces impossible monsters: United with her, she is the mother of the arts and the origin of their marvels."
BY LAUREN PURJE.

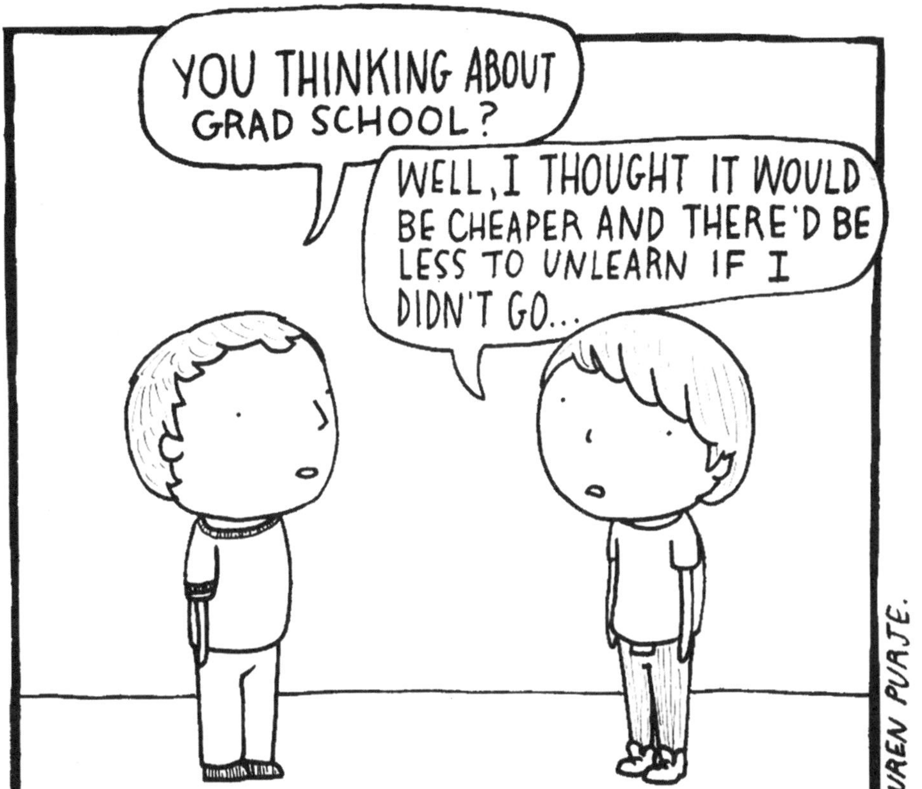
YOU THINKING ABOUT GRAD SCHOOL?
WELL, I THOUGHT IT WOULD BE CHEAPER AND THERE'D BE LESS TO UNLEARN IF I DIDN'T GO...
LAUREN PURJE.

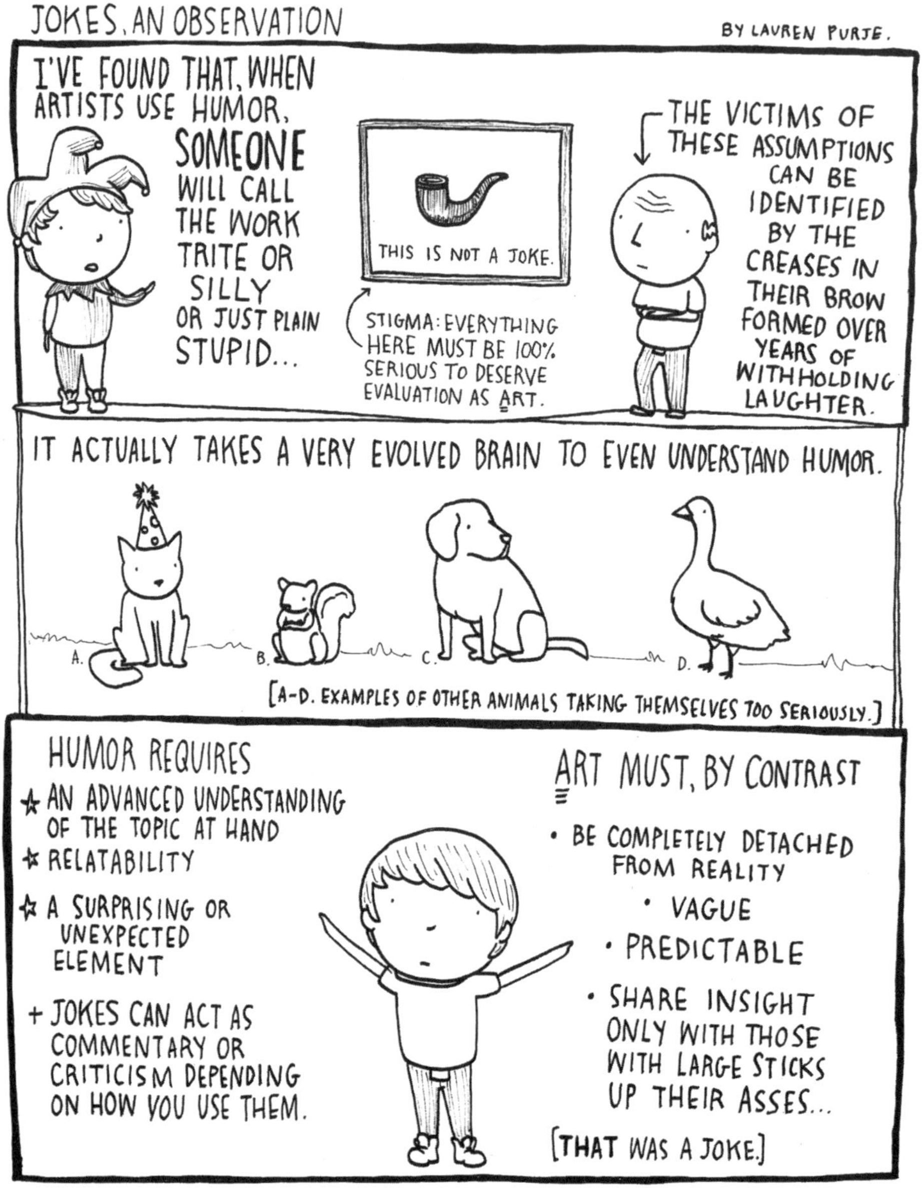
JOKES, AN OBSERVATION
BY LAUREN PURJE.
I'VE FOUND THAT, WHEN ARTISTS USE HUMOR,
SOMEONE WILL CALL THE WORK TRITE OR SILLY OR JUST PLAIN STUPID...
THIS IS NOT A JOKE.
STIGMA: EVERYTHING HERE MUST BE 100% SERIOUS TO DESERVE EVALUATION AS ART.
THE VICTIMS OF THESE ASSUMPTIONS CAN BE IDENTIFIED BY THE CREASES IN THEIR BROW FORMED OVER YEARS OF WITHHOLDING LAUGHTER.
IT ACTUALLY TAKES A VERY EVOLVED BRAIN TO EVEN UNDERSTAND HUMOR.
A.
B.
C.
D.
[A-D. EXAMPLES OF OTHER ANIMALS TAKING THEMSELVES TOO SERIOUSLY.]
HUMOR REQUIRES
AN ADVANCED UNDERSTANDING OF THE TOPIC AT HAND
RELATABILITY
A SURPRISING OR UNEXPECTED ELEMENT
+ JOKES CAN ACT AS COMMENTARY OR CRITICISM DEPENDING ON HOW YOU USE THEM.
ART MUST, BY CONTRAST
• BE COMPLETELY DETACHED FROM REALITY
• VAGUE
• PREDICTABLE
• SHARE INSIGHT ONLY WITH THOSE WITH LARGE STICKS UP THEIR ASSES...
[THAT WAS A JOKE.]

NEEDS BY LAUREN PURJE. AKA "THE ARTIST'S HIERARCHY OF NEEDS"

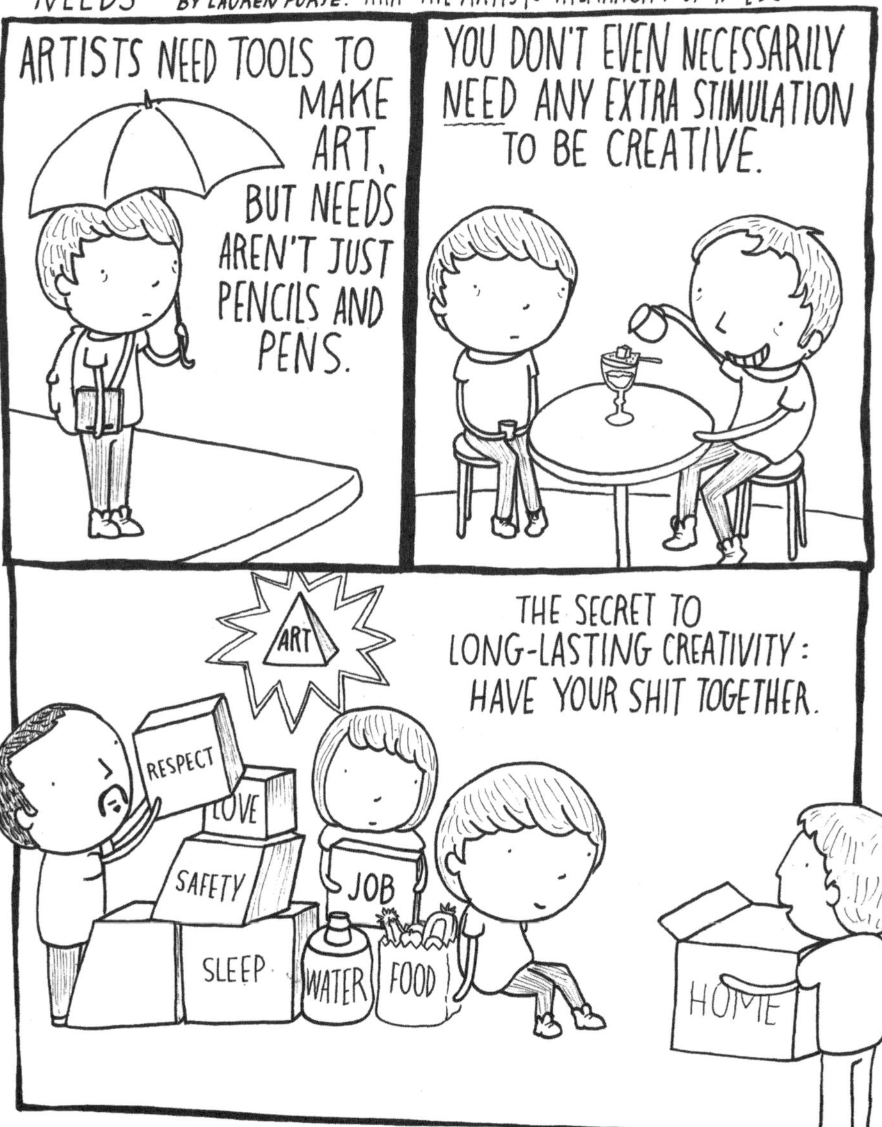

ARTISTS NEED TOOLS TO MAKE ART, BUT NEEDS AREN'T JUST PENCILS AND PENS.
YOU DON'T EVEN NECESSARILY NEED ANY EXTRA STIMULATION TO BE CREATIVE.
ART
THE SECRET TO LONG-LASTING CREATIVITY: HAVE YOUR SHIT TOGETHER.
RESPECT
LOVE
SAFETY
JOB
SLEEP
WATER
FOOD
HOME

DRAWING UNDER THE INFLUENCE BY LAUREN PURJE.

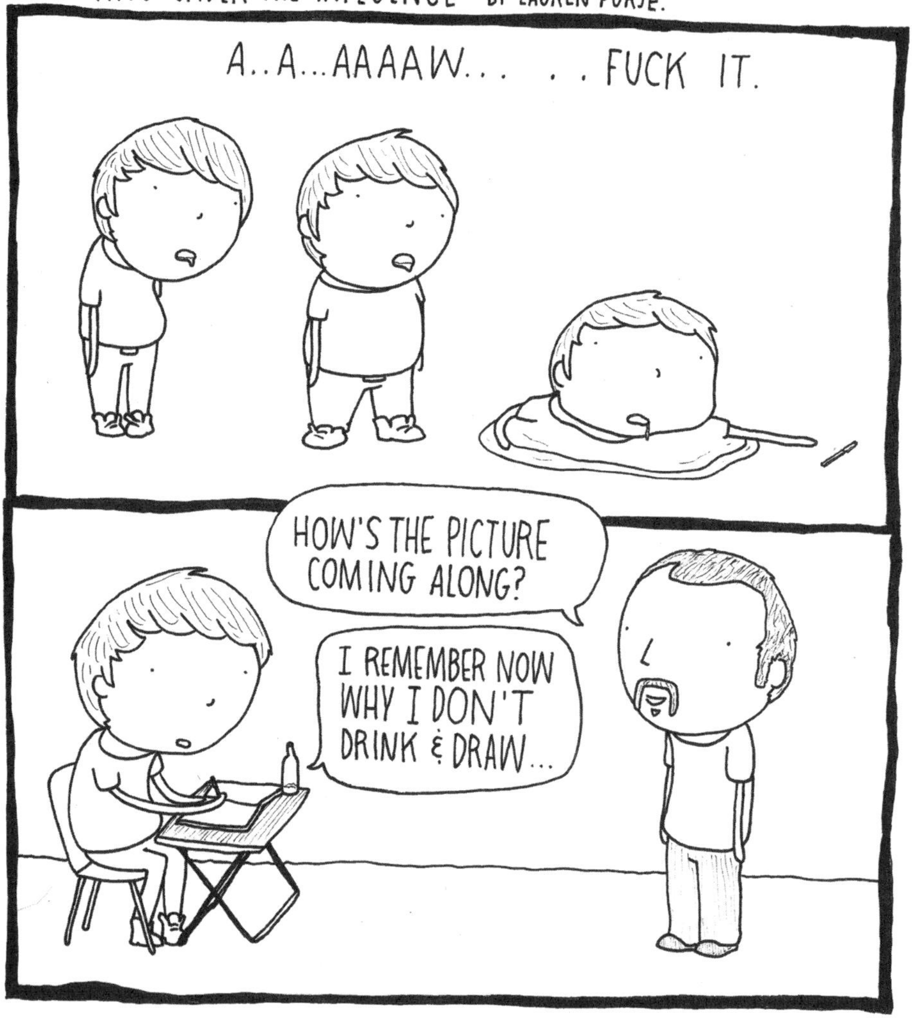
A..A...AAAAW... ..FUCK IT.
HOW'S THE PICTURE COMING ALONG?
I REMEMBER NOW WHY I DON'T DRINK & DRAW...

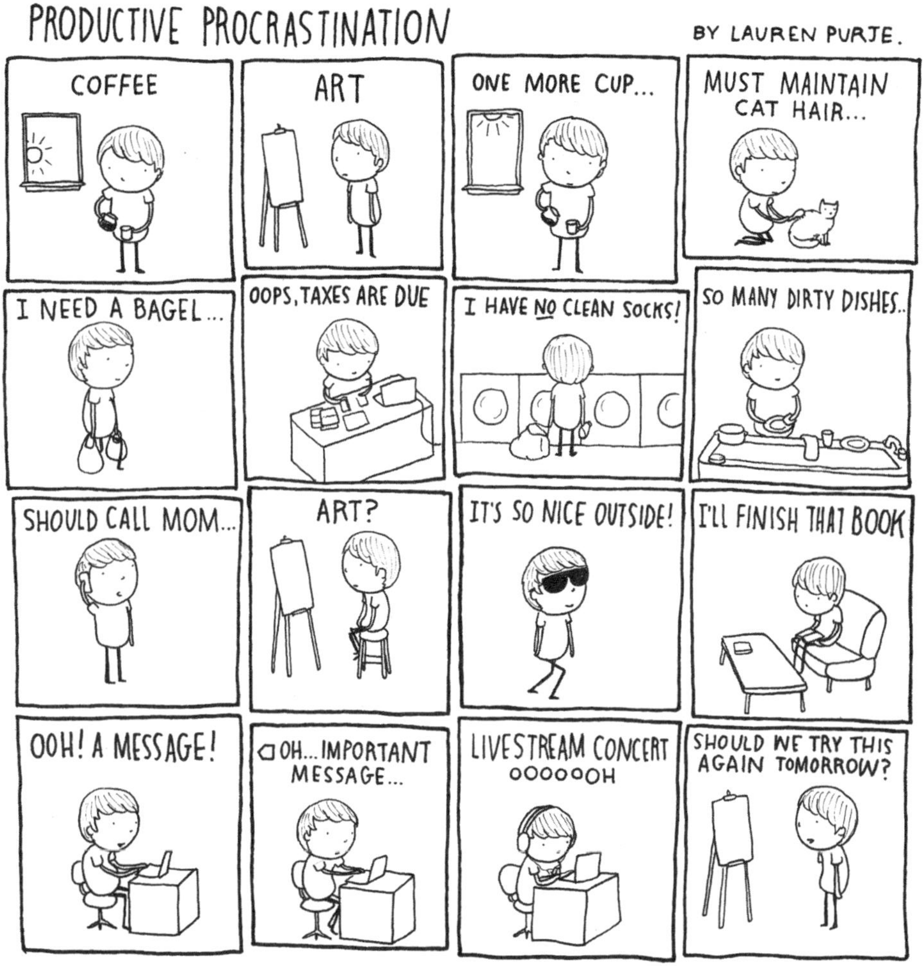
PRODUCTIVE PROCRASTINATION
BY LAUREN PURJE.
COFFEE
ART
ONE MORE CUP...
MUST MAINTAIN CAT HAIR...
I NEED A BAGEL...
OOPS, TAXES ARE DUE
I HAVE NO CLEAN SOCKS!
SO MANY DIRTY DISHES..
SHOULD CALL MOM...
ART?
IT'S SO NICE OUTSIDE!
I'LL FINISH THAT BOOK
OOH! A MESSAGE!
OH... IMPORTANT MESSAGE...
LIVESTREAM CONCERT OOOOOOH
SHOULD WE TRY THIS AGAIN TOMORROW?

FAKE IT TILL YOU MAKE IT BY LAUREN PURJE.

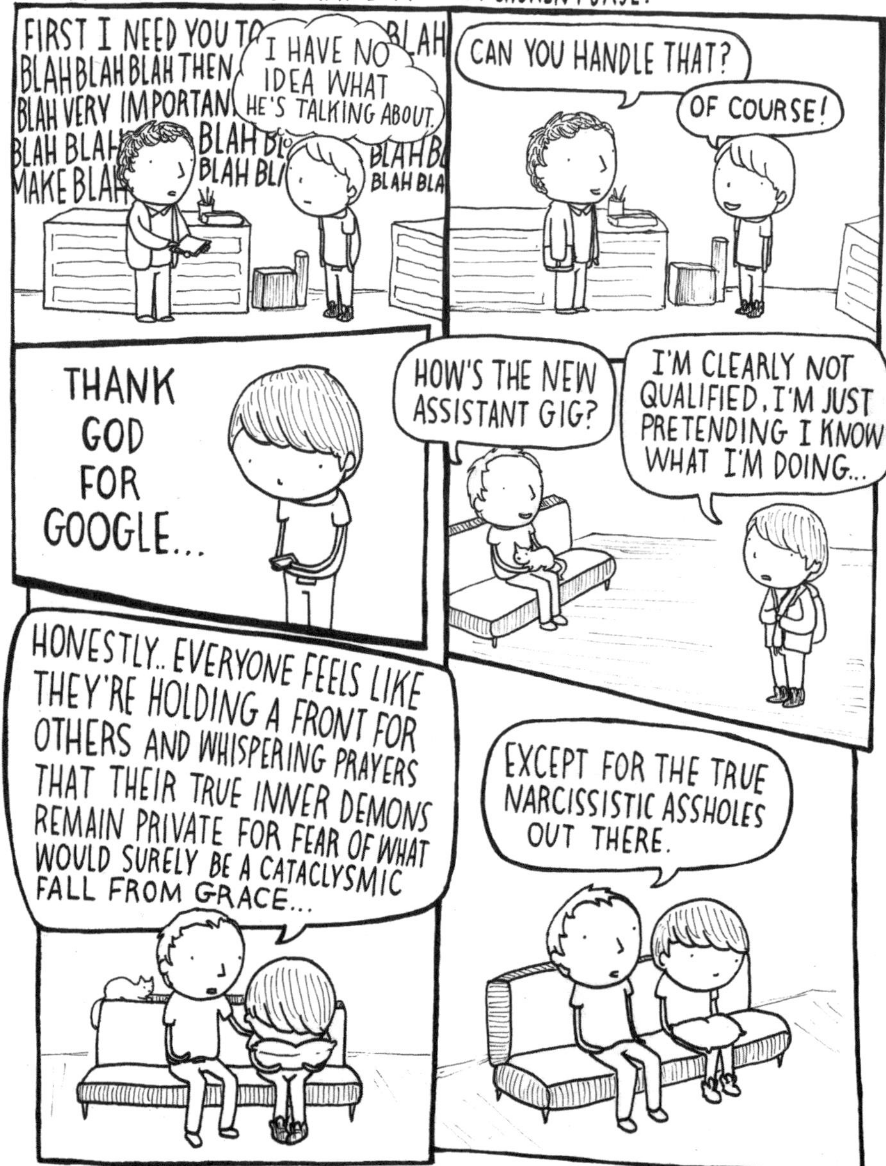
FIRST I NEED YOU TO BLAH BLAH BLAH BLAH THEN BLAH VERY IMPORTAN BLAH BLAH MAKE BLAH BLAH BLAH BLAH BLAH BLAH BLAH BLA
I HAVE NO IDEA WHAT HE'S TALKING ABOUT.
CAN YOU HANDLE THAT?
OF COURSE!
THANK GOD FOR GOOGLE...
HOW'S THE NEW ASSISTANT GIG?
I'M CLEARLY NOT QUALIFIED. I'M JUST PRETENDING I KNOW WHAT I'M DOING...
HONESTLY.. EVERYONE FEELS LIKE THEY'RE HOLDING A FRONT FOR OTHERS AND WHISPERING PRAYERS THAT THEIR TRUE INNER DEMONS REMAIN PRIVATE FOR FEAR OF WHAT WOULD SURELY BE A CATACLYSMIC FALL FROM GRACE...
EXCEPT FOR THE TRUE NARCISSISTIC ASSHOLES OUT THERE.

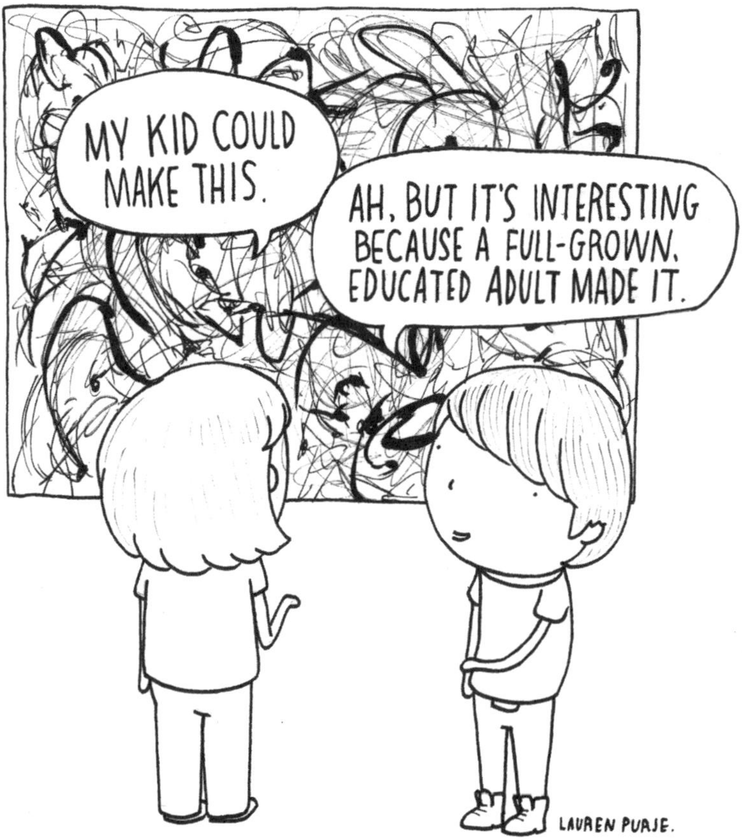
MY KID COULD MAKE THIS.
AH, BUT IT'S INTERESTING BECAUSE A FULL-GROWN, EDUCATED ADULT MADE IT.
LAUREN PURJE.

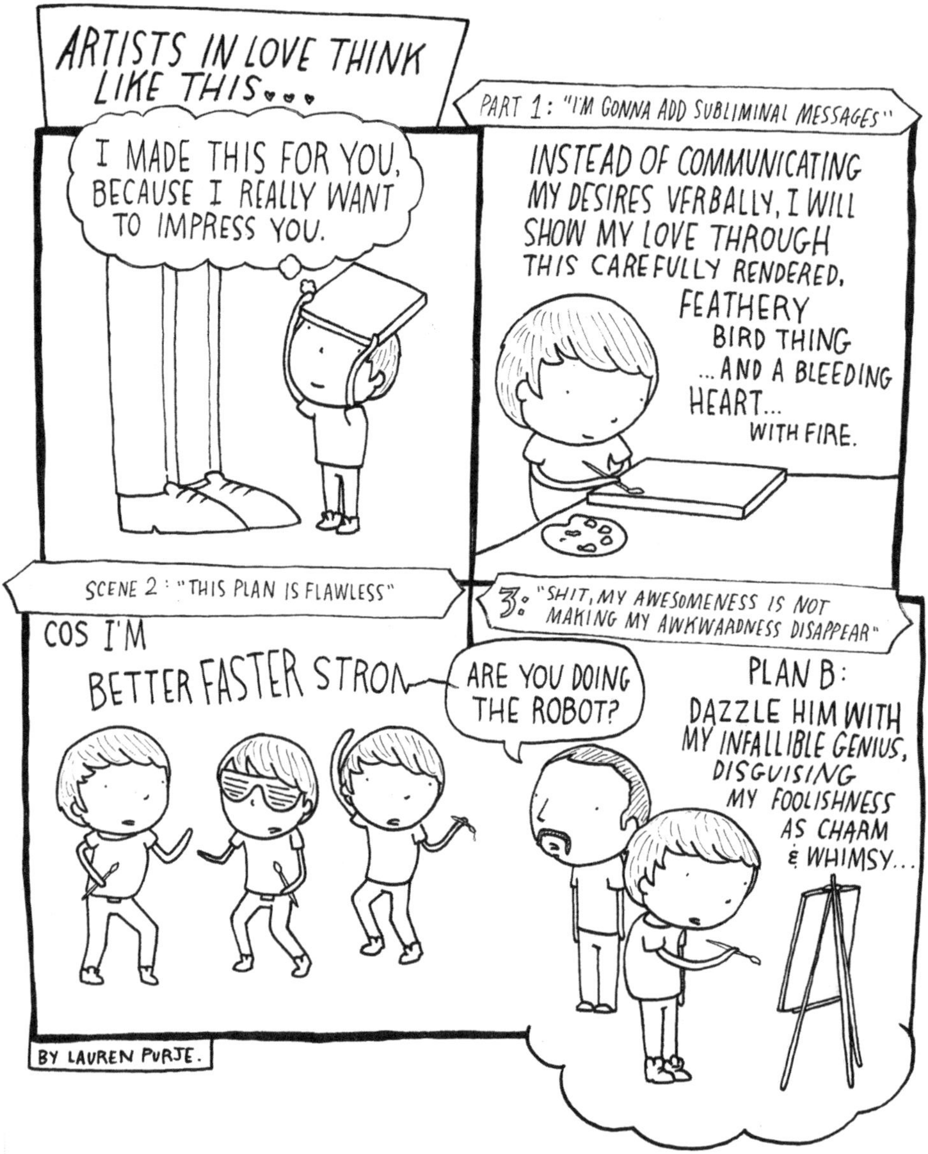
ARTISTS IN LOVE THINK LIKE THIS...
PART 1: "I'M GONNA ADD SUBLIMINAL MESSAGES"
I MADE THIS FOR YOU, BECAUSE I REALLY WANT TO IMPRESS YOU.
INSTEAD OF COMMUNICATING MY DESIRES VERBALLY, I WILL SHOW MY LOVE THROUGH THIS CAREFULLY RENDERED, FEATHERY BIRD THING ...AND A BLEEDING HEART... WITH FIRE.
SCENE 2: "THIS PLAN IS FLAWLESS"
COS I'M BETTER FASTER STRON
3: "SHIT, MY AWESOMENESS IS NOT MAKING MY AWKWARDNESS DISAPPEAR"
ARE YOU DOING THE ROBOT?
PLAN B: DAZZLE HIM WITH MY INFALLIBLE GENIUS, DISGUISING MY FOOLISHNESS AS CHARM & WHIMSY...
BY LAUREN PURJE.

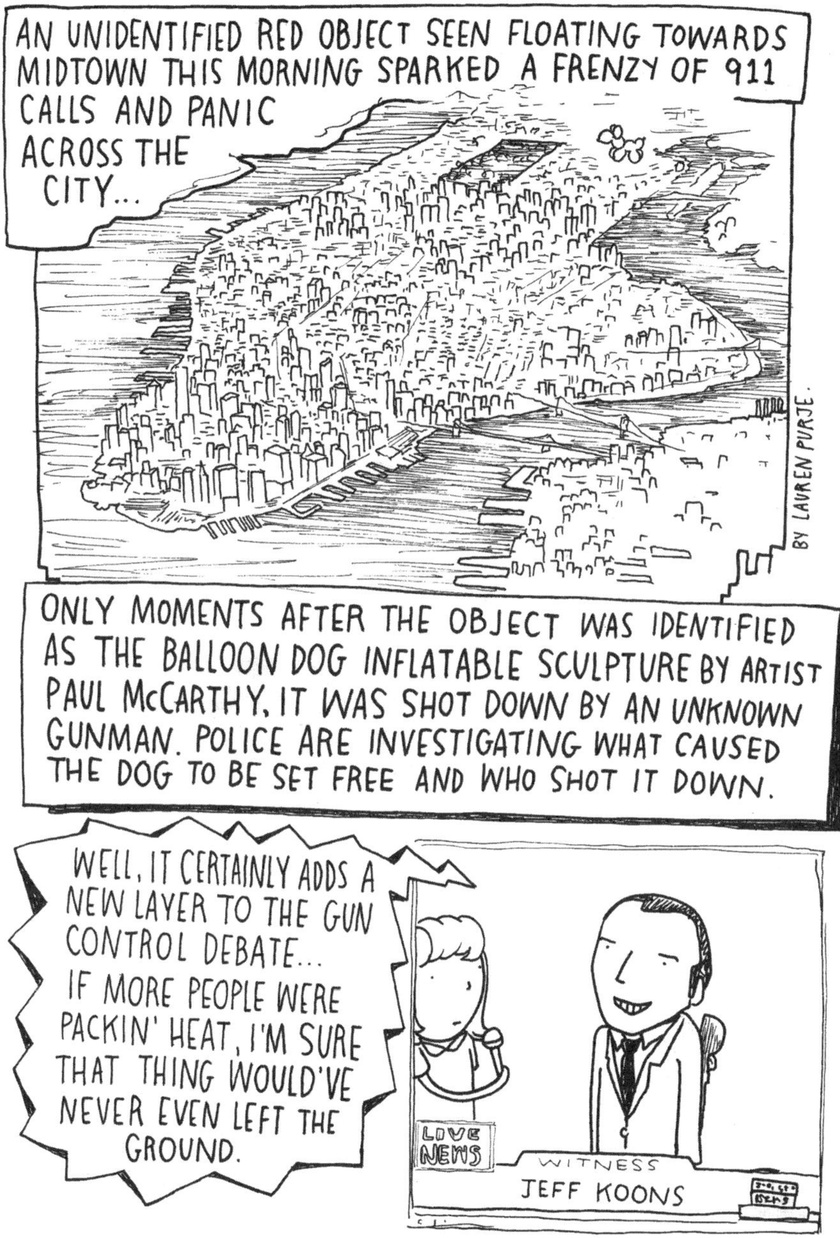
AN UNIDENTIFIED RED OBJECT SEEN FLOATING TOWARDS MIDTOWN THIS MORNING SPARKED A FRENZY OF 911 CALLS AND PANIC ACROSS THE CITY...
BY LAUREN PURJE.
ONLY MOMENTS AFTER THE OBJECT WAS IDENTIFIED AS THE BALLOON DOG INFLATABLE SCULPTURE BY ARTIST PAUL McCARTHY, IT WAS SHOT DOWN BY AN UNKNOWN GUNMAN. POLICE ARE INVESTIGATING WHAT CAUSED THE DOG TO BE SET FREE AND WHO SHOT IT DOWN.
WELL, IT CERTAINLY ADDS A NEW LAYER TO THE GUN CONTROL DEBATE... IF MORE PEOPLE WERE PACKIN' HEAT, I'M SURE THAT THING WOULD'VE NEVER EVEN LEFT THE GROUND.
LIVE NEWS
WITNESS
JEFF KOONS

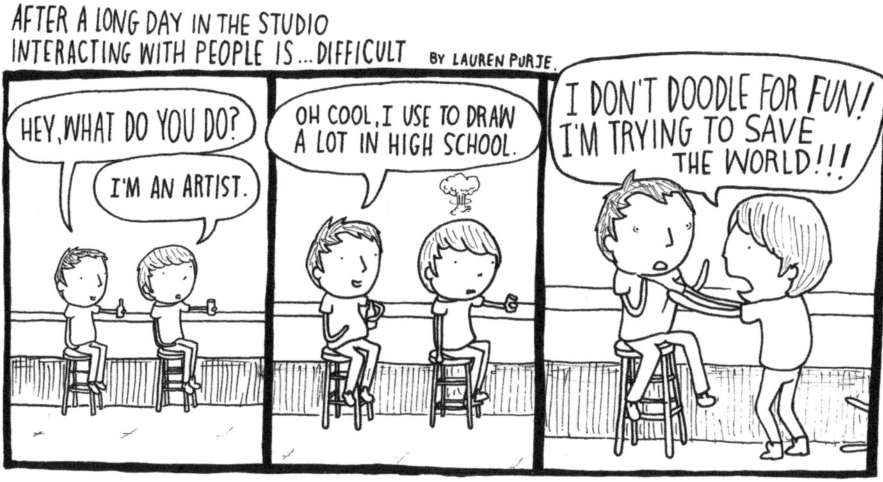
AFTER A LONG DAY IN THE STUDIO
INTERACTING WITH PEOPLE IS... DIFFICULT
BY LAUREN PURJE.
HEY, WHAT DO YOU DO?
I'M AN ARTIST.
OH COOL, I USE TO DRAW A LOT IN HIGH SCHOOL.
I DON'T DOODLE FOR FUN! I'M TRYING TO SAVE THE WORLD!!!

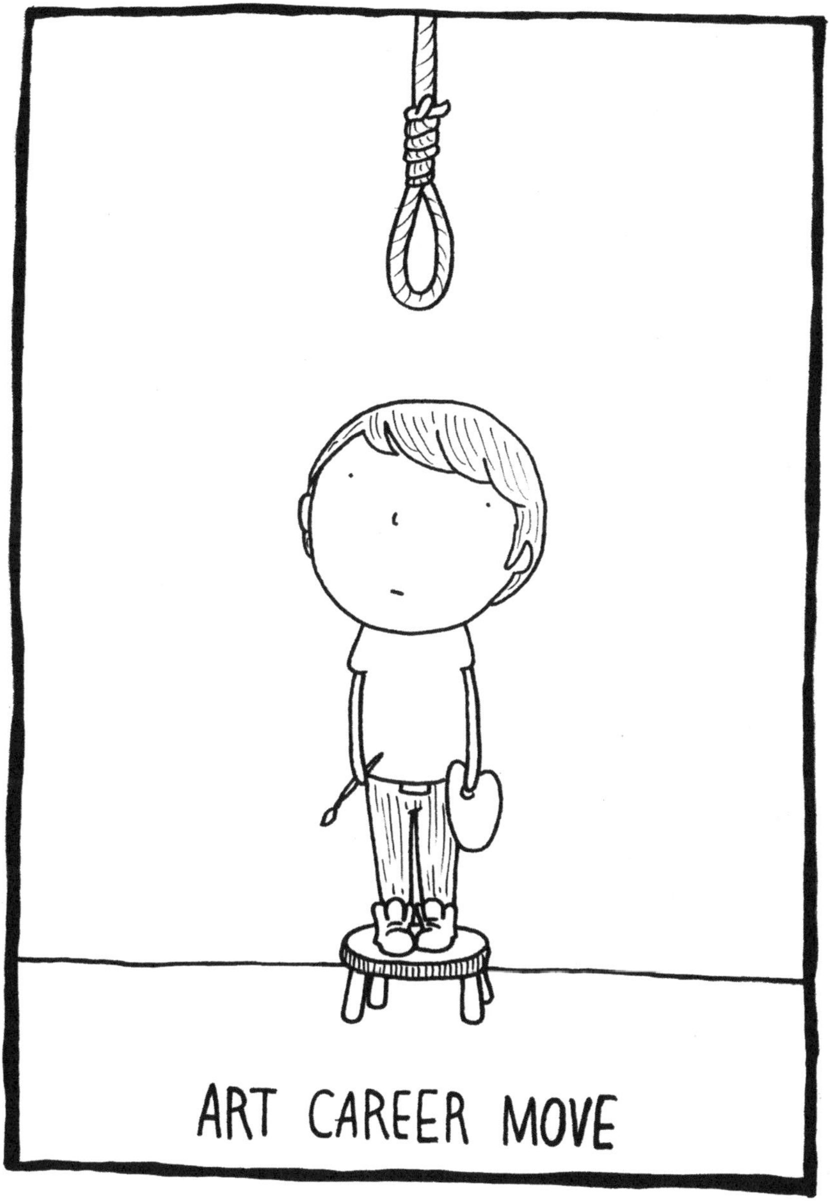
ART CAREER MOVE

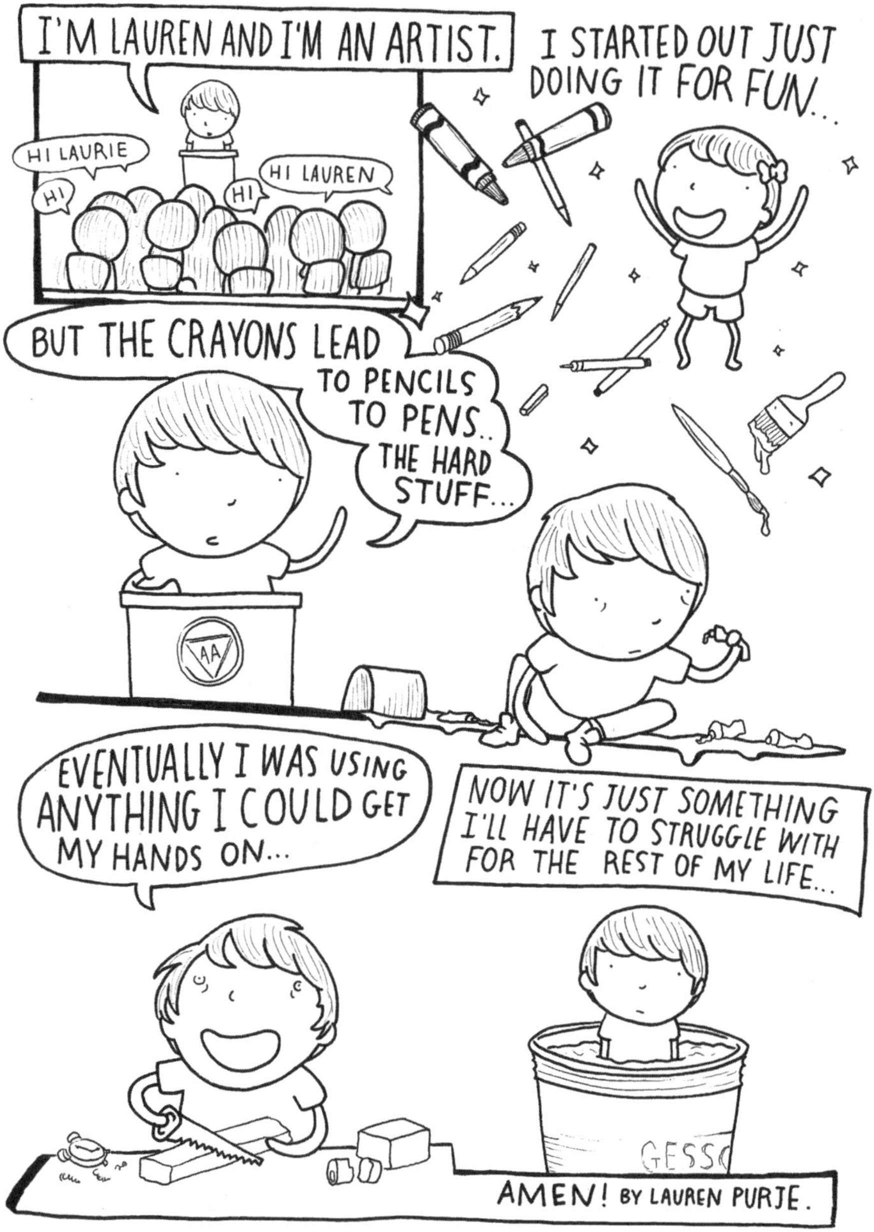
I'M LAUREN AND I'M AN ARTIST.
HI LAURIE
HI
HI
HI LAUREN
I STARTED OUT JUST DOING IT FOR FUN...
BUT THE CRAYONS LEAD
TO PENCILS TO PENS.. THE HARD STUFF...
AA
EVENTUALLY I WAS USING ANYTHING I COULD GET MY HANDS ON...
NOW IT'S JUST SOMETHING I'LL HAVE TO STRUGGLE WITH FOR THE REST OF MY LIFE...
GESSO
AMEN! BY LAUREN PURJE.

SOME EXCUSES
WHY AN ARTIST IS NOT MAKING ART

BY LAUREN PURJE.

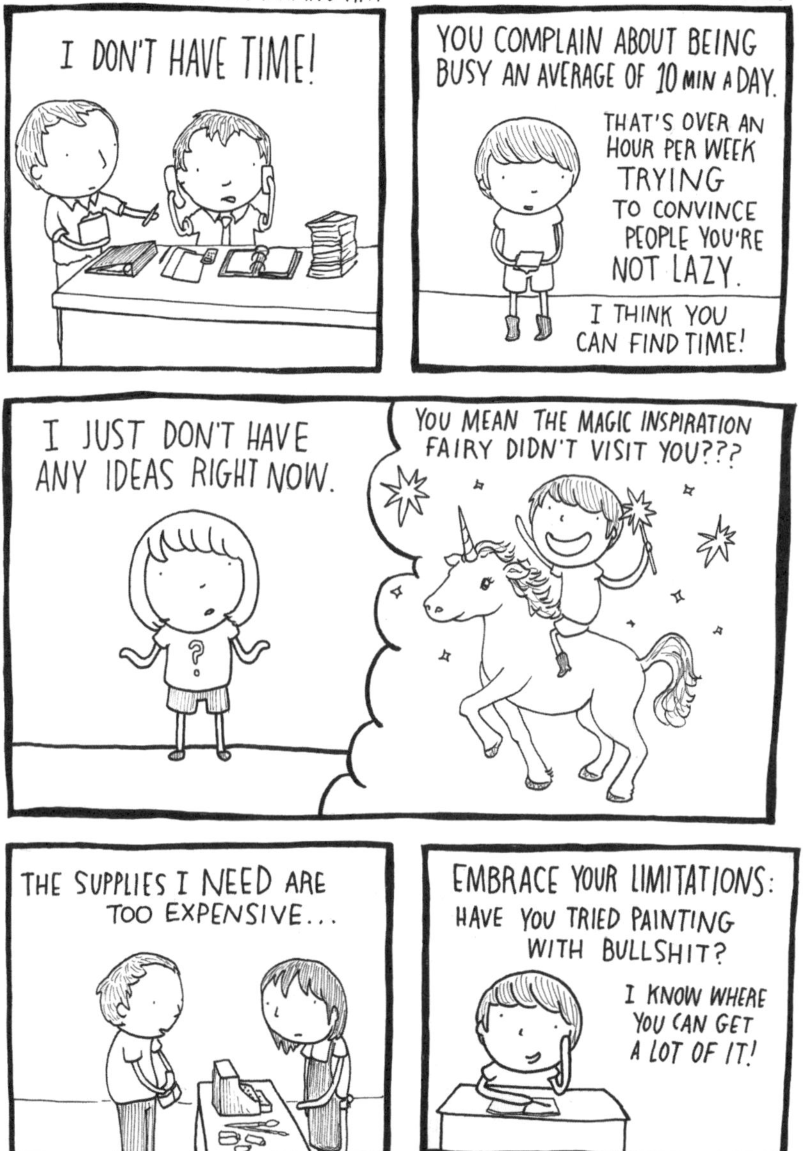
I DON'T HAVE TIME!
YOU COMPLAIN ABOUT BEING BUSY AN AVERAGE OF 10 MIN A DAY.
THAT'S OVER AN HOUR PER WEEK TRYING TO CONVINCE PEOPLE YOU'RE NOT LAZY.
I THINK YOU CAN FIND TIME!
I JUST DON'T HAVE ANY IDEAS RIGHT NOW.
YOU MEAN THE MAGIC INSPIRATION FAIRY DIDN'T VISIT YOU???
THE SUPPLIES I NEED ARE TOO EXPENSIVE...
EMBRACE YOUR LIMITATIONS: HAVE YOU TRIED PAINTING WITH BULLSHIT?
I KNOW WHERE YOU CAN GET A LOT OF IT!

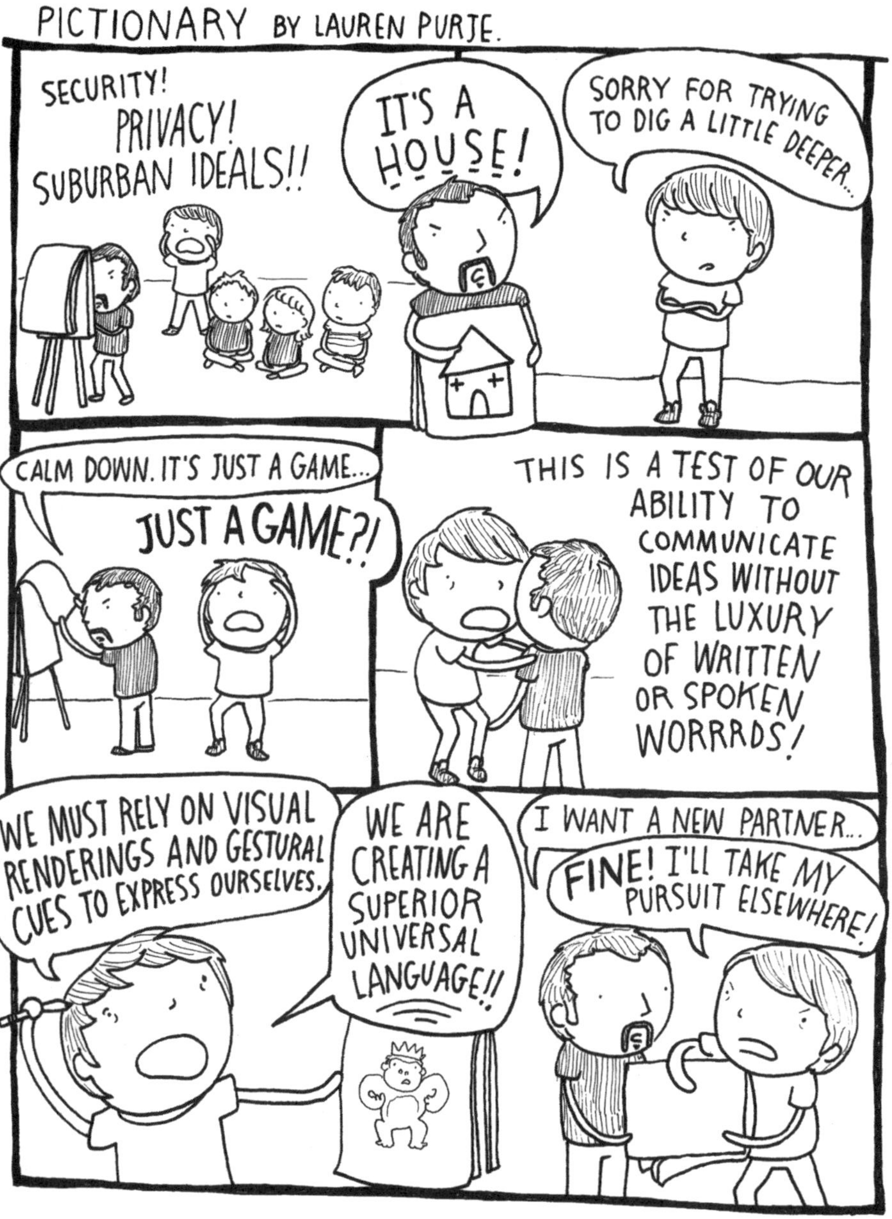
PICTIONARY BY LAUREN PURJE.
SECURITY! PRIVACY! SUBURBAN IDEALS!!
IT'S A HOUSE!
SORRY FOR TRYING TO DIG A LITTLE DEEPER...
CALM DOWN. IT'S JUST A GAME...
JUST A GAME?!
THIS IS A TEST OF OUR ABILITY TO COMMUNICATE IDEAS WITHOUT THE LUXURY OF WRITTEN OR SPOKEN WORRRDS!
WE MUST RELY ON VISUAL RENDERINGS AND GESTURAL CUES TO EXPRESS OURSELVES.
WE ARE CREATING A SUPERIOR UNIVERSAL LANGUAGE!!
I WANT A NEW PARTNER...
FINE! I'LL TAKE MY PURSUIT ELSEWHERE!

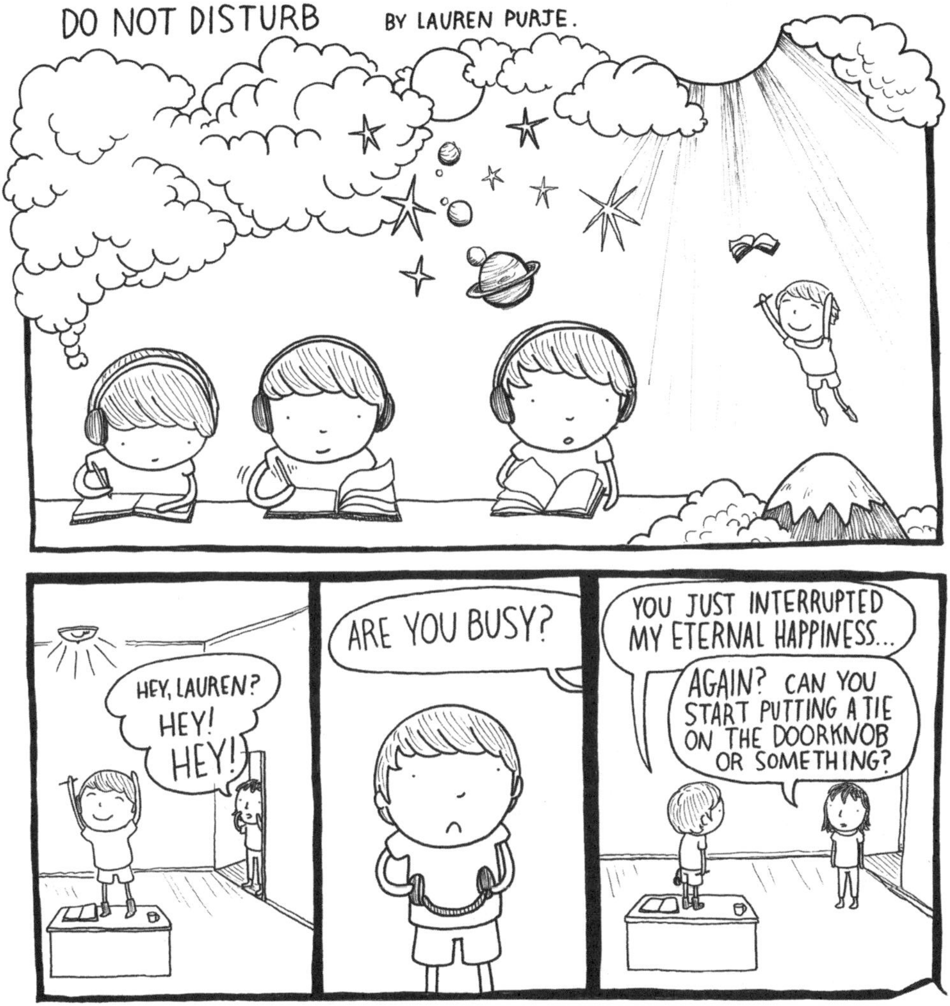
DO NOT DISTURB BY LAUREN PURJE.
HEY, LAUREN? HEY! HEY!
ARE YOU BUSY?
YOU JUST INTERRUPTED MY ETERNAL HAPPINESS...
AGAIN? CAN YOU START PUTTING A TIE ON THE DOORKNOB OR SOMETHING?

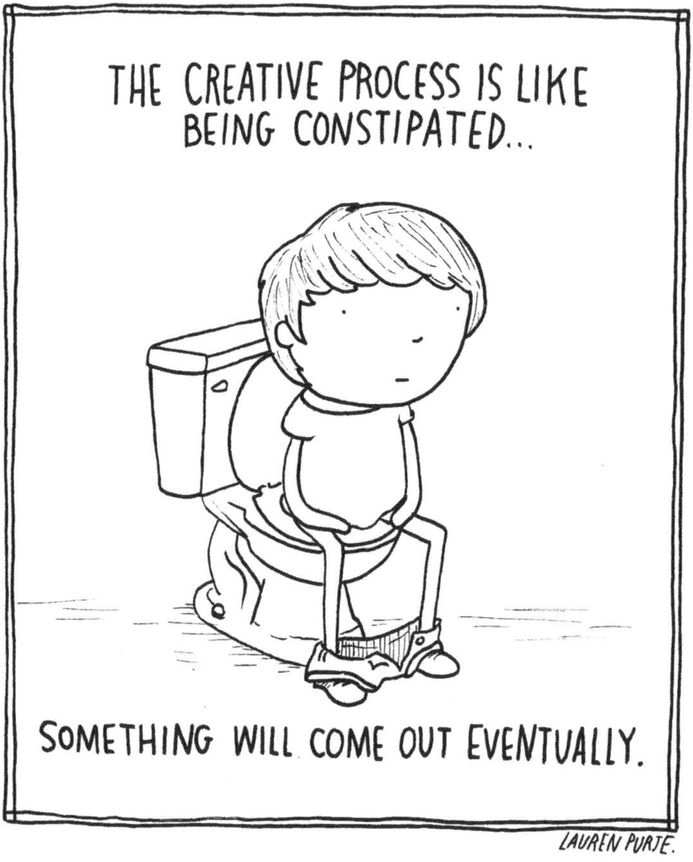
THE CREATIVE PROCESS IS LIKE BEING CONSTIPATED...
SOMETHING WILL COME OUT EVENTUALLY.
LAUREN PURJE.

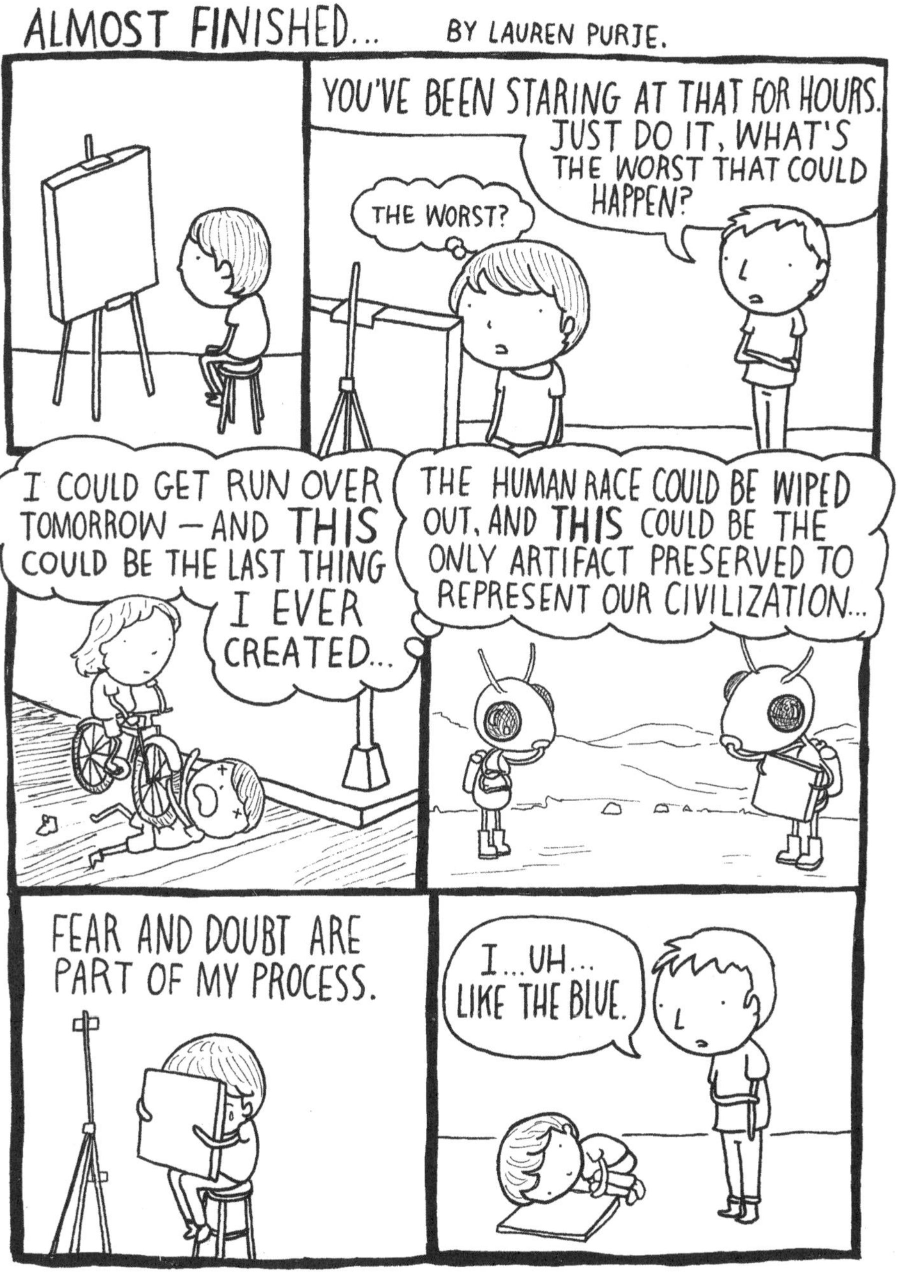
ALMOST FINISHED...
BY LAUREN PURJE.
YOU'VE BEEN STARING AT THAT FOR HOURS.
JUST DO IT, WHAT'S THE WORST THAT COULD HAPPEN?
THE WORST?
I COULD GET RUN OVER TOMORROW — AND THIS COULD BE THE LAST THING I EVER CREATED...
THE HUMAN RACE COULD BE WIPED OUT, AND THIS COULD BE THE ONLY ARTIFACT PRESERVED TO REPRESENT OUR CIVILIZATION...
FEAR AND DOUBT ARE PART OF MY PROCESS.
I...UH... LIKE THE BLUE.

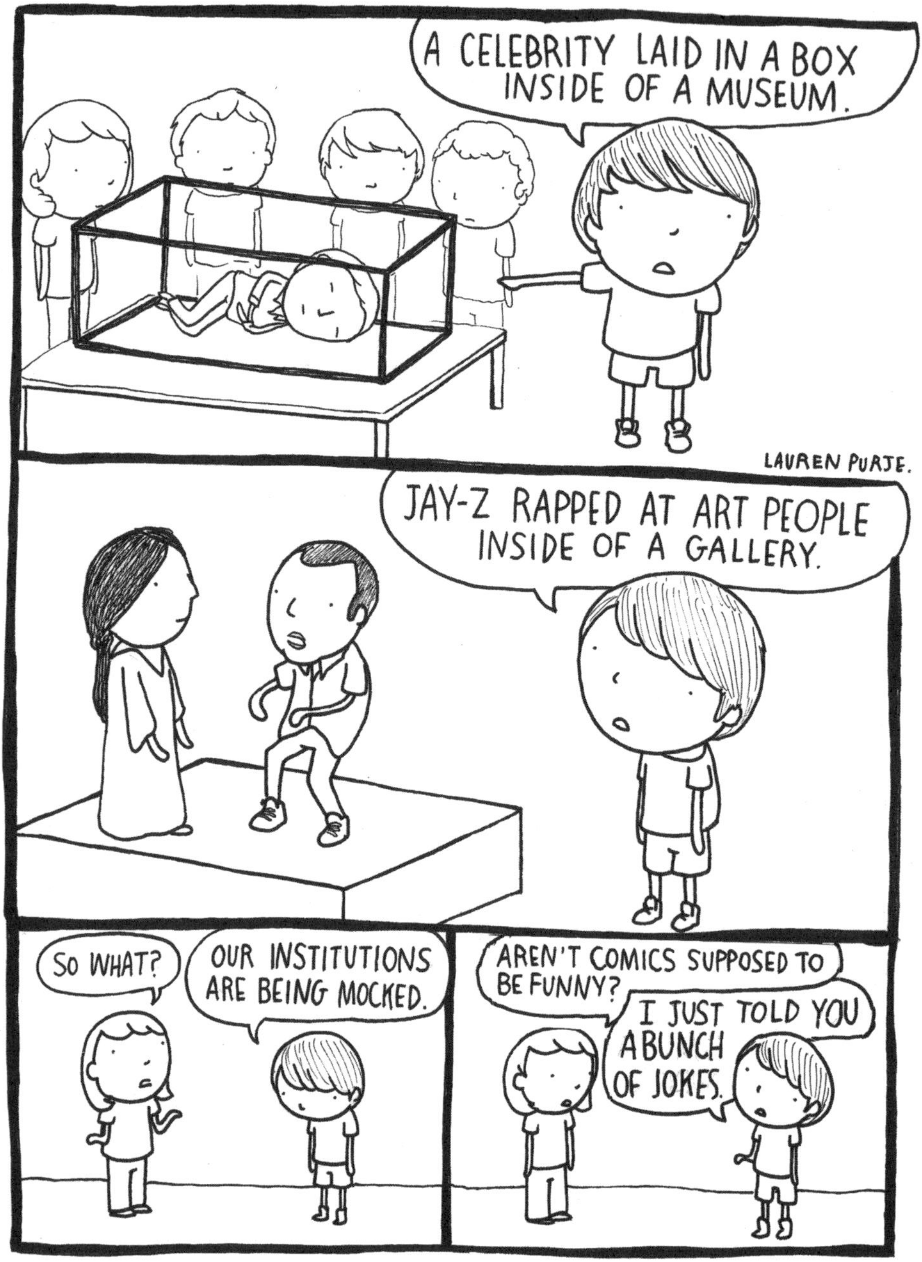
A CELEBRITY LAID IN A BOX INSIDE OF A MUSEUM.
LAUREN PURJE.
JAY-Z RAPPED AT ART PEOPLE INSIDE OF A GALLERY.
SO WHAT?
OUR INSTITUTIONS ARE BEING MOCKED.
AREN'T COMICS SUPPOSED TO BE FUNNY?
I JUST TOLD YOU A BUNCH OF JOKES.

HONORING THOSE WHO CAME BEFORE... BY LAUREN PURJE.

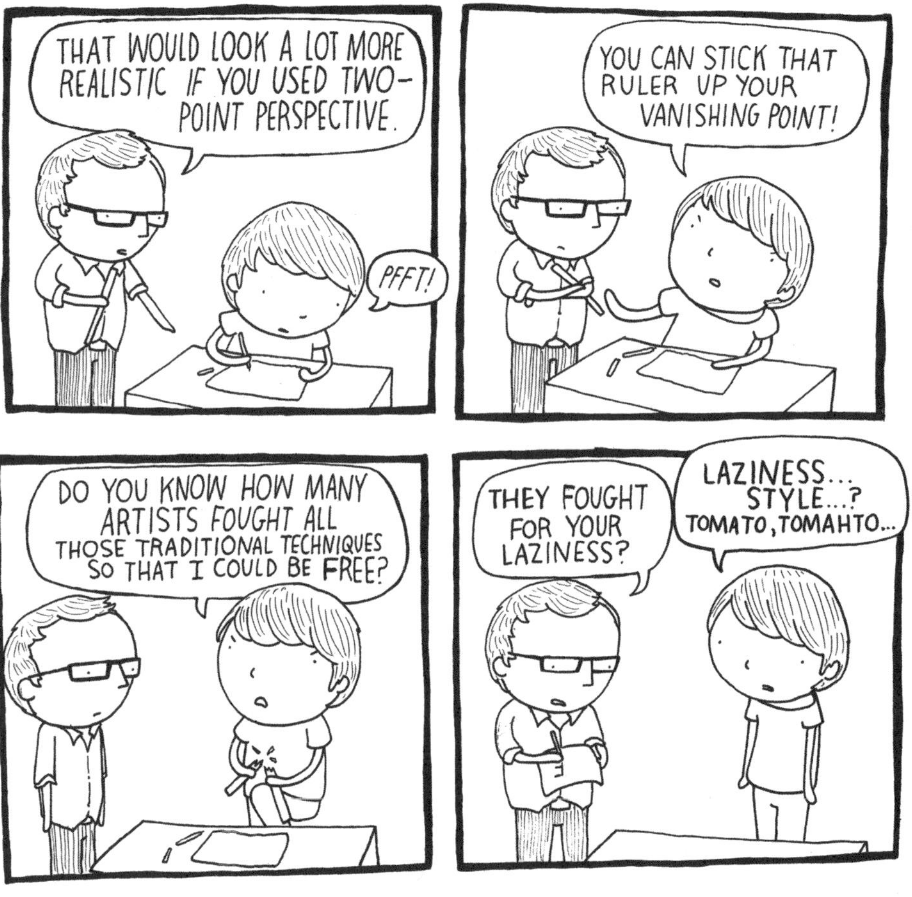
THAT WOULD LOOK A LOT MORE REALISTIC IF YOU USED TWO-POINT PERSPECTIVE.
PFFT!
YOU CAN STICK THAT RULER UP YOUR VANISHING POINT!
DO YOU KNOW HOW MANY ARTISTS FOUGHT ALL THOSE TRADITIONAL TECHNIQUES SO THAT I COULD BE FREE?
THEY FOUGHT FOR YOUR LAZINESS?
LAZINESS... STYLE...? TOMATO, TOMAHTO...

RITUALS OF SELF-TORTURE

BY LAUREN PURJE.

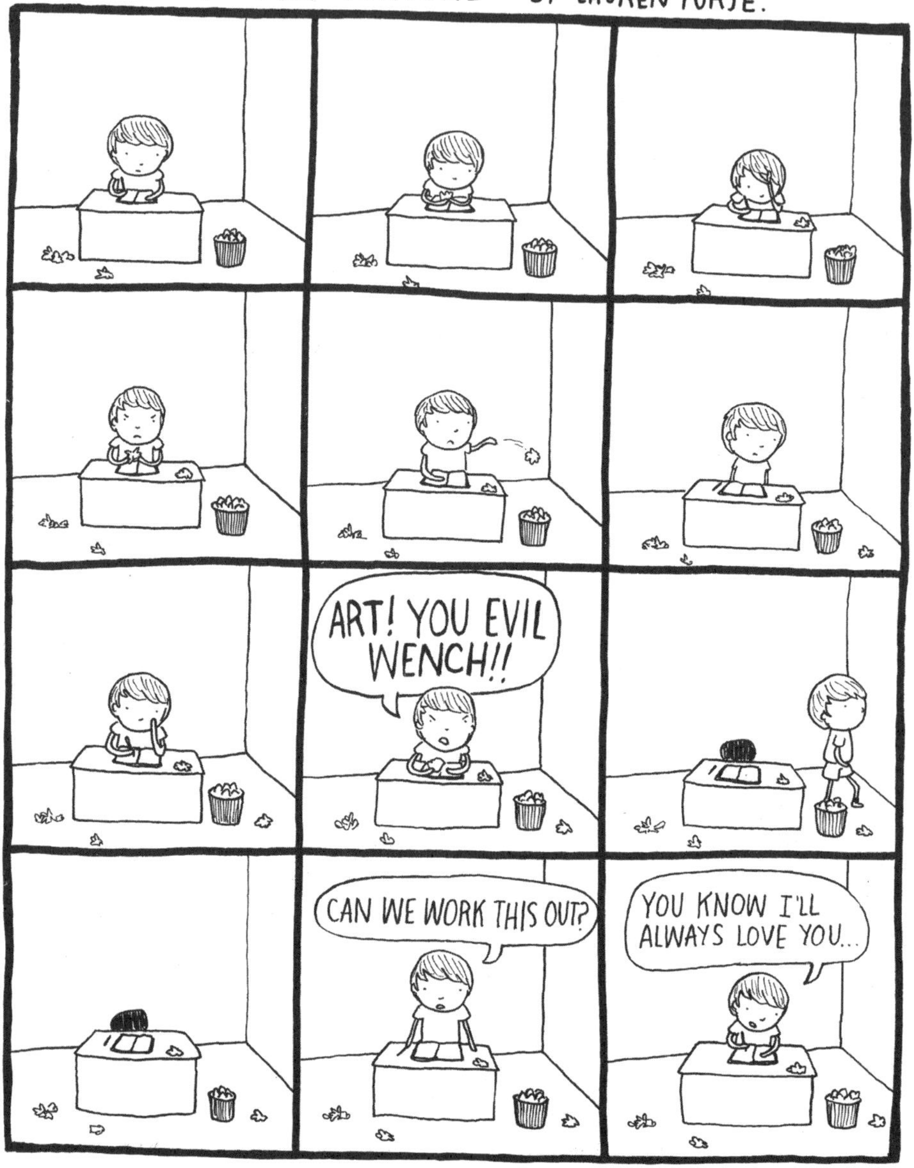

ART! YOU EVIL WENCH!!
CAN WE WORK THIS OUT?
YOU KNOW I'LL ALWAYS LOVE YOU...

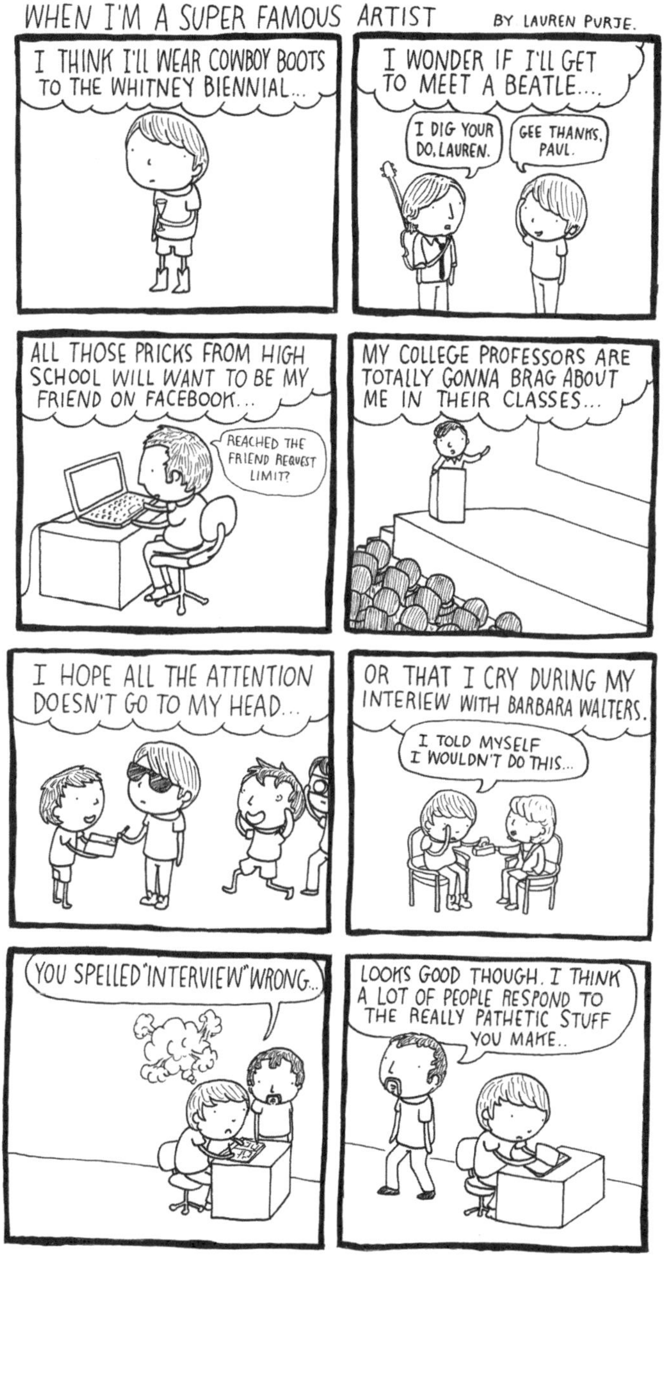
WHEN I'M A SUPER FAMOUS ARTIST
BY LAUREN PURJE.
I THINK I'LL WEAR COWBOY BOOTS TO THE WHITNEY BIENNIAL...
I WONDER IF I'LL GET TO MEET A BEATLE....
I DIG YOUR DO, LAUREN.
GEE THANKS, PAUL.
ALL THOSE PRICKS FROM HIGH SCHOOL WILL WANT TO BE MY FRIEND ON FACEBOOK...
REACHED THE FRIEND REQUEST LIMIT?
MY COLLEGE PROFESSORS ARE TOTALLY GONNA BRAG ABOUT ME IN THEIR CLASSES...
I HOPE ALL THE ATTENTION DOESN'T GO TO MY HEAD...
OR THAT I CRY DURING MY INTERIEW WITH BARBARA WALTERS.
I TOLD MYSELF I WOULDN'T DO THIS...
YOU SPELLED "INTERVIEW" WRONG..
LOOKS GOOD THOUGH. I THINK A LOT OF PEOPLE RESPOND TO THE REALLY PATHETIC STUFF YOU MAKE..

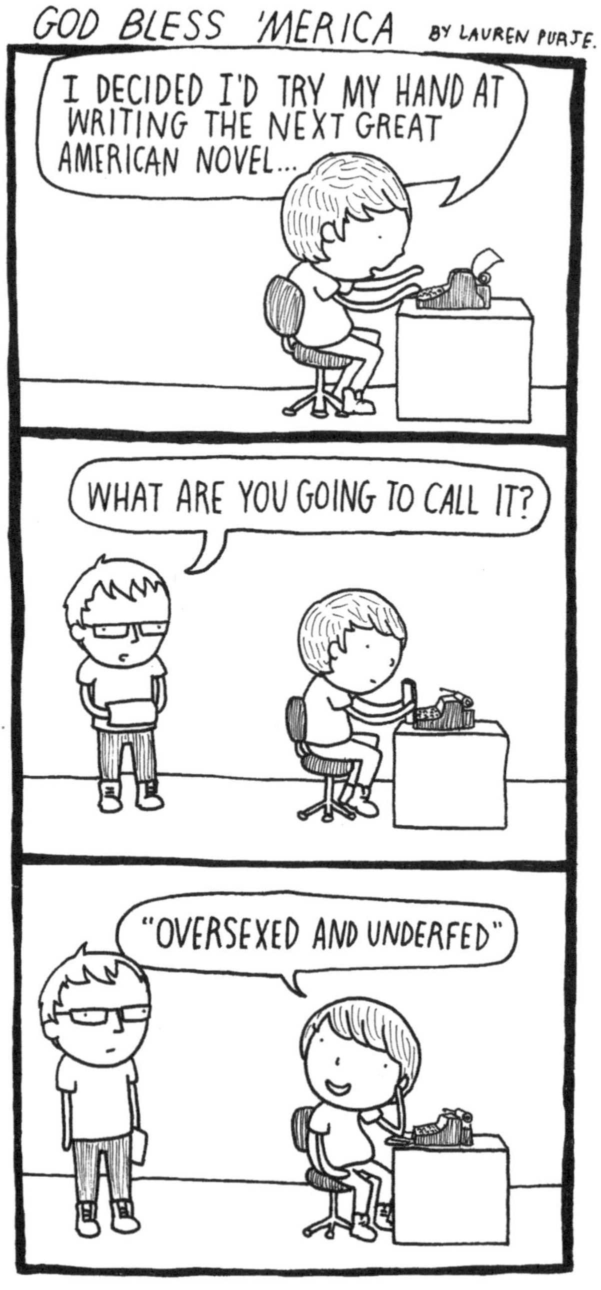
GOD BLESS 'MERICA
BY LAUREN PURJE.
I DECIDED I'D TRY MY HAND AT WRITING THE NEXT GREAT AMERICAN NOVEL...
WHAT ARE YOU GOING TO CALL IT?
"OVERSEXED AND UNDERFED"

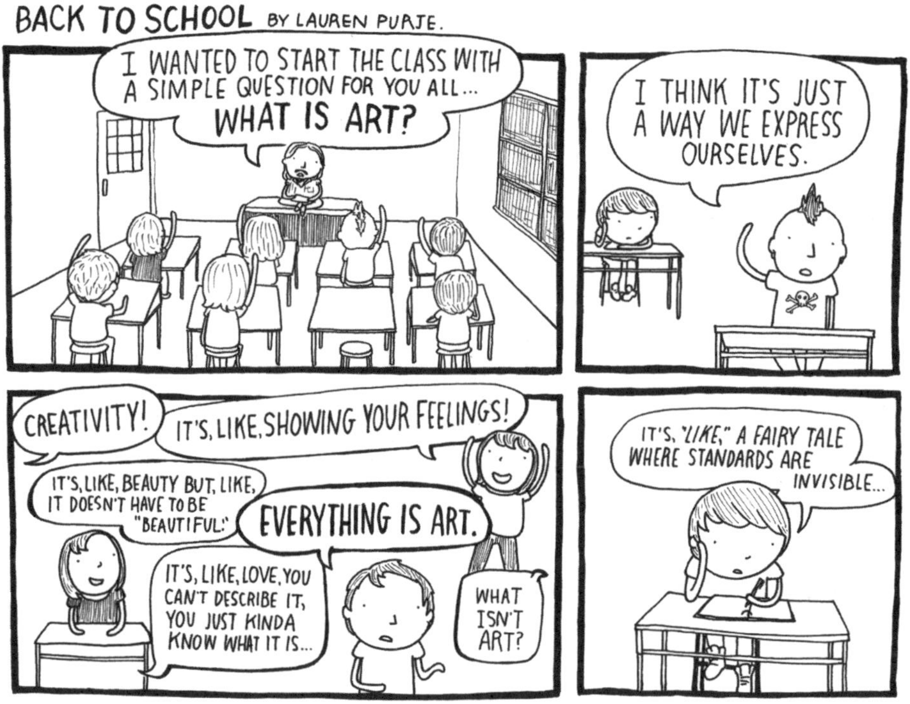
BACK TO SCHOOL BY LAUREN PURJE.
I WANTED TO START THE CLASS WITH A SIMPLE QUESTION FOR YOU ALL... WHAT IS ART?
I THINK IT'S JUST A WAY WE EXPRESS OURSELVES.
CREATIVITY!
IT'S, LIKE, SHOWING YOUR FEELINGS!
IT'S, LIKE, BEAUTY BUT, LIKE, IT DOESN'T HAVE TO BE "BEAUTIFUL."
EVERYTHING IS ART.
IT'S, LIKE, LOVE, YOU CAN'T DESCRIBE IT, YOU JUST KINDA KNOW WHAT IT IS...
WHAT ISN'T ART?
IT'S, "LIKE," A FAIRY TALE WHERE STANDARDS ARE INVISIBLE...

THANK YOU, YOU'RE UNWELCOME ✧ LAUREN PURJE ✧

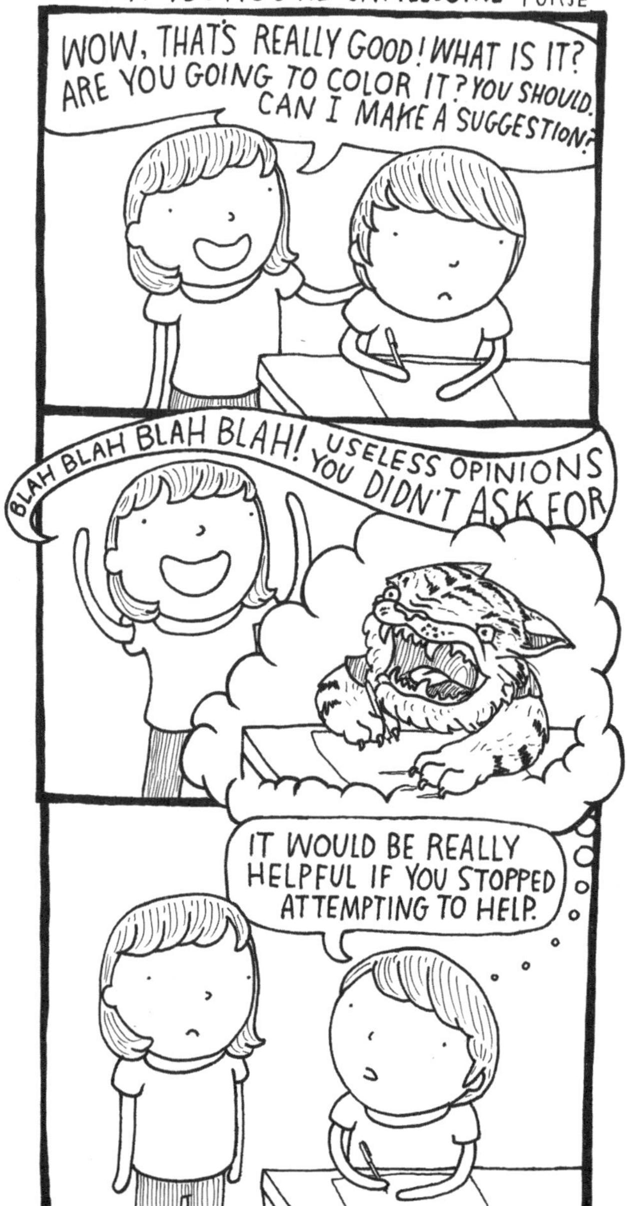
WOW, THAT'S REALLY GOOD! WHAT IS IT? ARE YOU GOING TO COLOR IT? YOU SHOULD. CAN I MAKE A SUGGESTION?
BLAH BLAH BLAH BLAH! USELESS OPINIONS YOU DIDN'T ASK FOR
IT WOULD BE REALLY HELPFUL IF YOU STOPPED ATTEMPTING TO HELP.

NOTHING IS SACRED...

BY LAUREN PURJE.

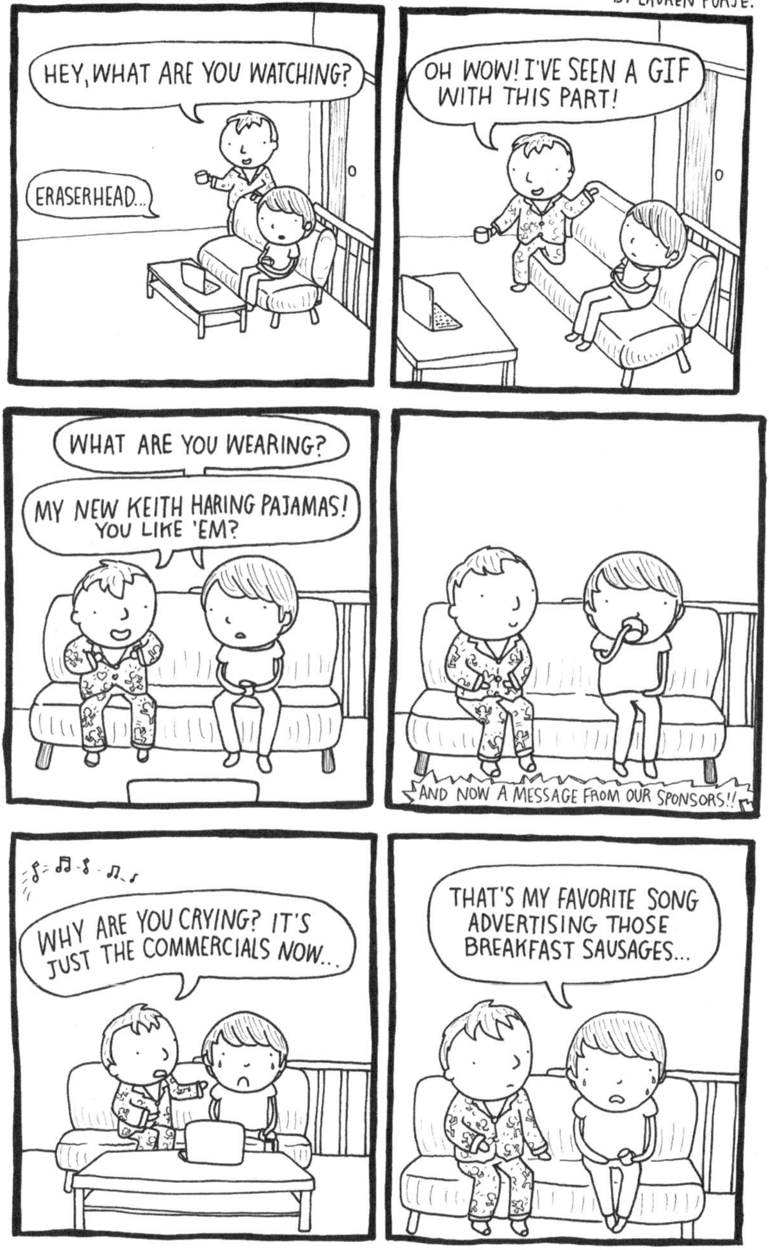
HEY, WHAT ARE YOU WATCHING?
ERASERHEAD...
OH WOW! I'VE SEEN A GIF WITH THIS PART!
WHAT ARE YOU WEARING?
MY NEW KEITH HARING PAJAMAS! YOU LIKE 'EM?
AND NOW A MESSAGE FROM OUR SPONSORS!!
WHY ARE YOU CRYING? IT'S JUST THE COMMERCIALS NOW...
THAT'S MY FAVORITE SONG ADVERTISING THOSE BREAKFAST SAUSAGES...

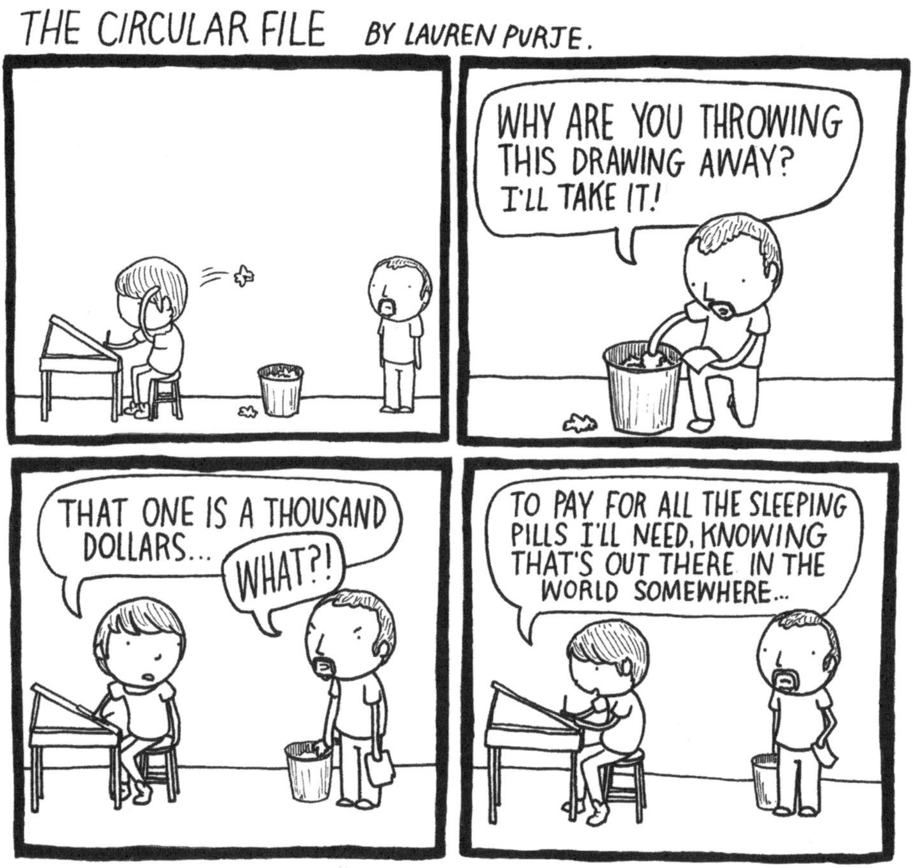
THE CIRCULAR FILE BY LAUREN PURJE.
WHY ARE YOU THROWING THIS DRAWING AWAY? I'LL TAKE IT!
THAT ONE IS A THOUSAND DOLLARS...
WHAT?!
TO PAY FOR ALL THE SLEEPING PILLS I'LL NEED, KNOWING THAT'S OUT THERE IN THE WORLD SOMEWHERE...

DEADLINES BY LAUREN PURJE.

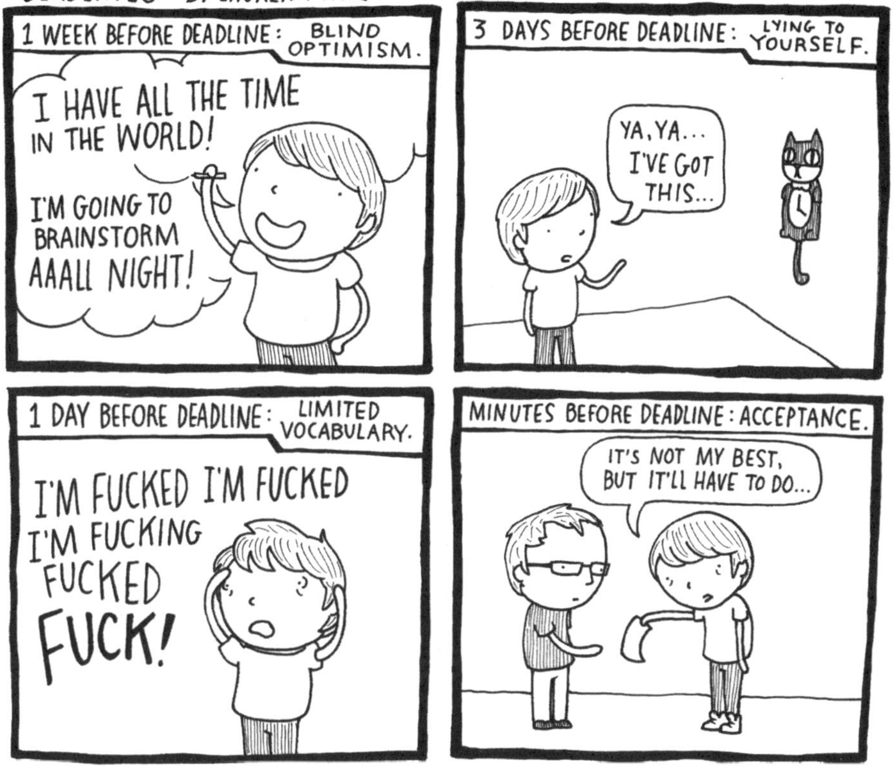

1 WEEK BEFORE DEADLINE: BLIND OPTIMISM.
I HAVE ALL THE TIME IN THE WORLD!
I'M GOING TO BRAINSTORM AAALL NIGHT!
3 DAYS BEFORE DEADLINE: LYING TO YOURSELF.
YA, YA... I'VE GOT THIS...
1 DAY BEFORE DEADLINE: LIMITED VOCABULARY.
I'M FUCKED I'M FUCKED I'M FUCKING FUCKED FUCK!
MINUTES BEFORE DEADLINE: ACCEPTANCE.
IT'S NOT MY BEST, BUT IT'LL HAVE TO DO...

SELF-PROMOTION

BY LAUREN PURJE.

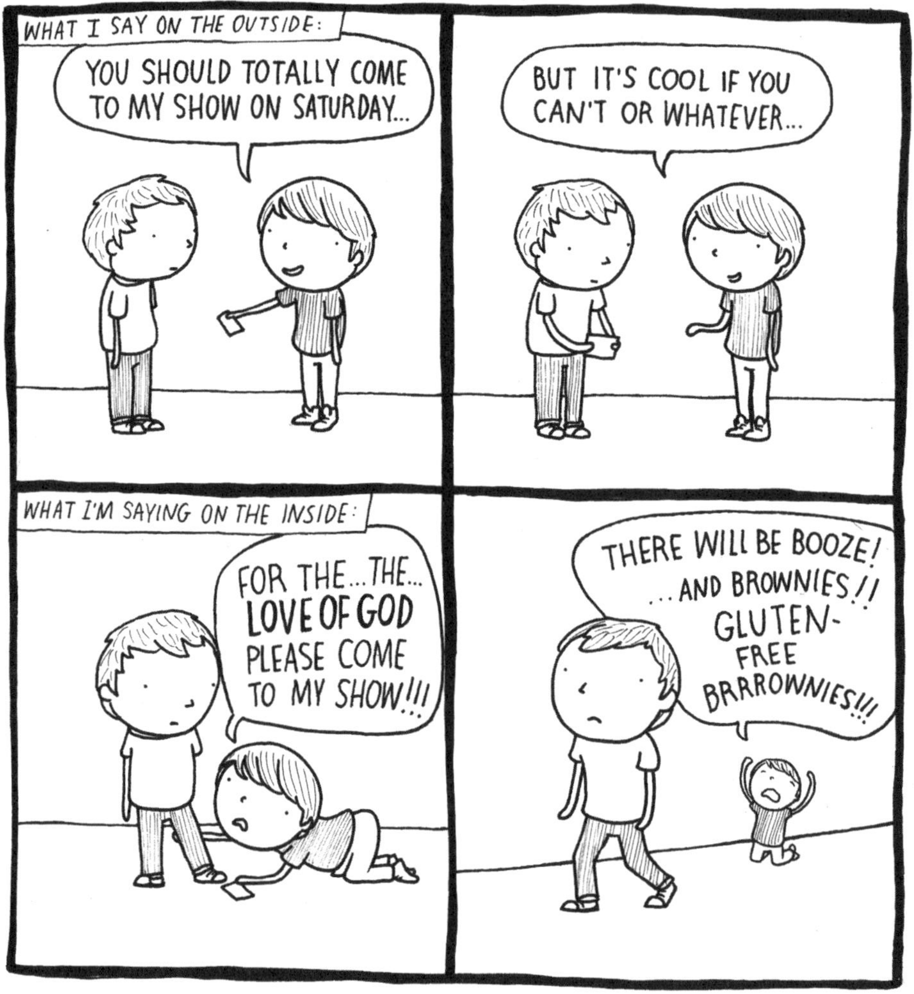
WHAT I SAY ON THE OUTSIDE:
YOU SHOULD TOTALLY COME TO MY SHOW ON SATURDAY...
BUT IT'S COOL IF YOU CAN'T OR WHATEVER...
WHAT I'M SAYING ON THE INSIDE:
FOR THE...THE... LOVE OF GOD PLEASE COME TO MY SHOW!!!
THERE WILL BE BOOZE! ...AND BROWNIES!! GLUTEN-FREE BRRROWNIES!!!

EXPECTATIONS BY LAUREN PURJE.

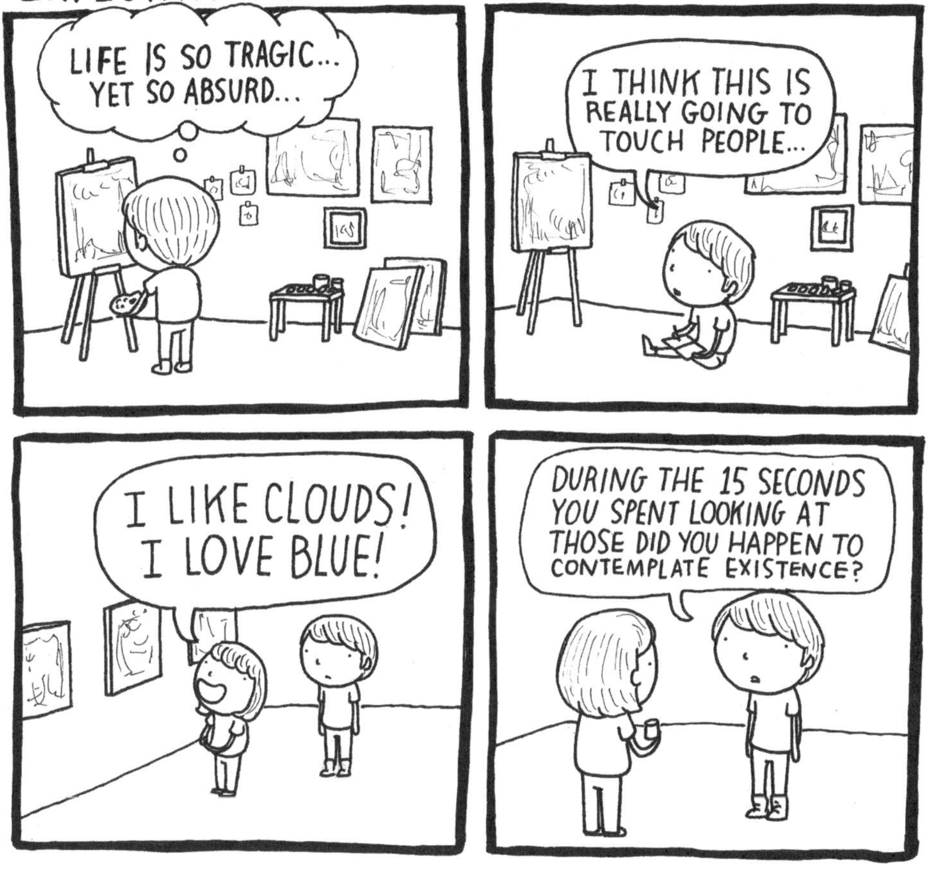

LIFE IS SO TRAGIC... YET SO ABSURD...
I THINK THIS IS REALLY GOING TO TOUCH PEOPLE...
I LIKE CLOUDS! I LOVE BLUE!
DURING THE 15 SECONDS YOU SPENT LOOKING AT THOSE DID YOU HAPPEN TO CONTEMPLATE EXISTENCE?

BY LAUREN PURJE.

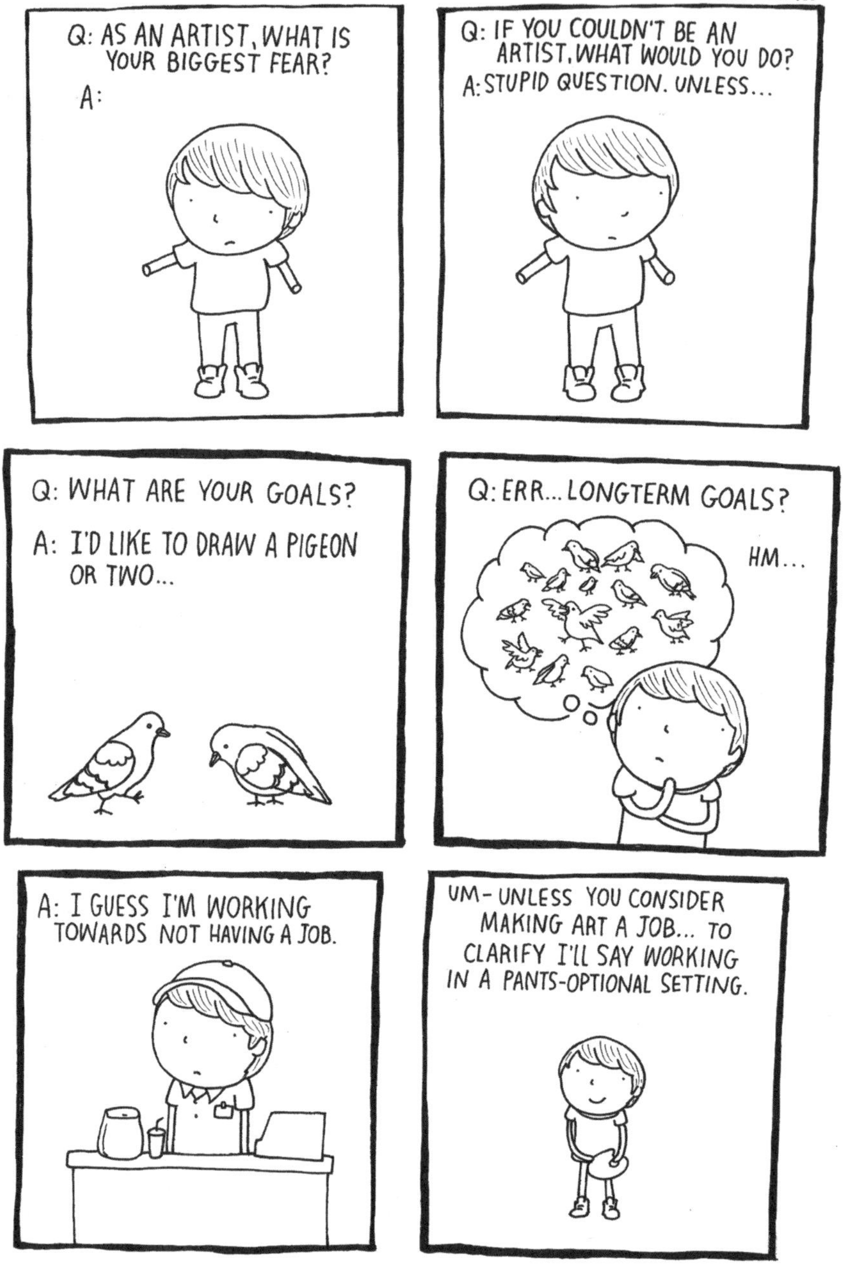
Q: AS AN ARTIST, WHAT IS YOUR BIGGEST FEAR?
A:
Q: IF YOU COULDN'T BE AN ARTIST, WHAT WOULD YOU DO?
A: STUPID QUESTION. UNLESS...
Q: WHAT ARE YOUR GOALS?
A: I'D LIKE TO DRAW A PIGEON OR TWO...
Q: ERR... LONGTERM GOALS?
HM...
A: I GUESS I'M WORKING TOWARDS NOT HAVING A JOB.
UM- UNLESS YOU CONSIDER MAKING ART A JOB... TO CLARIFY I'LL SAY WORKING IN A PANTS-OPTIONAL SETTING.

THE UNLEARNING PROCESS

BY LAUREN PURJE.

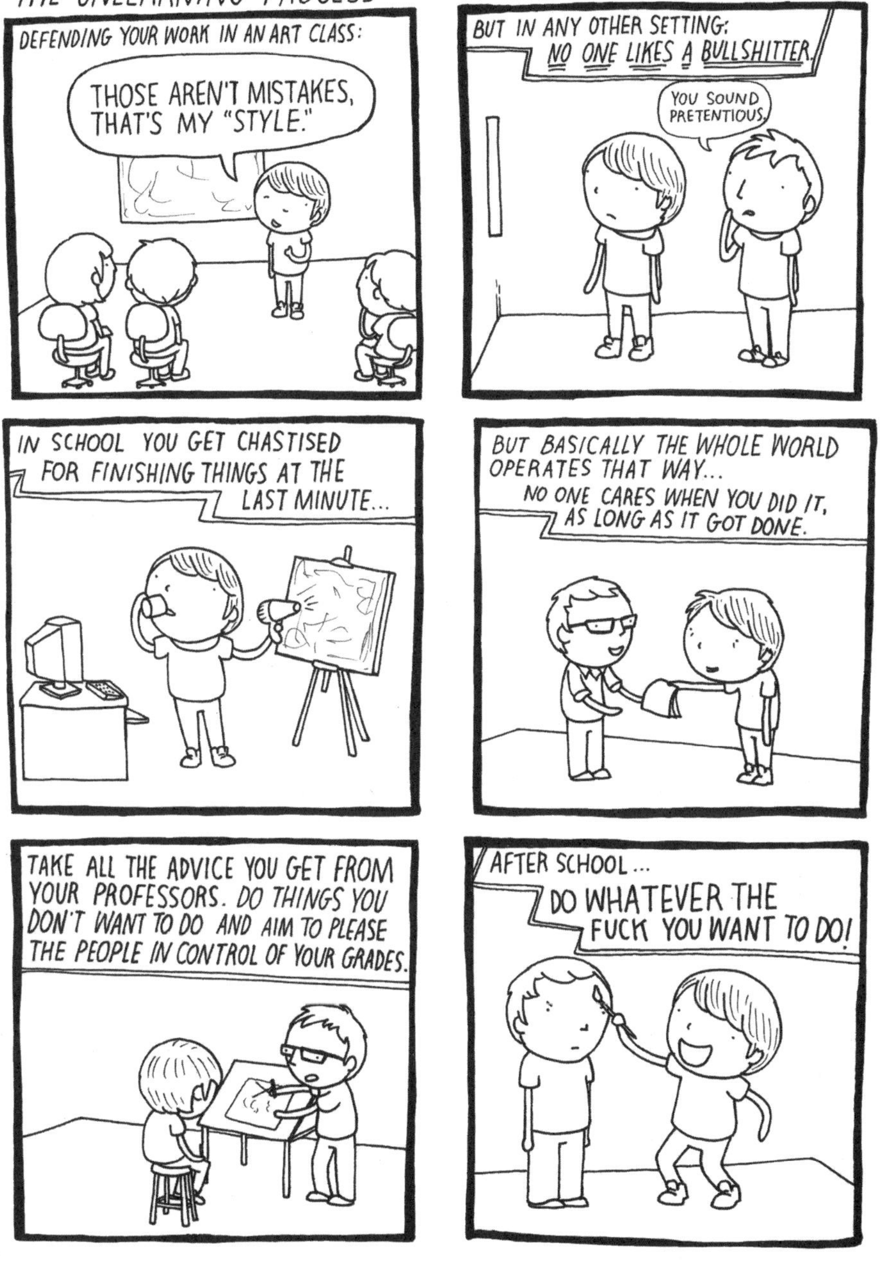

DEFENDING YOUR WORK IN AN ART CLASS:
THOSE AREN'T MISTAKES, THAT'S MY "STYLE."
BUT IN ANY OTHER SETTING: NO ONE LIKES A BULLSHITTER.
YOU SOUND PRETENTIOUS.
IN SCHOOL YOU GET CHASTISED FOR FINISHING THINGS AT THE LAST MINUTE...
BUT BASICALLY THE WHOLE WORLD OPERATES THAT WAY... NO ONE CARES WHEN YOU DID IT, AS LONG AS IT GOT DONE.
TAKE ALL THE ADVICE YOU GET FROM YOUR PROFESSORS. DO THINGS YOU DON'T WANT TO DO AND AIM TO PLEASE THE PEOPLE IN CONTROL OF YOUR GRADES.
AFTER SCHOOL... DO WHATEVER THE FUCK YOU WANT TO DO!

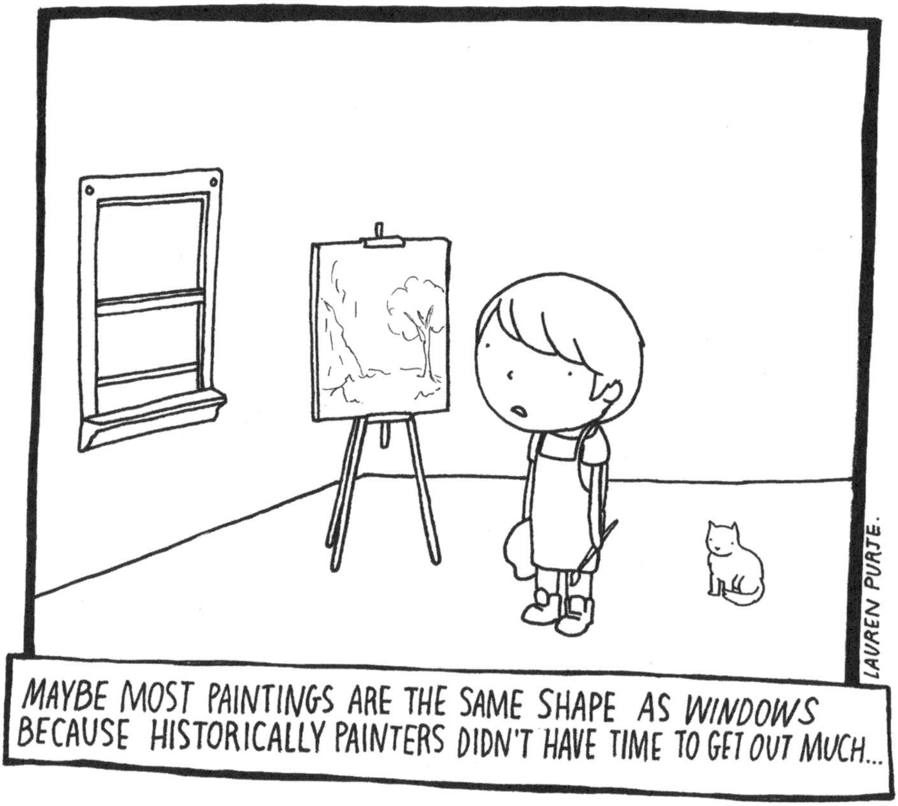
LAUREN PURJE.
MAYBE MOST PAINTINGS ARE THE SAME SHAPE AS WINDOWS BECAUSE HISTORICALLY PAINTERS DIDN'T HAVE TIME TO GET OUT MUCH...

HOW ARTISTS CAN TAKE ADVANTAGE OF HOLIDAY SPENDING

BY LAUREN PURJE.

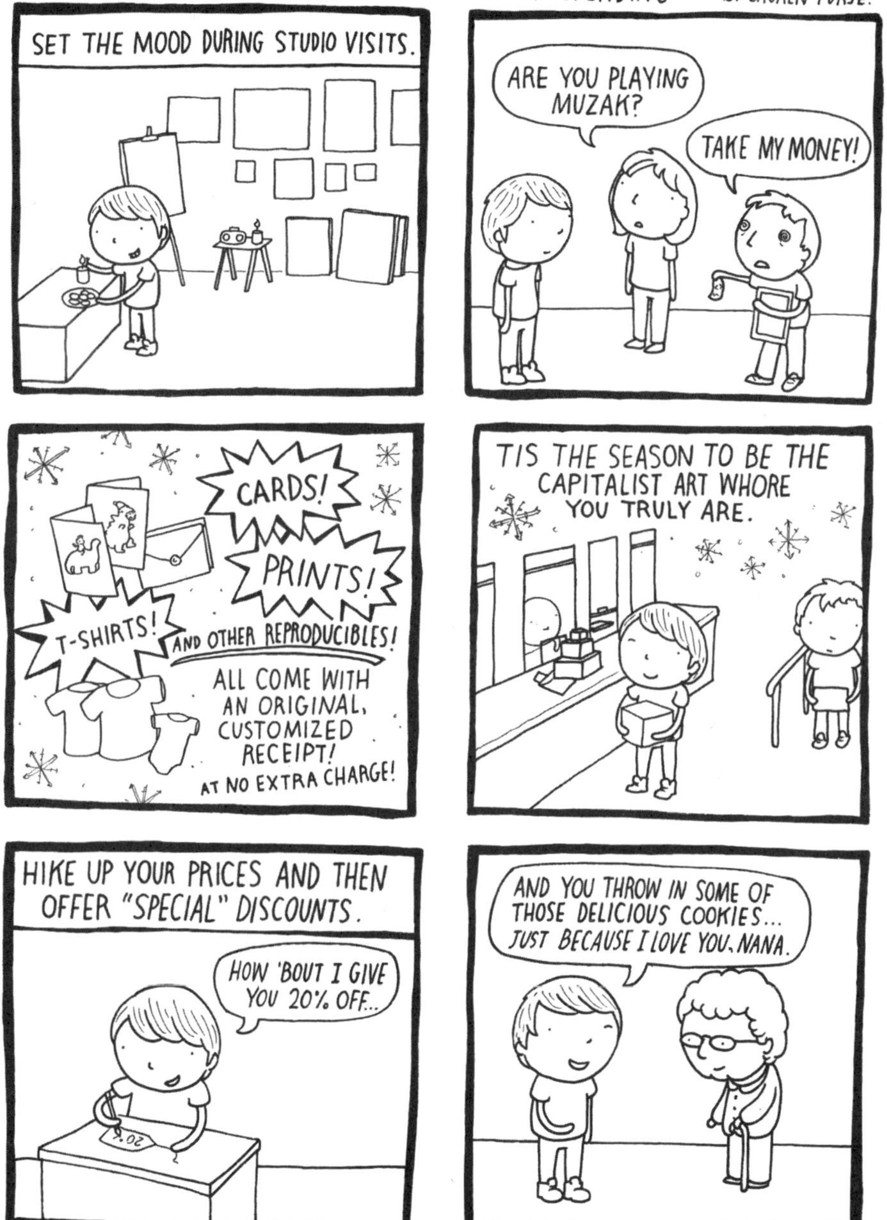
SET THE MOOD DURING STUDIO VISITS.
ARE YOU PLAYING MUZAK?
TAKE MY MONEY!
CARDS!
PRINTS!
T-SHIRTS!
AND OTHER REPRODUCIBLES!
ALL COME WITH AN ORIGINAL, CUSTOMIZED RECEIPT!
AT NO EXTRA CHARGE!
TIS THE SEASON TO BE THE CAPITALIST ART WHORE YOU TRULY ARE.
HIKE UP YOUR PRICES AND THEN OFFER "SPECIAL" DISCOUNTS.
HOW 'BOUT I GIVE YOU 20% OFF...
20%
AND YOU THROW IN SOME OF THOSE DELICIOUS COOKIES... JUST BECAUSE I LOVE YOU, NANA.

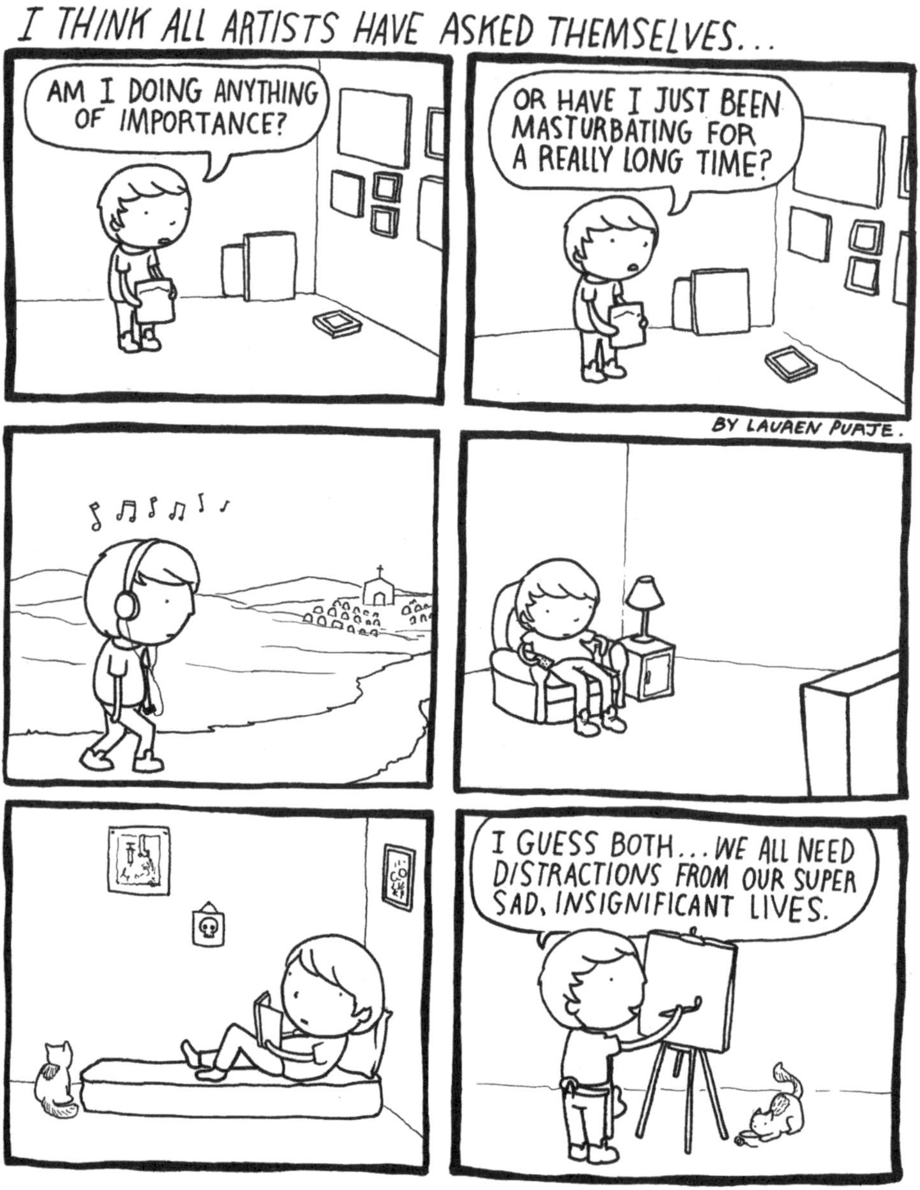
I THINK ALL ARTISTS HAVE ASKED THEMSELVES...
AM I DOING ANYTHING OF IMPORTANCE?
OR HAVE I JUST BEEN MASTURBATING FOR A REALLY LONG TIME?
BY LAUREN PURJE.
I GUESS BOTH... WE ALL NEED DISTRACTIONS FROM OUR SUPER SAD, INSIGNIFICANT LIVES.

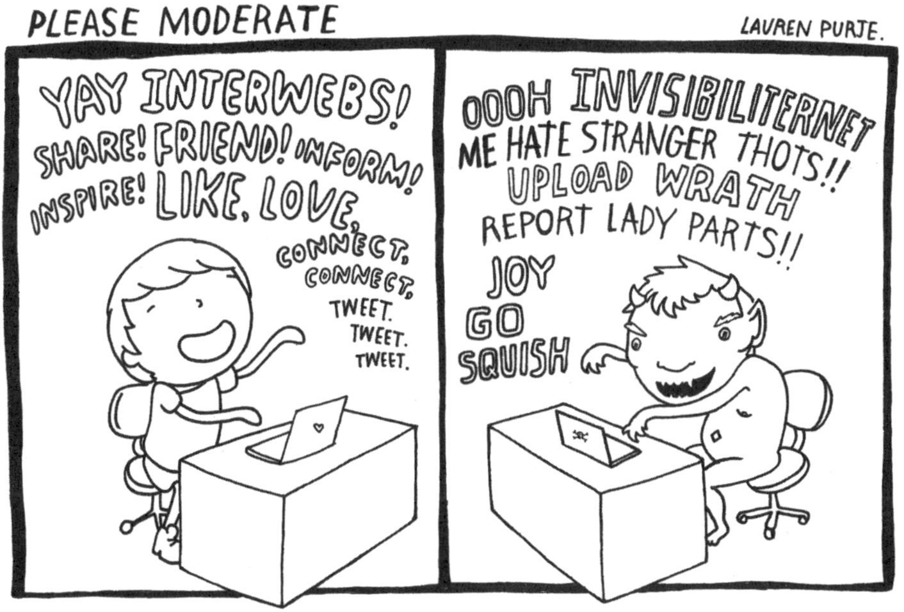
PLEASE MODERATE
LAUREN PURJE.
YAY INTERWEBS!
SHARE! FRIEND! INFORM!
INSPIRE! LIKE, LOVE,
CONNECT, CONNECT,
TWEET. TWEET. TWEET.
OOOH INVISIBILITERNET
ME HATE STRANGER THOTS!!
UPLOAD WRATH
REPORT LADY PARTS!!
JOY
GO
SQUISH

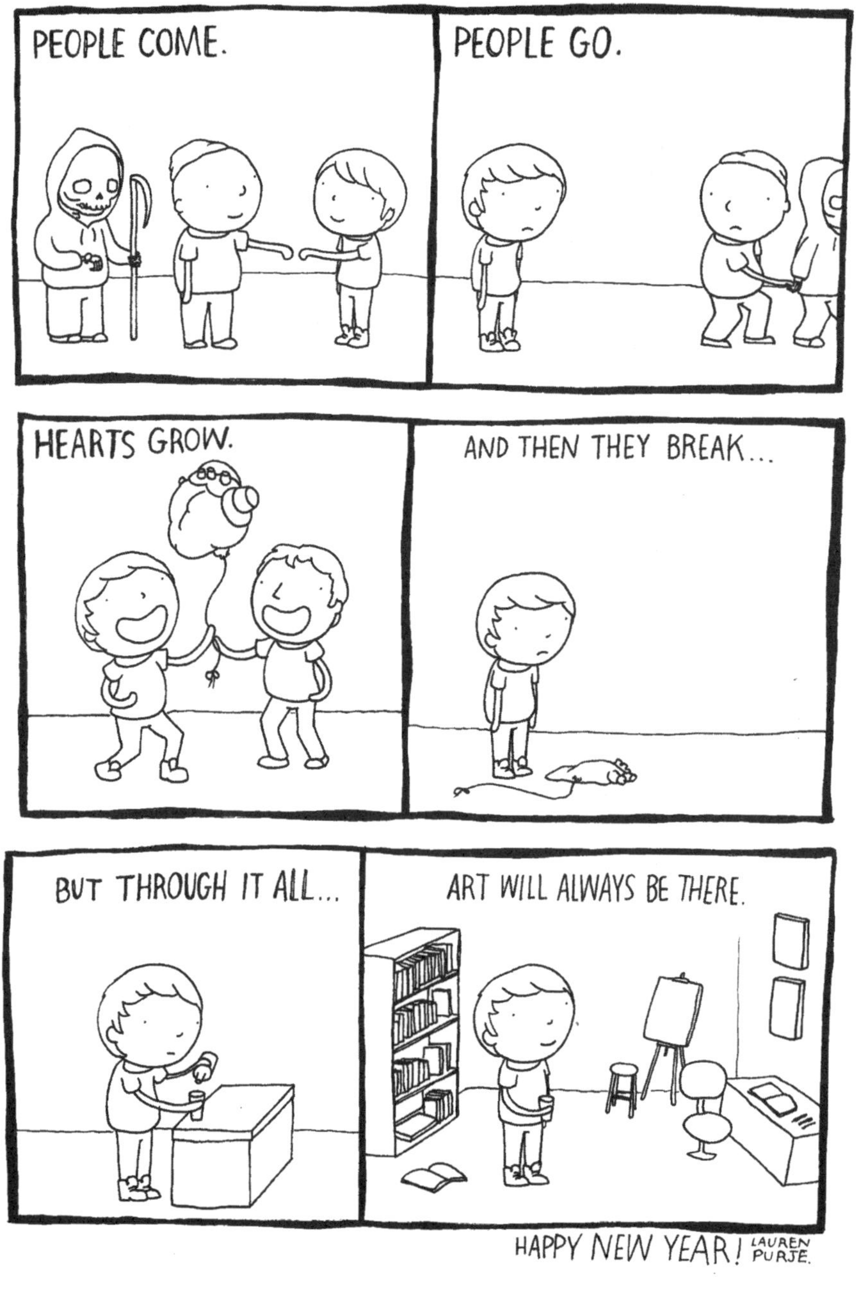
PEOPLE COME.
PEOPLE GO.
HEARTS GROW.
AND THEN THEY BREAK...
BUT THROUGH IT ALL...
ART WILL ALWAYS BE THERE.
HAPPY NEW YEAR!
LAUREN PURJE.

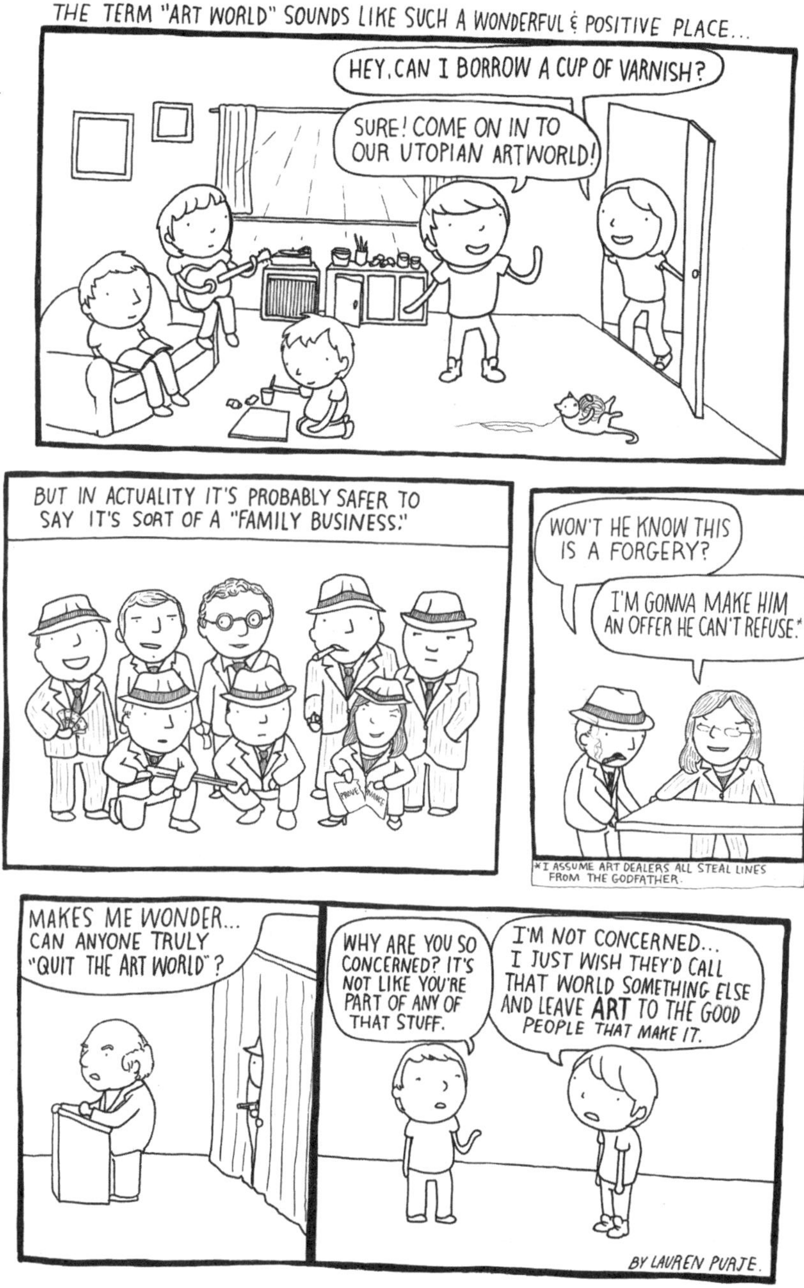
THE TERM "ART WORLD" SOUNDS LIKE SUCH A WONDERFUL & POSITIVE PLACE...
HEY, CAN I BORROW A CUP OF VARNISH?
SURE! COME ON IN TO OUR UTOPIAN ARTWORLD!
BUT IN ACTUALITY IT'S PROBABLY SAFER TO SAY IT'S SORT OF A "FAMILY BUSINESS."
WON'T HE KNOW THIS IS A FORGERY?
I'M GONNA MAKE HIM AN OFFER HE CAN'T REFUSE.*
*I ASSUME ART DEALERS ALL STEAL LINES FROM THE GODFATHER.
MAKES ME WONDER... CAN ANYONE TRULY "QUIT THE ART WORLD"?
WHY ARE YOU SO CONCERNED? IT'S NOT LIKE YOU'RE PART OF ANY OF THAT STUFF.
I'M NOT CONCERNED... I JUST WISH THEY'D CALL THAT WORLD SOMETHING ELSE AND LEAVE ART TO THE GOOD PEOPLE THAT MAKE IT.
BY LAUREN PURJE.

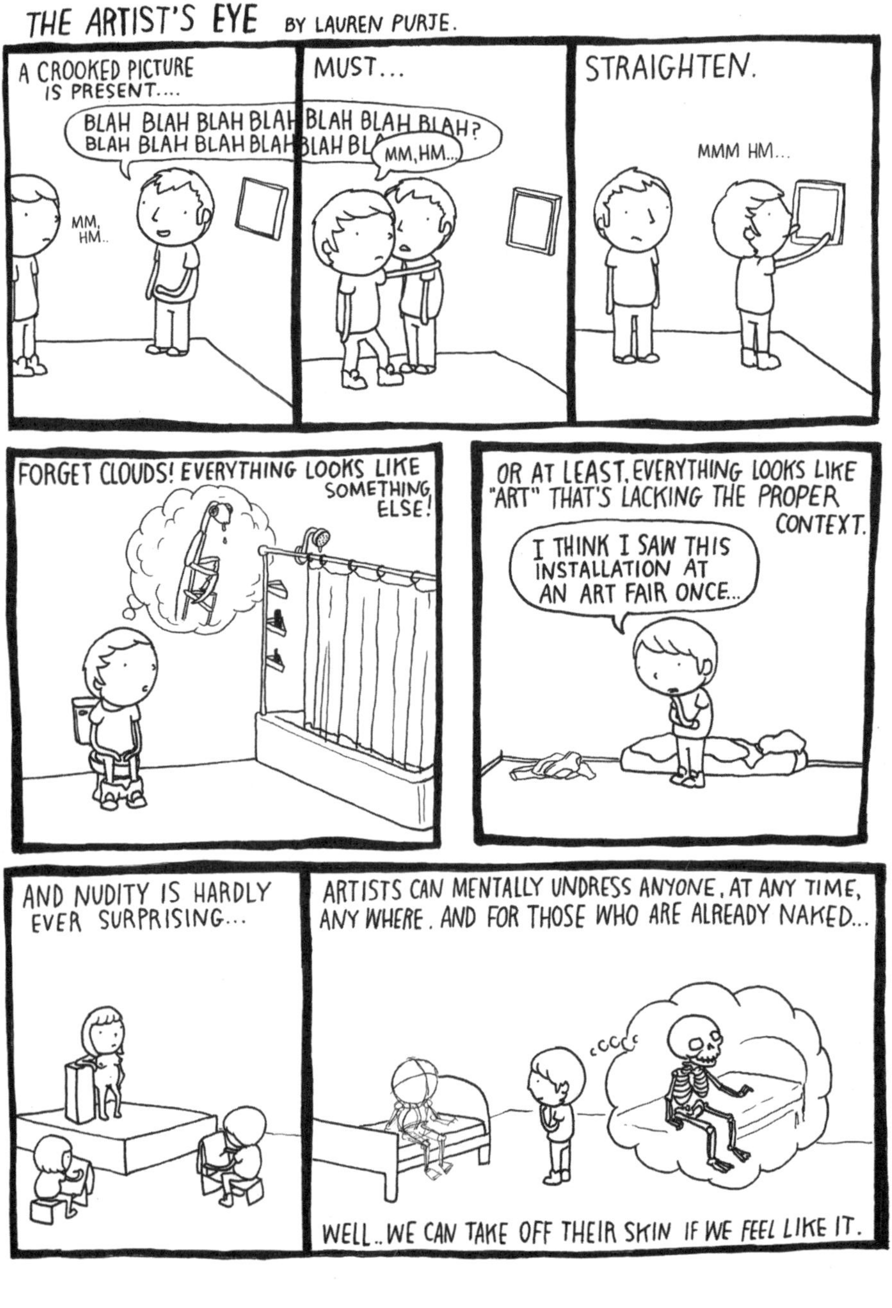
THE ARTIST'S EYE BY LAUREN PURJE.
A CROOKED PICTURE IS PRESENT....
BLAH BLAH BLAH BLAH BLAH BLAH BLAH? BLAH BLAH BLAH BLAH BLAH BL
MM, HM..
MUST...
MM, HM...
STRAIGHTEN.
MMM HM...
FORGET CLOUDS! EVERYTHING LOOKS LIKE SOMETHING ELSE!
OR AT LEAST, EVERYTHING LOOKS LIKE "ART" THAT'S LACKING THE PROPER CONTEXT.
I THINK I SAW THIS INSTALLATION AT AN ART FAIR ONCE...
AND NUDITY IS HARDLY EVER SURPRISING...
ARTISTS CAN MENTALLY UNDRESS ANYONE, AT ANY TIME, ANY WHERE. AND FOR THOSE WHO ARE ALREADY NAKED...
WELL.. WE CAN TAKE OFF THEIR SKIN IF WE FEEL LIKE IT.

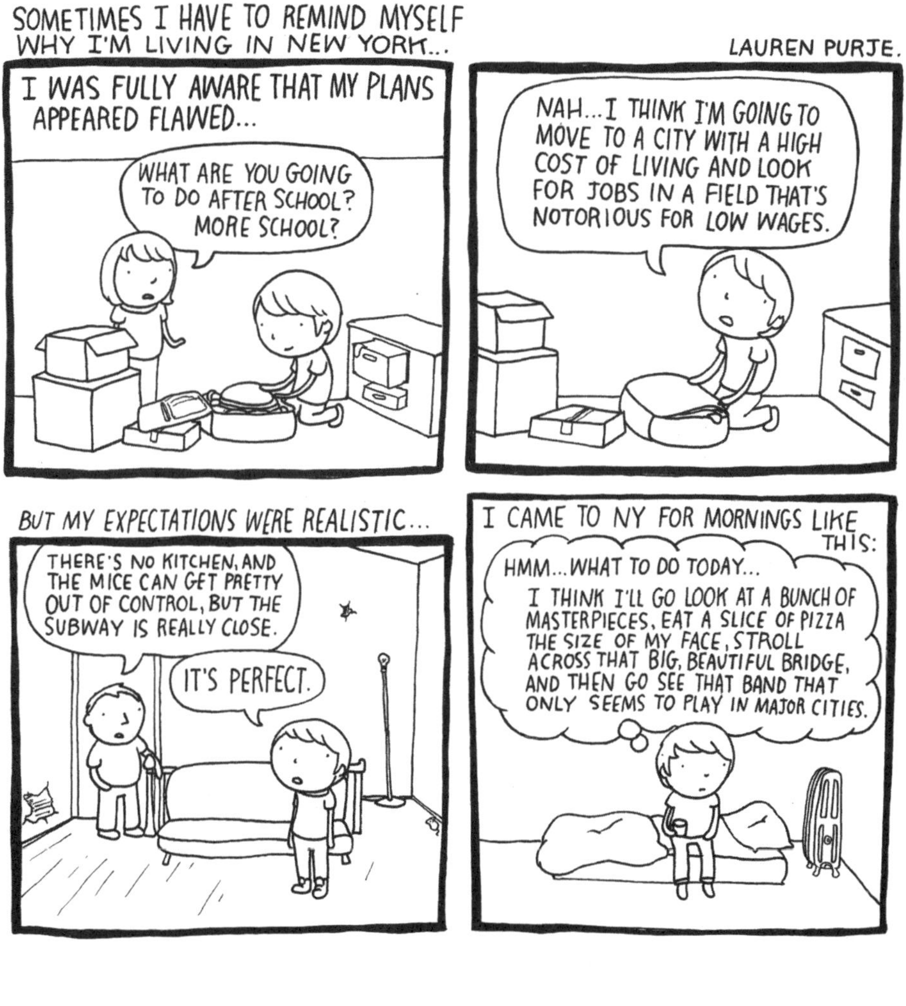
SOMETIMES I HAVE TO REMIND MYSELF WHY I'M LIVING IN NEW YORK...
LAUREN PURJE.
I WAS FULLY AWARE THAT MY PLANS APPEARED FLAWED...
WHAT ARE YOU GOING TO DO AFTER SCHOOL? MORE SCHOOL?
NAH...I THINK I'M GOING TO MOVE TO A CITY WITH A HIGH COST OF LIVING AND LOOK FOR JOBS IN A FIELD THAT'S NOTORIOUS FOR LOW WAGES.
BUT MY EXPECTATIONS WERE REALISTIC...
THERE'S NO KITCHEN, AND THE MICE CAN GET PRETTY OUT OF CONTROL, BUT THE SUBWAY IS REALLY CLOSE.
IT'S PERFECT.
I CAME TO NY FOR MORNINGS LIKE THIS:
HMM...WHAT TO DO TODAY...
I THINK I'LL GO LOOK AT A BUNCH OF MASTERPIECES, EAT A SLICE OF PIZZA THE SIZE OF MY FACE, STROLL ACROSS THAT BIG, BEAUTIFUL BRIDGE, AND THEN GO SEE THAT BAND THAT ONLY SEEMS TO PLAY IN MAJOR CITIES.

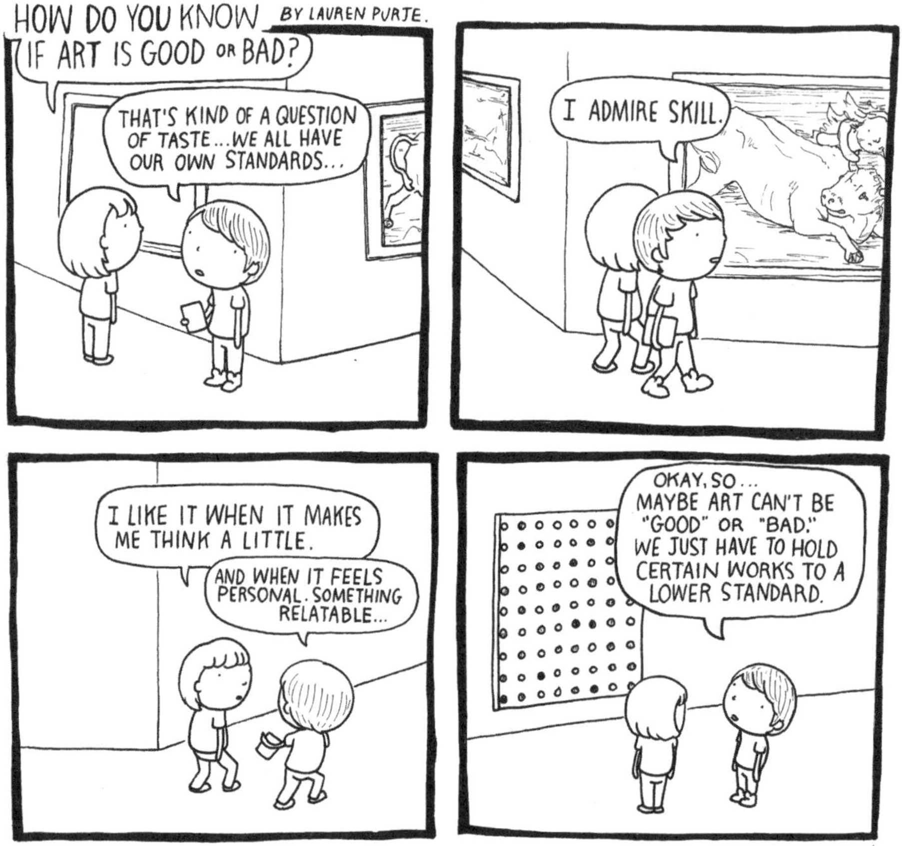
HOW DO YOU KNOW IF ART IS GOOD OR BAD?
BY LAUREN PURJE.
THAT'S KIND OF A QUESTION OF TASTE...WE ALL HAVE OUR OWN STANDARDS...
I ADMIRE SKILL.
I LIKE IT WHEN IT MAKES ME THINK A LITTLE.
AND WHEN IT FEELS PERSONAL. SOMETHING RELATABLE...
OKAY, SO... MAYBE ART CAN'T BE "GOOD" OR "BAD." WE JUST HAVE TO HOLD CERTAIN WORKS TO A LOWER STANDARD.

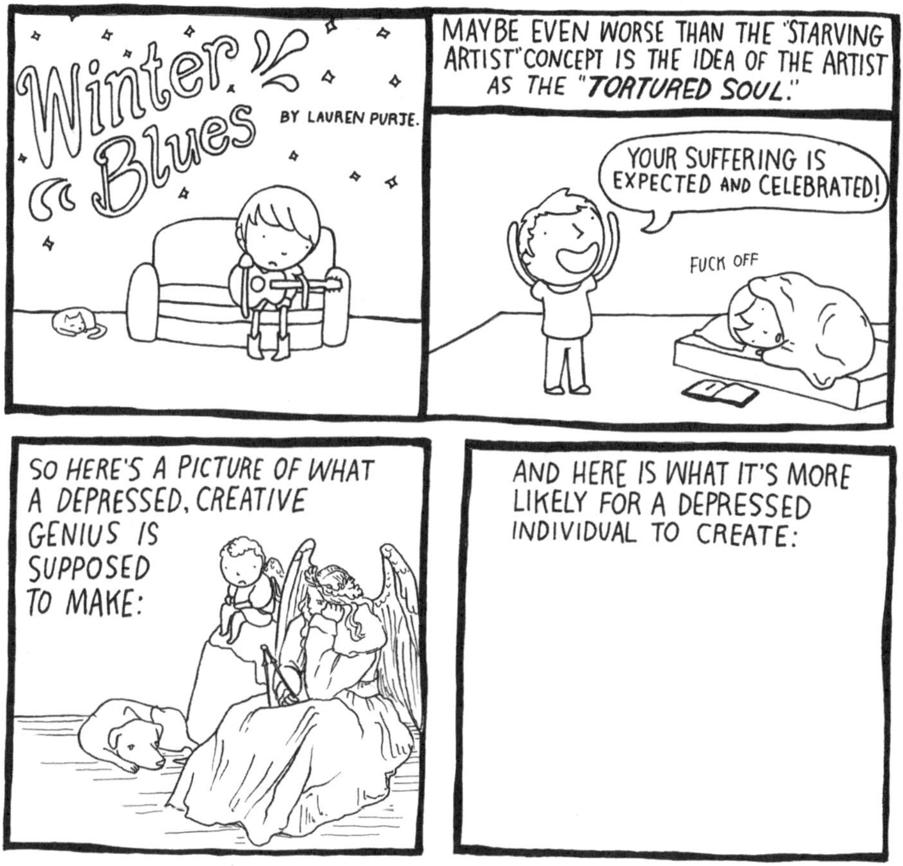
Winter Blues
BY LAUREN PURJE.
MAYBE EVEN WORSE THAN THE "STARVING ARTIST" CONCEPT IS THE IDEA OF THE ARTIST AS THE "TORTURED SOUL."
YOUR SUFFERING IS EXPECTED AND CELEBRATED!
FUCK OFF
SO HERE'S A PICTURE OF WHAT A DEPRESSED, CREATIVE GENIUS IS SUPPOSED TO MAKE:
AND HERE IS WHAT IT'S MORE LIKELY FOR A DEPRESSED INDIVIDUAL TO CREATE:

I WAS SO MUCH OLDER THEN... BY LAUREN PURJE.

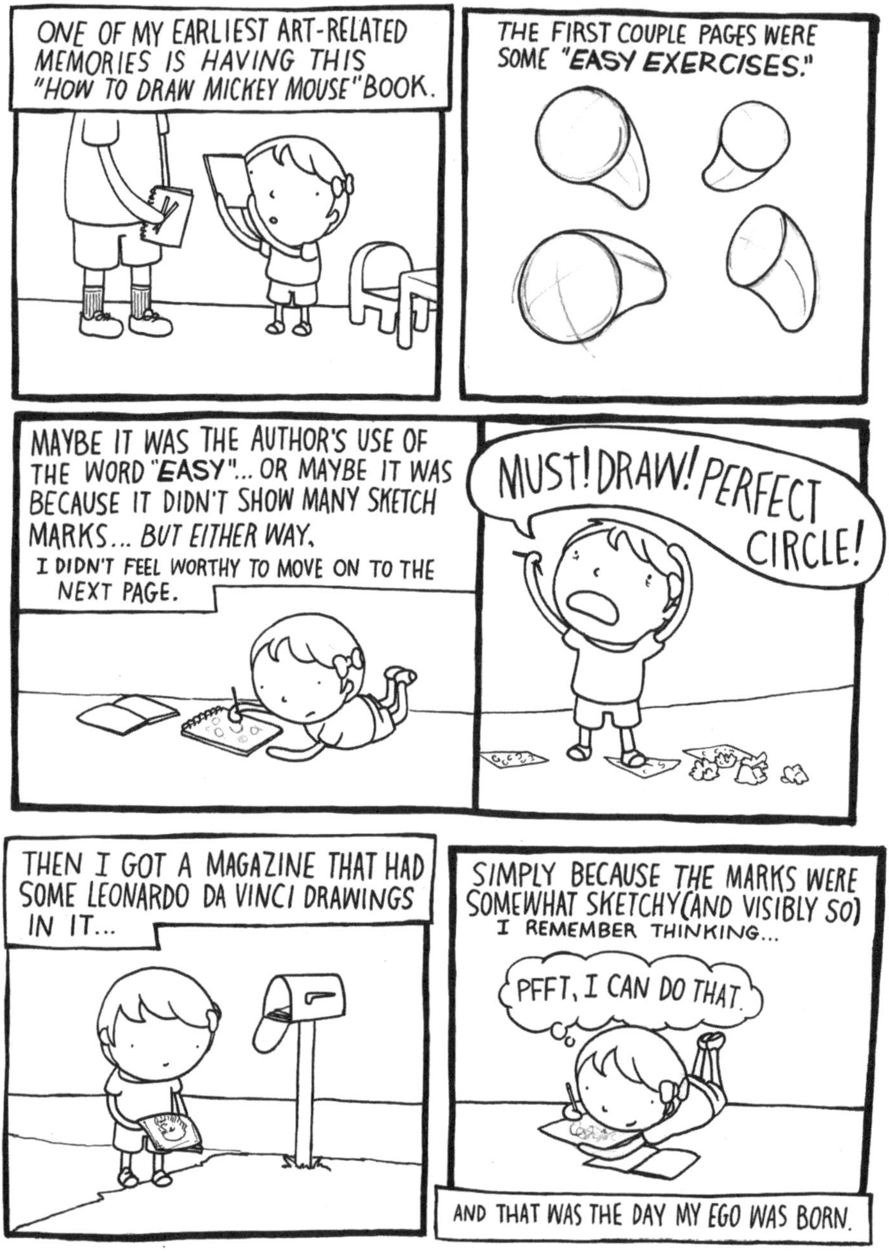
ONE OF MY EARLIEST ART-RELATED MEMORIES IS HAVING THIS "HOW TO DRAW MICKEY MOUSE" BOOK.
THE FIRST COUPLE PAGES WERE SOME "EASY EXERCISES."
MAYBE IT WAS THE AUTHOR'S USE OF THE WORD "EASY"... OR MAYBE IT WAS BECAUSE IT DIDN'T SHOW MANY SKETCH MARKS... BUT EITHER WAY,
I DIDN'T FEEL WORTHY TO MOVE ON TO THE NEXT PAGE.
MUST! DRAW! PERFECT CIRCLE!
THEN I GOT A MAGAZINE THAT HAD SOME LEONARDO DA VINCI DRAWINGS IN IT...
SIMPLY BECAUSE THE MARKS WERE SOMEWHAT SKETCHY (AND VISIBLY SO)
I REMEMBER THINKING...
PFFT, I CAN DO THAT.
AND THAT WAS THE DAY MY EGO WAS BORN.

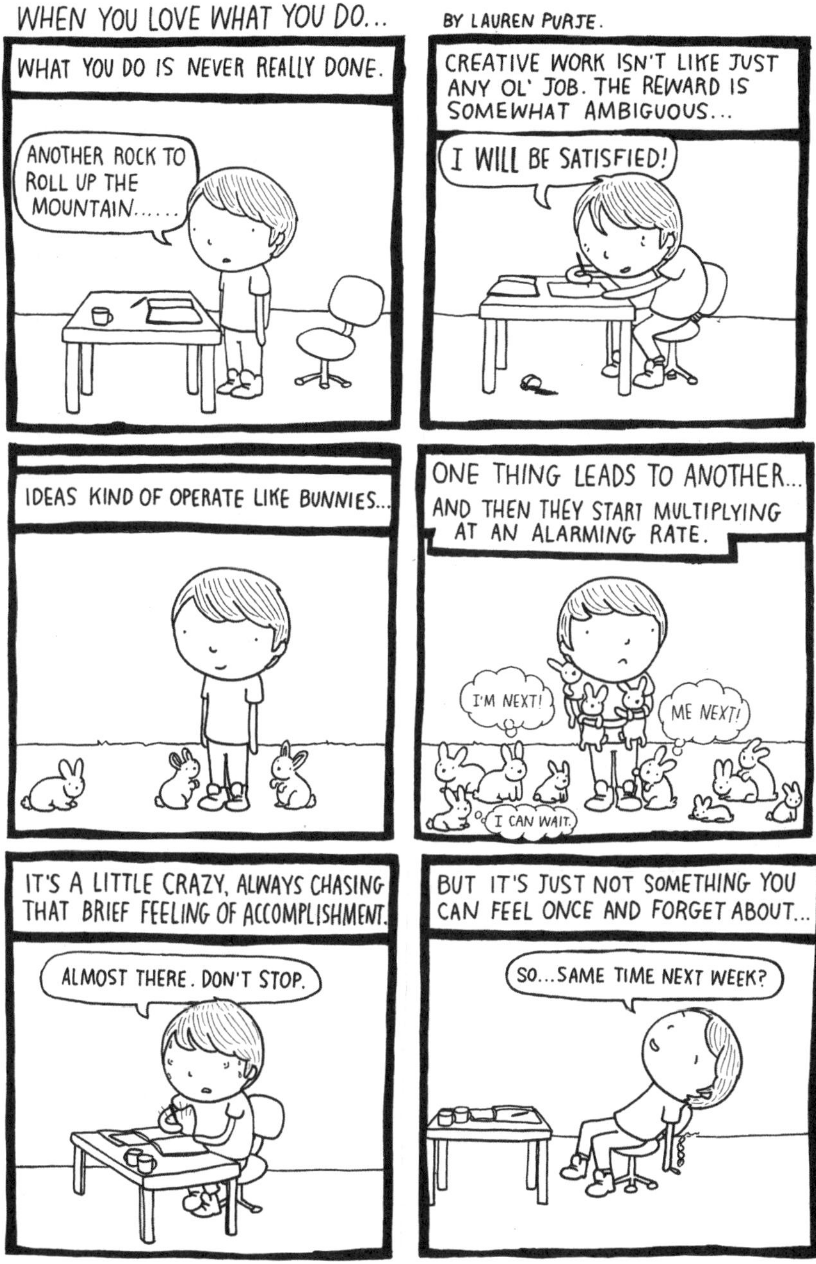
WHEN YOU LOVE WHAT YOU DO...
BY LAUREN PURJE.
WHAT YOU DO IS NEVER REALLY DONE.
ANOTHER ROCK TO ROLL UP THE MOUNTAIN......
CREATIVE WORK ISN'T LIKE JUST ANY OL' JOB. THE REWARD IS SOMEWHAT AMBIGUOUS...
I WILL BE SATISFIED!
IDEAS KIND OF OPERATE LIKE BUNNIES...
ONE THING LEADS TO ANOTHER...
AND THEN THEY START MULTIPLYING AT AN ALARMING RATE.
I'M NEXT!
ME NEXT!
I CAN WAIT.
IT'S A LITTLE CRAZY, ALWAYS CHASING THAT BRIEF FEELING OF ACCOMPLISHMENT.
ALMOST THERE. DON'T STOP.
BUT IT'S JUST NOT SOMETHING YOU CAN FEEL ONCE AND FORGET ABOUT...
SO...SAME TIME NEXT WEEK?

DISCONNECTED BY LAUREN PURJE.

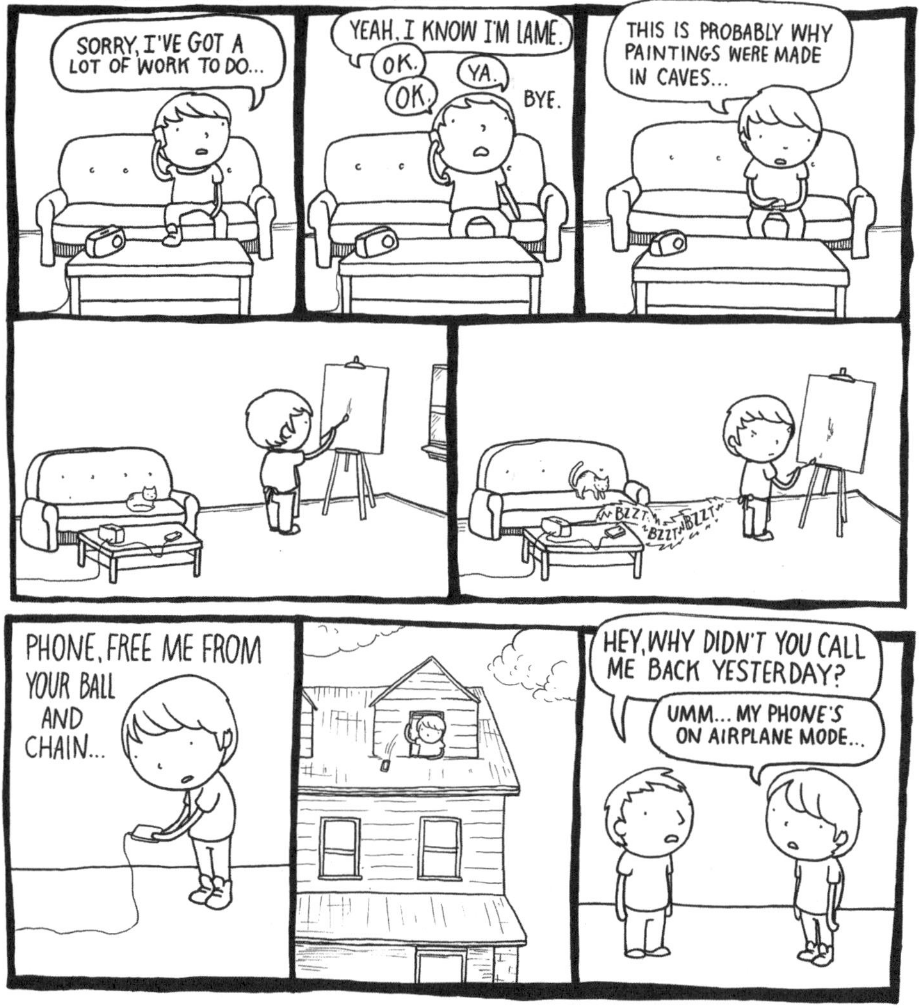
SORRY, I'VE GOT A LOT OF WORK TO DO...
YEAH. I KNOW I'M LAME.
OK.
OK.
YA.
BYE.
THIS IS PROBABLY WHY PAINTINGS WERE MADE IN CAVES...
BZZT
BZZT
BZZT
PHONE, FREE ME FROM YOUR BALL AND CHAIN...
HEY, WHY DIDN'T YOU CALL ME BACK YESTERDAY?
UMM... MY PHONE'S ON AIRPLANE MODE...

SHHHAADDUP BY LAUREN PURJE.

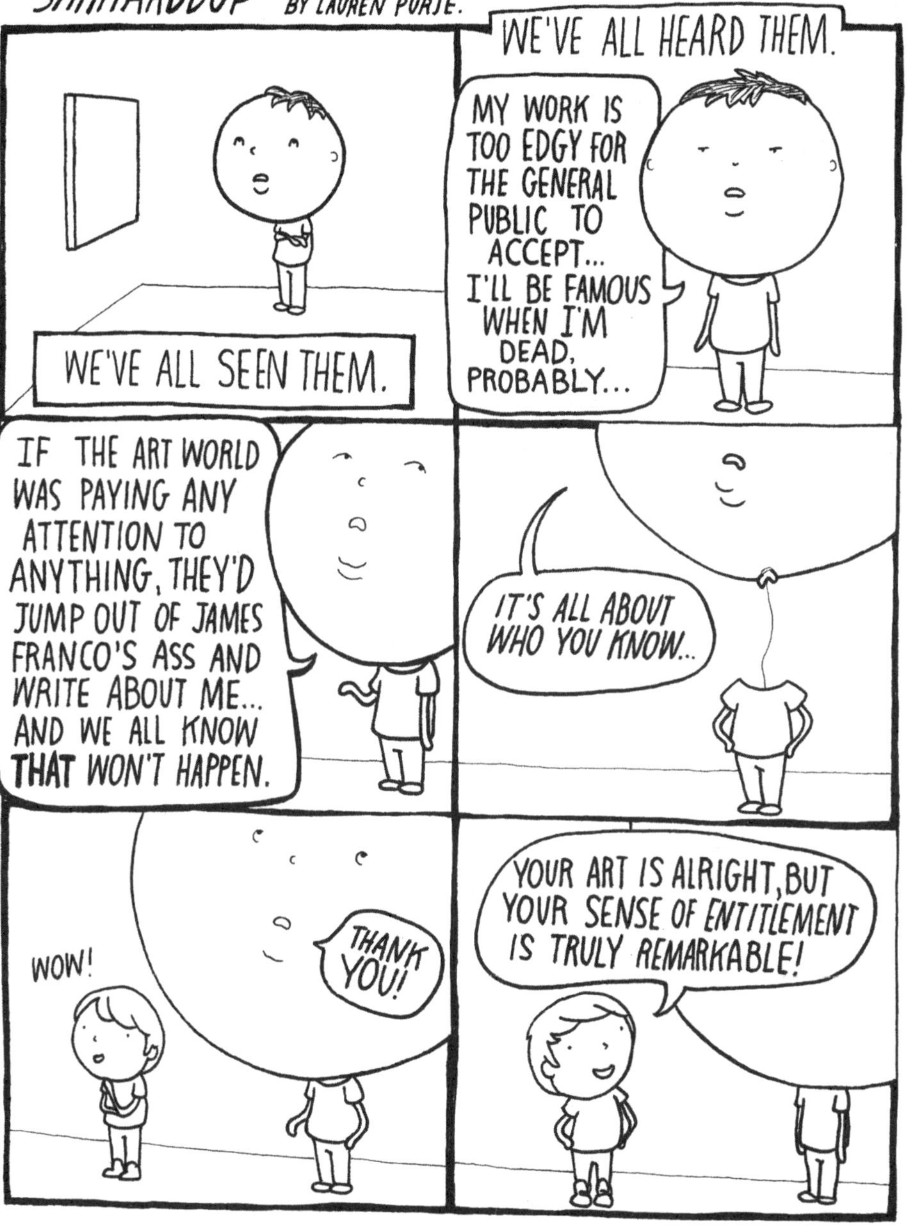
WE'VE ALL SEEN THEM.
WE'VE ALL HEARD THEM.
MY WORK IS TOO EDGY FOR THE GENERAL PUBLIC TO ACCEPT... I'LL BE FAMOUS WHEN I'M DEAD, PROBABLY...
IF THE ART WORLD WAS PAYING ANY ATTENTION TO ANYTHING, THEY'D JUMP OUT OF JAMES FRANCO'S ASS AND WRITE ABOUT ME... AND WE ALL KNOW THAT WON'T HAPPEN.
IT'S ALL ABOUT WHO YOU KNOW...
WOW!
THANK YOU!
YOUR ART IS ALRIGHT, BUT YOUR SENSE OF ENTITLEMENT IS TRULY REMARKABLE!

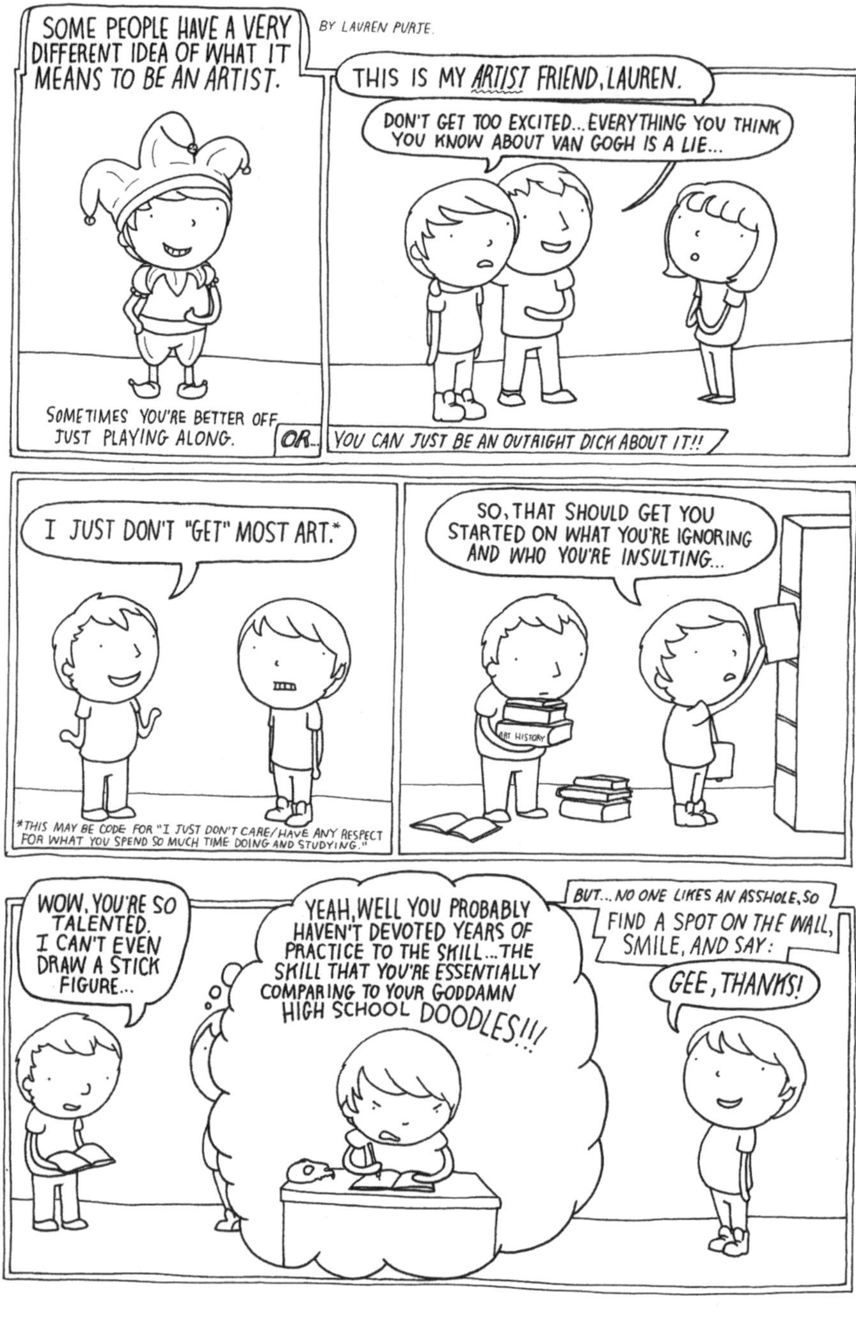
SOME PEOPLE HAVE A VERY DIFFERENT IDEA OF WHAT IT MEANS TO BE AN ARTIST.
BY LAUREN PURJE.
SOMETIMES YOU'RE BETTER OFF JUST PLAYING ALONG.
OR...
THIS IS MY ARTIST FRIEND, LAUREN.
DON'T GET TOO EXCITED... EVERYTHING YOU THINK YOU KNOW ABOUT VAN GOGH IS A LIE...
YOU CAN JUST BE AN OUTRIGHT DICK ABOUT IT!!
I JUST DON'T "GET" MOST ART.*
*THIS MAY BE CODE FOR "I JUST DON'T CARE/HAVE ANY RESPECT FOR WHAT YOU SPEND SO MUCH TIME DOING AND STUDYING."
SO, THAT SHOULD GET YOU STARTED ON WHAT YOU'RE IGNORING AND WHO YOU'RE INSULTING...
ART HISTORY
WOW, YOU'RE SO TALENTED. I CAN'T EVEN DRAW A STICK FIGURE...
YEAH, WELL YOU PROBABLY HAVEN'T DEVOTED YEARS OF PRACTICE TO THE SKILL... THE SKILL THAT YOU'RE ESSENTIALLY COMPARING TO YOUR GODDAMN HIGH SCHOOL DOODLES!!!
BUT... NO ONE LIKES AN ASSHOLE, SO
FIND A SPOT ON THE WALL, SMILE, AND SAY:
GEE, THANKS!

SELF-REFLECTION BY LAUREN PURJE.

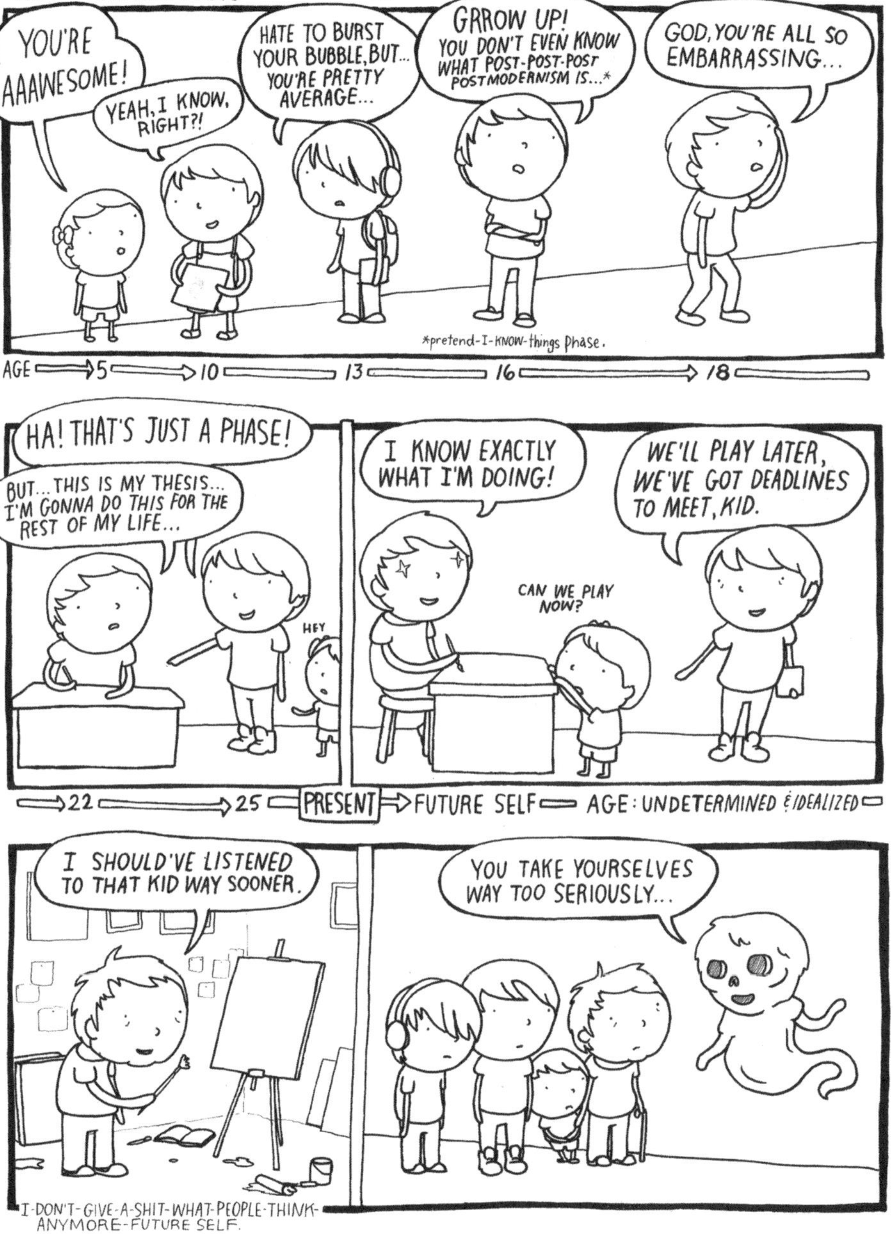
YOU'RE AAAWESOME!
YEAH, I KNOW, RIGHT?!
HATE TO BURST YOUR BUBBLE, BUT... YOU'RE PRETTY AVERAGE...
GRROW UP! YOU DON'T EVEN KNOW WHAT POST-POST-POST POSTMODERNISM IS...*
GOD, YOU'RE ALL SO EMBARRASSING...
*pretend-I-KNOW-things phase.
AGE 5 10 13 16 18
HA! THAT'S JUST A PHASE!
BUT... THIS IS MY THESIS... I'M GONNA DO THIS FOR THE REST OF MY LIFE...
HEY
I KNOW EXACTLY WHAT I'M DOING!
CAN WE PLAY NOW?
WE'LL PLAY LATER, WE'VE GOT DEADLINES TO MEET, KID.
22 25 PRESENT FUTURE SELF AGE: UNDETERMINED & IDEALIZED
I SHOULD'VE LISTENED TO THAT KID WAY SOONER.
YOU TAKE YOURSELVES WAY TOO SERIOUSLY...
I-DON'T-GIVE-A-SHIT-WHAT-PEOPLE-THINK-ANYMORE-FUTURE SELF.

WORKING HARD/HARDLY WORKING

BY LAUREN PURJE.

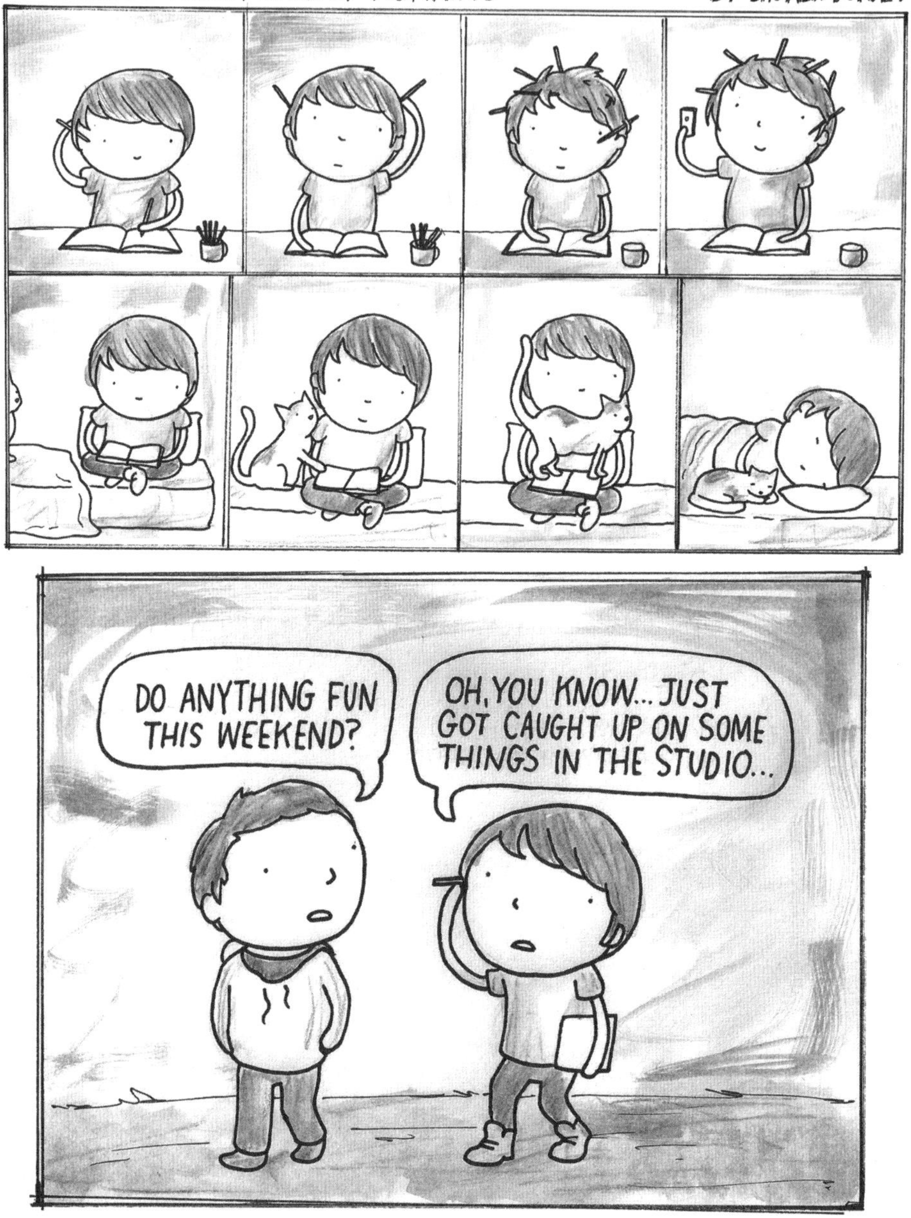
DO ANYTHING FUN THIS WEEKEND?
OH, YOU KNOW... JUST GOT CAUGHT UP ON SOME THINGS IN THE STUDIO...

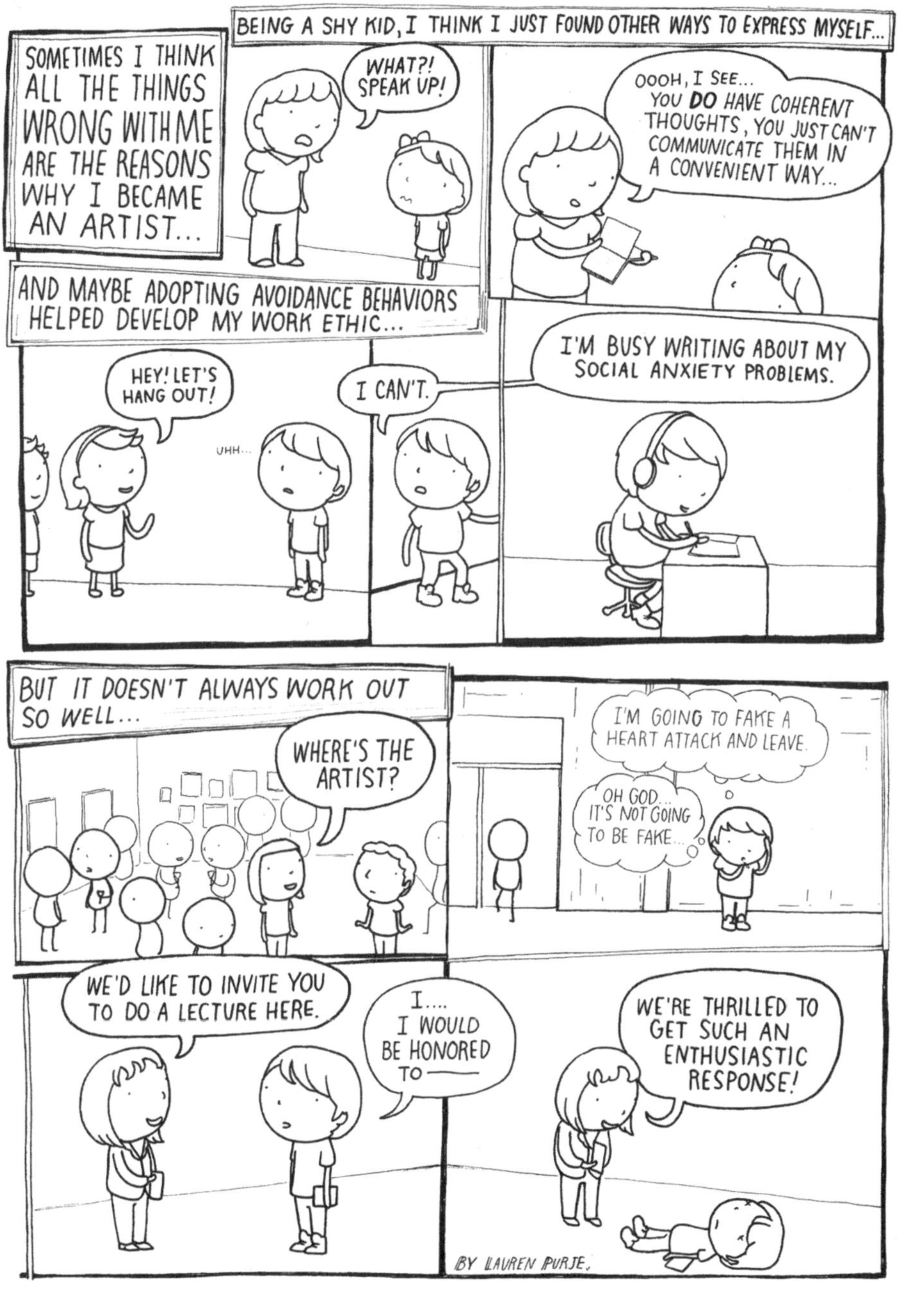

SOMETIMES I THINK ALL THE THINGS WRONG WITH ME ARE THE REASONS WHY I BECAME AN ARTIST...
BEING A SHY KID, I THINK I JUST FOUND OTHER WAYS TO EXPRESS MYSELF...
WHAT?! SPEAK UP!
OOOH, I SEE... YOU DO HAVE COHERENT THOUGHTS, YOU JUST CAN'T COMMUNICATE THEM IN A CONVENIENT WAY...
AND MAYBE ADOPTING AVOIDANCE BEHAVIORS HELPED DEVELOP MY WORK ETHIC...
HEY! LET'S HANG OUT!
UHH...
I CAN'T.
I'M BUSY WRITING ABOUT MY SOCIAL ANXIETY PROBLEMS.
BUT IT DOESN'T ALWAYS WORK OUT SO WELL...
WHERE'S THE ARTIST?
I'M GOING TO FAKE A HEART ATTACK AND LEAVE.
OH GOD... IT'S NOT GOING TO BE FAKE...
WE'D LIKE TO INVITE YOU TO DO A LECTURE HERE.
I.... I WOULD BE HONORED TO——
WE'RE THRILLED TO GET SUCH AN ENTHUSIASTIC RESPONSE!
BY LAUREN PURJE.

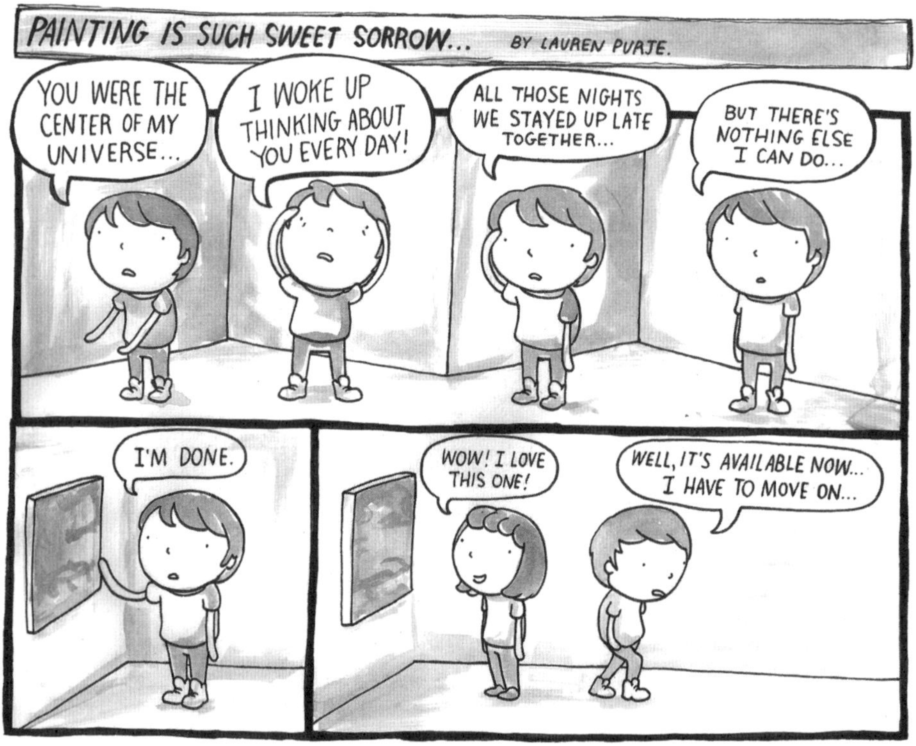
PAINTING IS SUCH SWEET SORROW... BY LAUREN PURJE.
YOU WERE THE CENTER OF MY UNIVERSE...
I WOKE UP THINKING ABOUT YOU EVERY DAY!
ALL THOSE NIGHTS WE STAYED UP LATE TOGETHER...
BUT THERE'S NOTHING ELSE I CAN DO...
I'M DONE.
WOW! I LOVE THIS ONE!
WELL, IT'S AVAILABLE NOW... I HAVE TO MOVE ON...

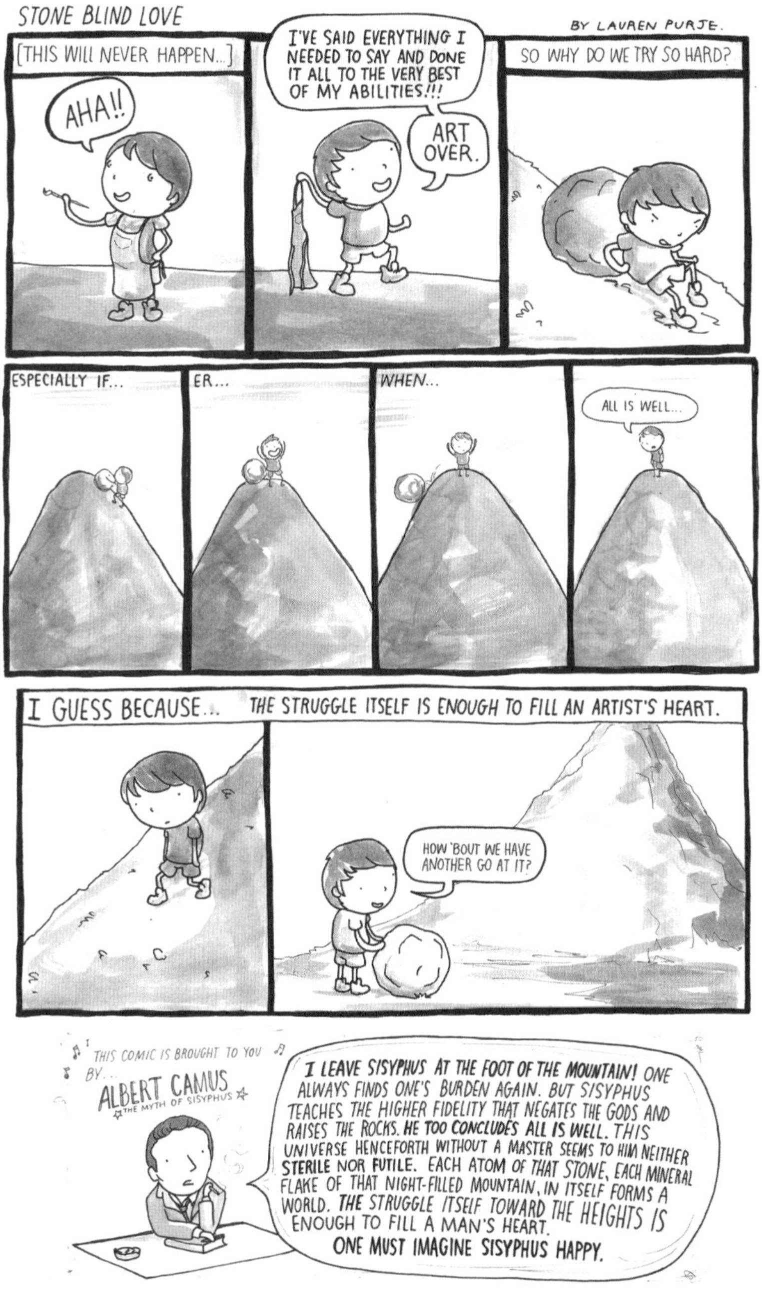
STONE BLIND LOVE
BY LAUREN PURJE.
[THIS WILL NEVER HAPPEN...]
AHA!!
I'VE SAID EVERYTHING I NEEDED TO SAY AND DONE IT ALL TO THE VERY BEST OF MY ABILITIES!!!
ART OVER.
SO WHY DO WE TRY SO HARD?
ESPECIALLY IF...
ER...
WHEN...
ALL IS WELL...
I GUESS BECAUSE...
THE STRUGGLE ITSELF IS ENOUGH TO FILL AN ARTIST'S HEART.
HOW 'BOUT WE HAVE ANOTHER GO AT IT?
THIS COMIC IS BROUGHT TO YOU BY...
ALBERT CAMUS
THE MYTH OF SISYPHUS
I LEAVE SISYPHUS AT THE FOOT OF THE MOUNTAIN! ONE ALWAYS FINDS ONE'S BURDEN AGAIN. BUT SISYPHUS TEACHES THE HIGHER FIDELITY THAT NEGATES THE GODS AND RAISES THE ROCKS. HE TOO CONCLUDES ALL IS WELL. THIS UNIVERSE HENCEFORTH WITHOUT A MASTER SEEMS TO HIM NEITHER STERILE NOR FUTILE. EACH ATOM OF THAT STONE, EACH MINERAL FLAKE OF THAT NIGHT-FILLED MOUNTAIN, IN ITSELF FORMS A WORLD. THE STRUGGLE ITSELF TOWARD THE HEIGHTS IS ENOUGH TO FILL A MAN'S HEART.
ONE MUST IMAGINE SISYPHUS HAPPY.

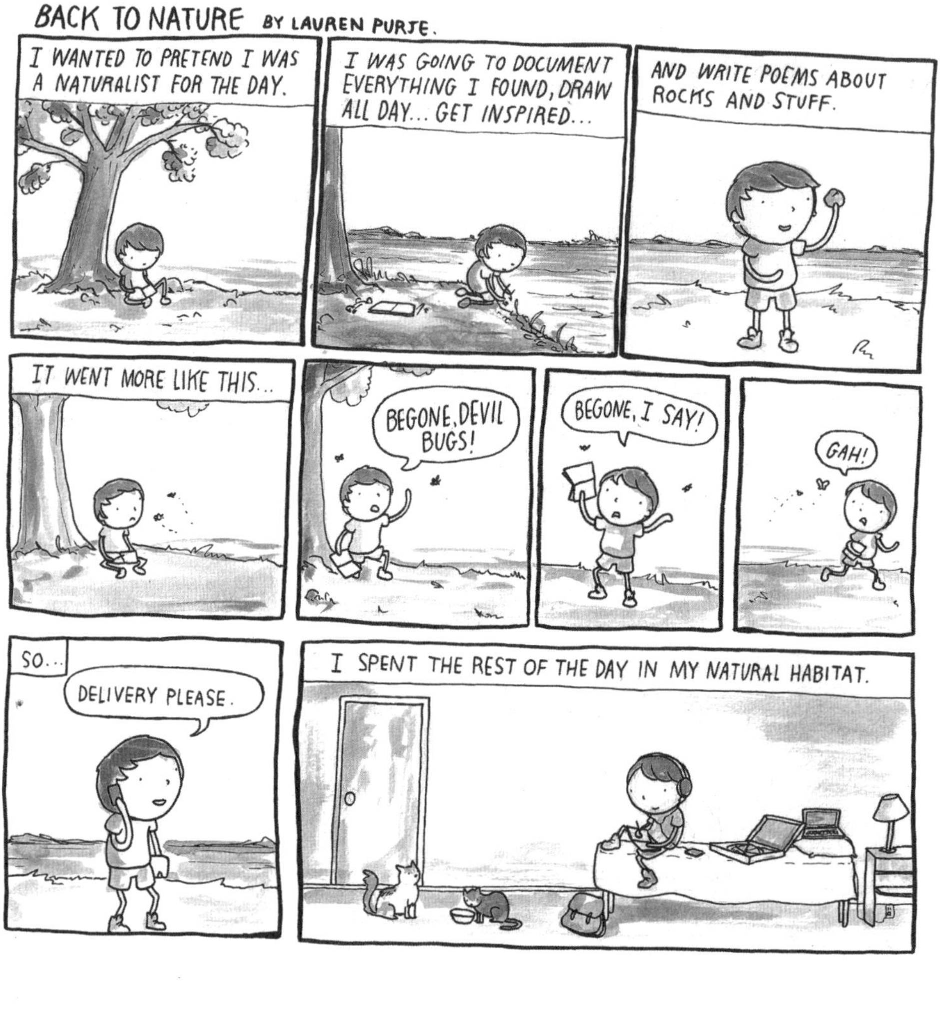
BACK TO NATURE BY LAUREN PURJE.
I WANTED TO PRETEND I WAS A NATURALIST FOR THE DAY.
I WAS GOING TO DOCUMENT EVERYTHING I FOUND, DRAW ALL DAY... GET INSPIRED...
AND WRITE POEMS ABOUT ROCKS AND STUFF.
IT WENT MORE LIKE THIS...
BEGONE, DEVIL BUGS!
BEGONE, I SAY!
GAH!
SO...
DELIVERY PLEASE.
I SPENT THE REST OF THE DAY IN MY NATURAL HABITAT.

DO'S AND DON'T'S BY LAUREN PURJE.

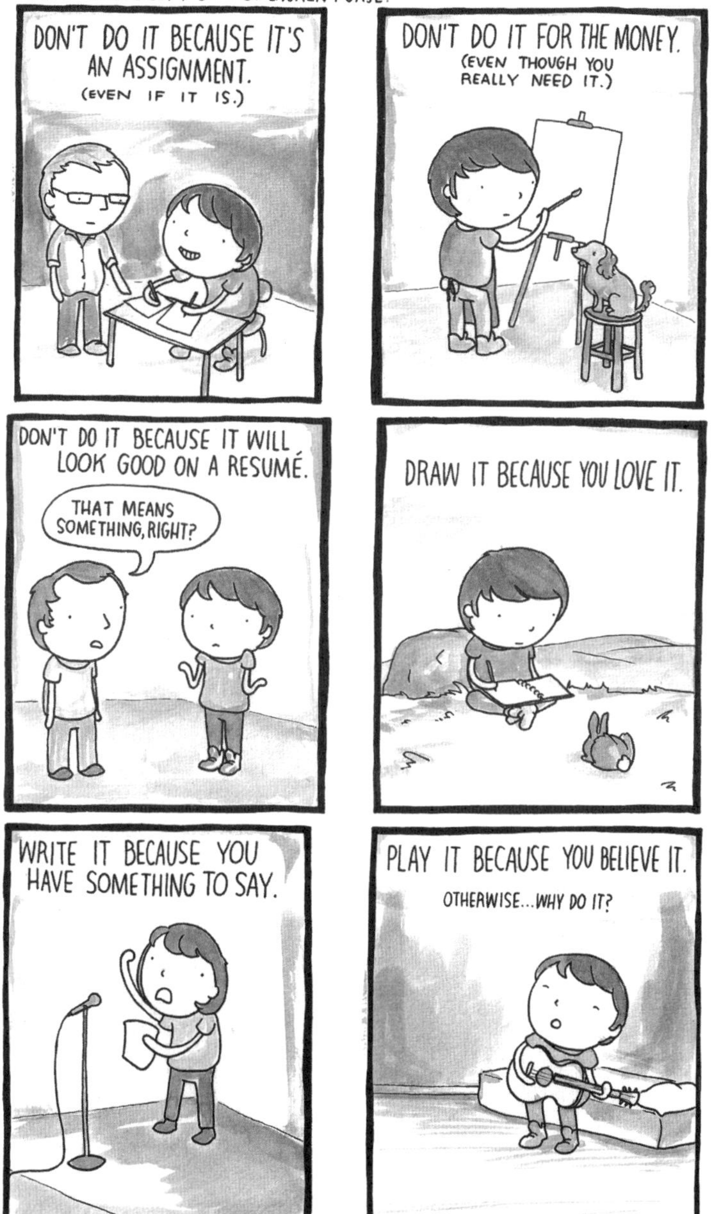
DON'T DO IT BECAUSE IT'S AN ASSIGNMENT.
(EVEN IF IT IS.)
DON'T DO IT FOR THE MONEY.
(EVEN THOUGH YOU REALLY NEED IT.)
DON'T DO IT BECAUSE IT WILL LOOK GOOD ON A RESUMÉ.
THAT MEANS SOMETHING, RIGHT?
DRAW IT BECAUSE YOU LOVE IT.
WRITE IT BECAUSE YOU HAVE SOMETHING TO SAY.
PLAY IT BECAUSE YOU BELIEVE IT.
OTHERWISE...WHY DO IT?

HELLO, STUDENTS! BY LAUREN PURJE.

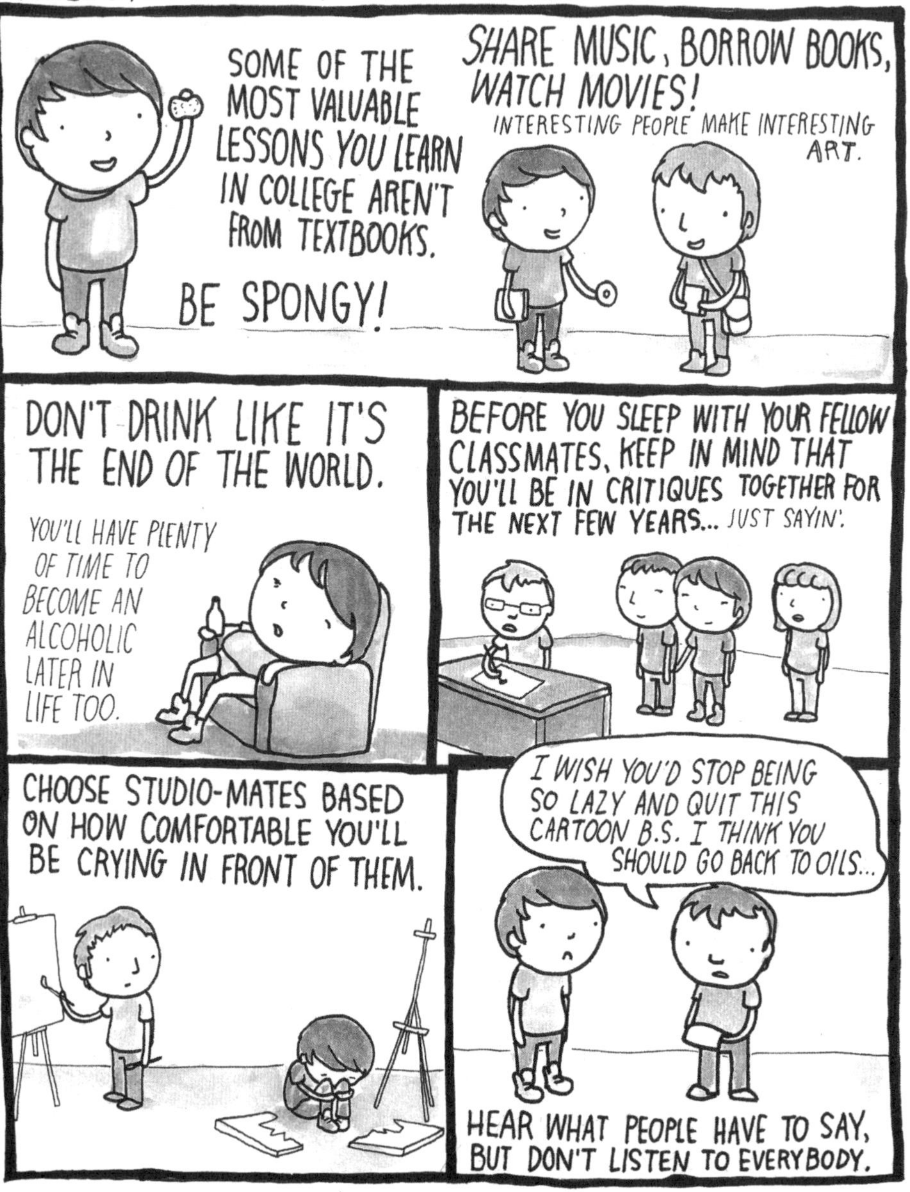
SOME OF THE MOST VALUABLE LESSONS YOU LEARN IN COLLEGE AREN'T FROM TEXTBOOKS.
BE SPONGY!
SHARE MUSIC, BORROW BOOKS, WATCH MOVIES!
INTERESTING PEOPLE MAKE INTERESTING ART.
DON'T DRINK LIKE IT'S THE END OF THE WORLD.
YOU'LL HAVE PLENTY OF TIME TO BECOME AN ALCOHOLIC LATER IN LIFE TOO.
BEFORE YOU SLEEP WITH YOUR FELLOW CLASSMATES, KEEP IN MIND THAT YOU'LL BE IN CRITIQUES TOGETHER FOR THE NEXT FEW YEARS... JUST SAYIN'.
CHOOSE STUDIO-MATES BASED ON HOW COMFORTABLE YOU'LL BE CRYING IN FRONT OF THEM.
I WISH YOU'D STOP BEING SO LAZY AND QUIT THIS CARTOON B.S. I THINK YOU SHOULD GO BACK TO OILS...
HEAR WHAT PEOPLE HAVE TO SAY, BUT DON'T LISTEN TO EVERYBODY.

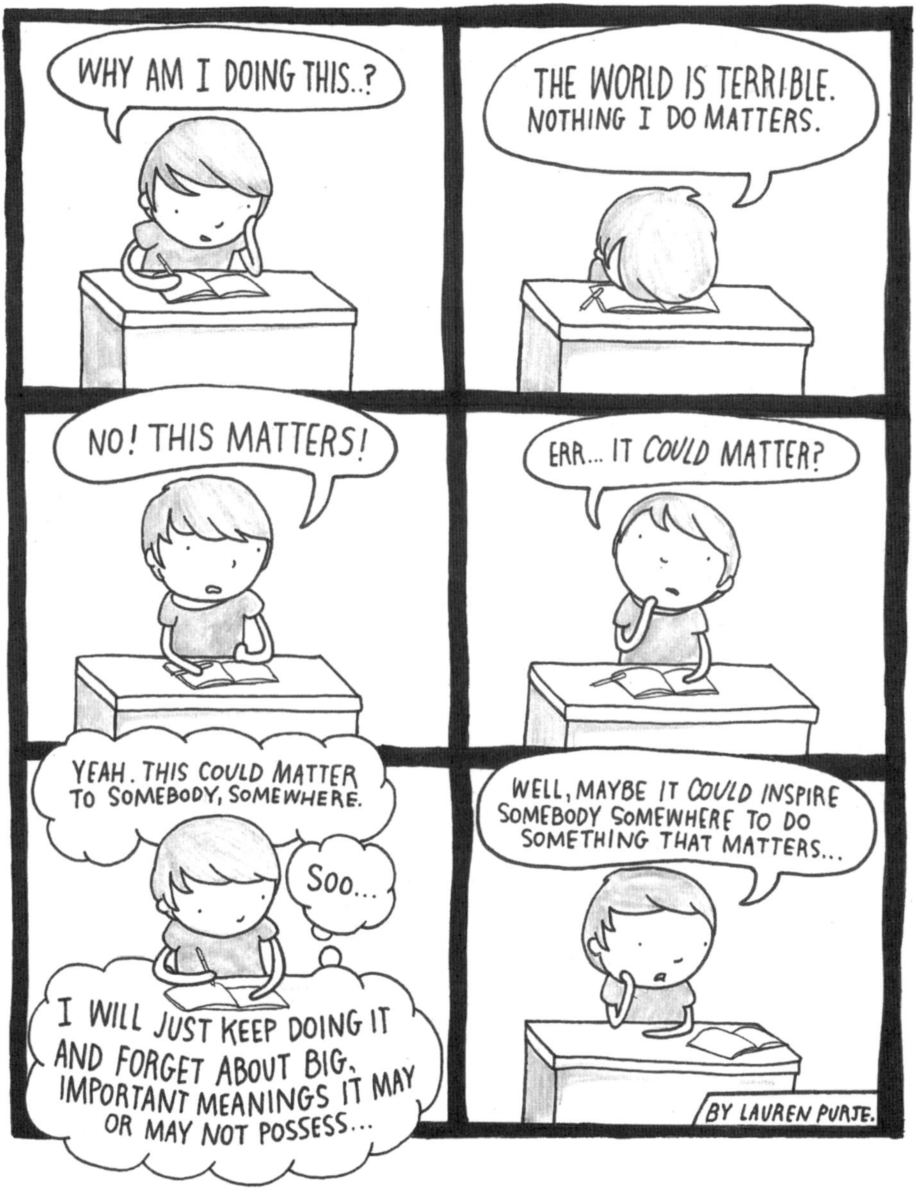
WHY AM I DOING THIS..?
THE WORLD IS TERRIBLE. NOTHING I DO MATTERS.
NO! THIS MATTERS!
ERR... IT COULD MATTER?
YEAH. THIS COULD MATTER TO SOMEBODY, SOMEWHERE.
Soo...
I WILL JUST KEEP DOING IT AND FORGET ABOUT BIG, IMPORTANT MEANINGS IT MAY OR MAY NOT POSSESS...
WELL, MAYBE IT COULD INSPIRE SOMEBODY SOMEWHERE TO DO SOMETHING THAT MATTERS...
BY LAUREN PURJE.

YOU'RE NOT THAT SPECIAL (AND THAT'S WONDERFUL.) BY LAUREN PURJE.

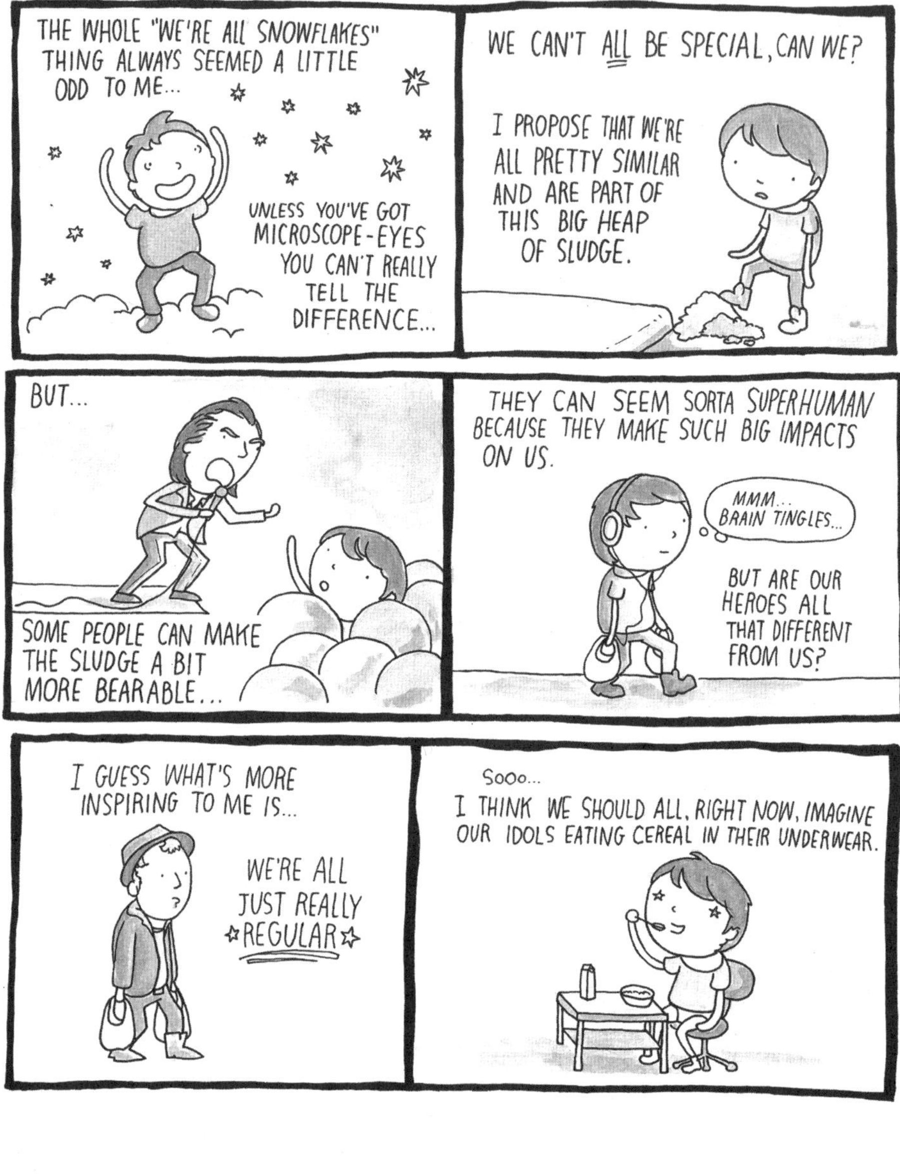
THE WHOLE "WE'RE ALL SNOWFLAKES" THING ALWAYS SEEMED A LITTLE ODD TO ME...
UNLESS YOU'VE GOT MICROSCOPE-EYES YOU CAN'T REALLY TELL THE DIFFERENCE...
WE CAN'T ALL BE SPECIAL, CAN WE?
I PROPOSE THAT WE'RE ALL PRETTY SIMILAR AND ARE PART OF THIS BIG HEAP OF SLUDGE.
BUT...
SOME PEOPLE CAN MAKE THE SLUDGE A BIT MORE BEARABLE...
THEY CAN SEEM SORTA SUPERHUMAN BECAUSE THEY MAKE SUCH BIG IMPACTS ON US.
MMM... BRAIN TINGLES...
BUT ARE OUR HEROES ALL THAT DIFFERENT FROM US?
I GUESS WHAT'S MORE INSPIRING TO ME IS...
WE'RE ALL JUST REALLY REGULAR
Sooo...
I THINK WE SHOULD ALL, RIGHT NOW, IMAGINE OUR IDOLS EATING CEREAL IN THEIR UNDERWEAR.

MY SPIRIT ANIMAL

BY LAUREN PURJE.

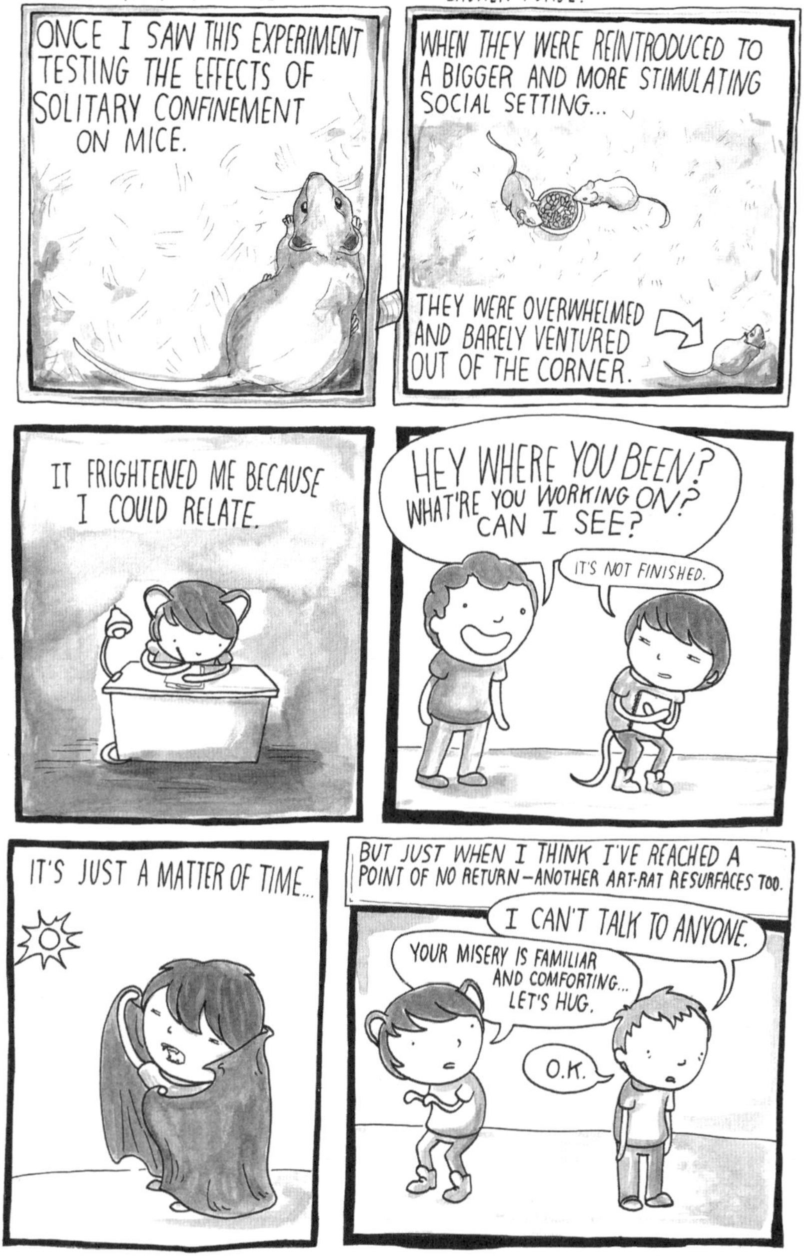
ONCE I SAW THIS EXPERIMENT TESTING THE EFFECTS OF SOLITARY CONFINEMENT ON MICE.
WHEN THEY WERE REINTRODUCED TO A BIGGER AND MORE STIMULATING SOCIAL SETTING...
THEY WERE OVERWHELMED AND BARELY VENTURED OUT OF THE CORNER.
IT FRIGHTENED ME BECAUSE I COULD RELATE.
HEY WHERE YOU BEEN? WHAT'RE YOU WORKING ON? CAN I SEE?
IT'S NOT FINISHED.
IT'S JUST A MATTER OF TIME...
BUT JUST WHEN I THINK I'VE REACHED A POINT OF NO RETURN—ANOTHER ART-RAT RESURFACES TOO.
I CAN'T TALK TO ANYONE.
YOUR MISERY IS FAMILIAR AND COMFORTING... LET'S HUG.
O.K.

ART BABY

BY LAUREN PURJE.

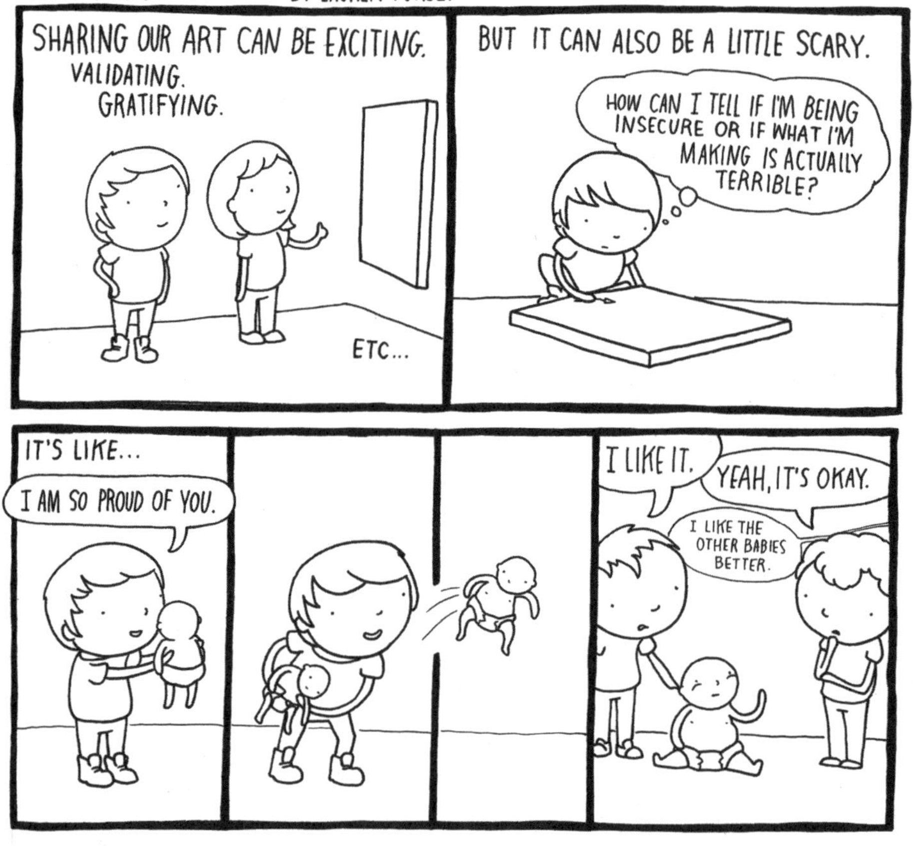

SHARING OUR ART CAN BE EXCITING.
VALIDATING.
GRATIFYING.
ETC...
BUT IT CAN ALSO BE A LITTLE SCARY.
HOW CAN I TELL IF I'M BEING INSECURE OR IF WHAT I'M MAKING IS ACTUALLY TERRIBLE?
IT'S LIKE...
I AM SO PROUD OF YOU.
I LIKE IT.
YEAH, IT'S OKAY.
I LIKE THE OTHER BABIES BETTER.

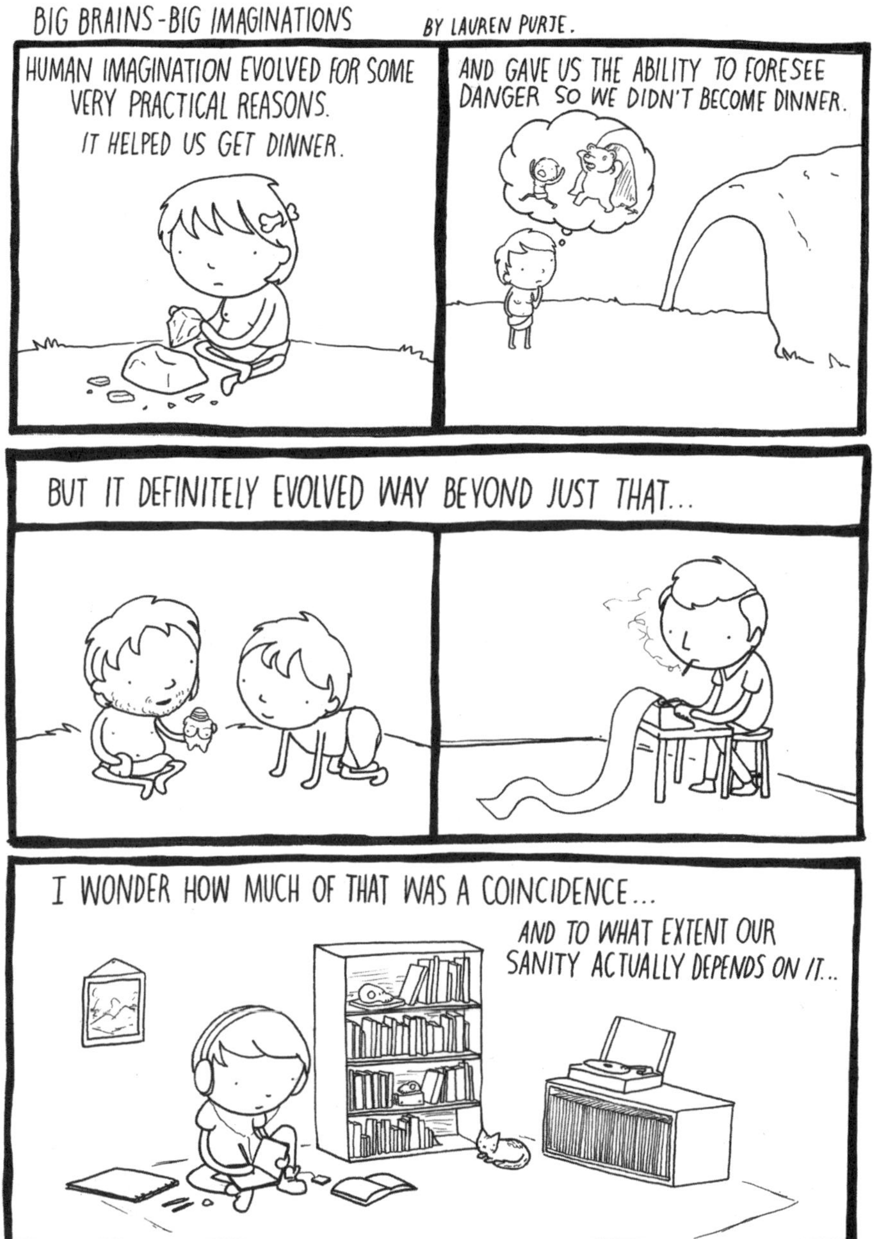
BIG BRAINS-BIG IMAGINATIONS
BY LAUREN PURJE.
HUMAN IMAGINATION EVOLVED FOR SOME VERY PRACTICAL REASONS.
IT HELPED US GET DINNER.
AND GAVE US THE ABILITY TO FORESEE DANGER SO WE DIDN'T BECOME DINNER.
BUT IT DEFINITELY EVOLVED WAY BEYOND JUST THAT...
I WONDER HOW MUCH OF THAT WAS A COINCIDENCE...
AND TO WHAT EXTENT OUR SANITY ACTUALLY DEPENDS ON IT...

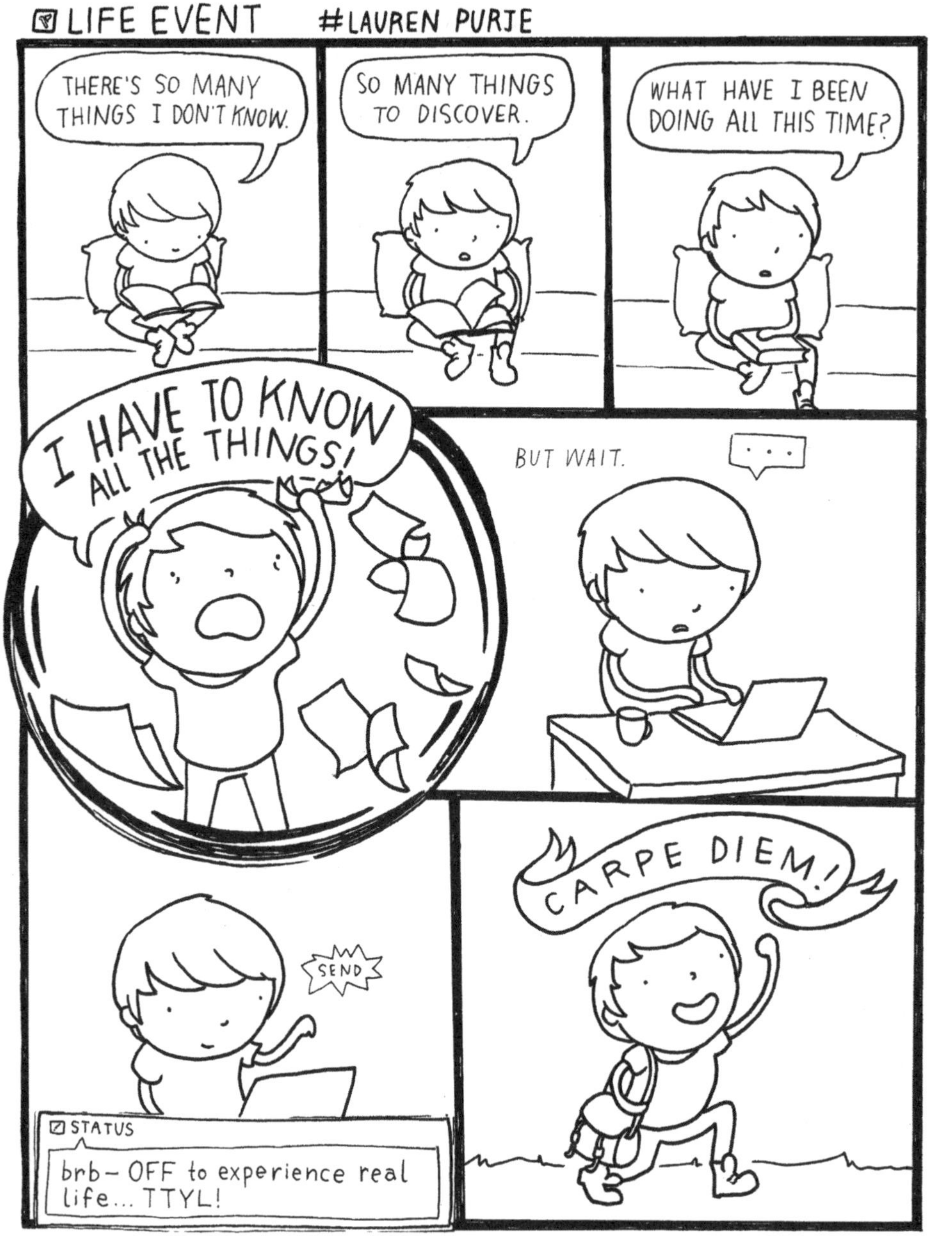
LIFE EVENT
#LAUREN PURJE
THERE'S SO MANY THINGS I DON'T KNOW.
SO MANY THINGS TO DISCOVER.
WHAT HAVE I BEEN DOING ALL THIS TIME?
I HAVE TO KNOW ALL THE THINGS!
BUT WAIT.
. . .
SEND
STATUS
brb – OFF to experience real life... TTYL!
CARPE DIEM!

I'M NEVER READY BY LAUREN PURJE.

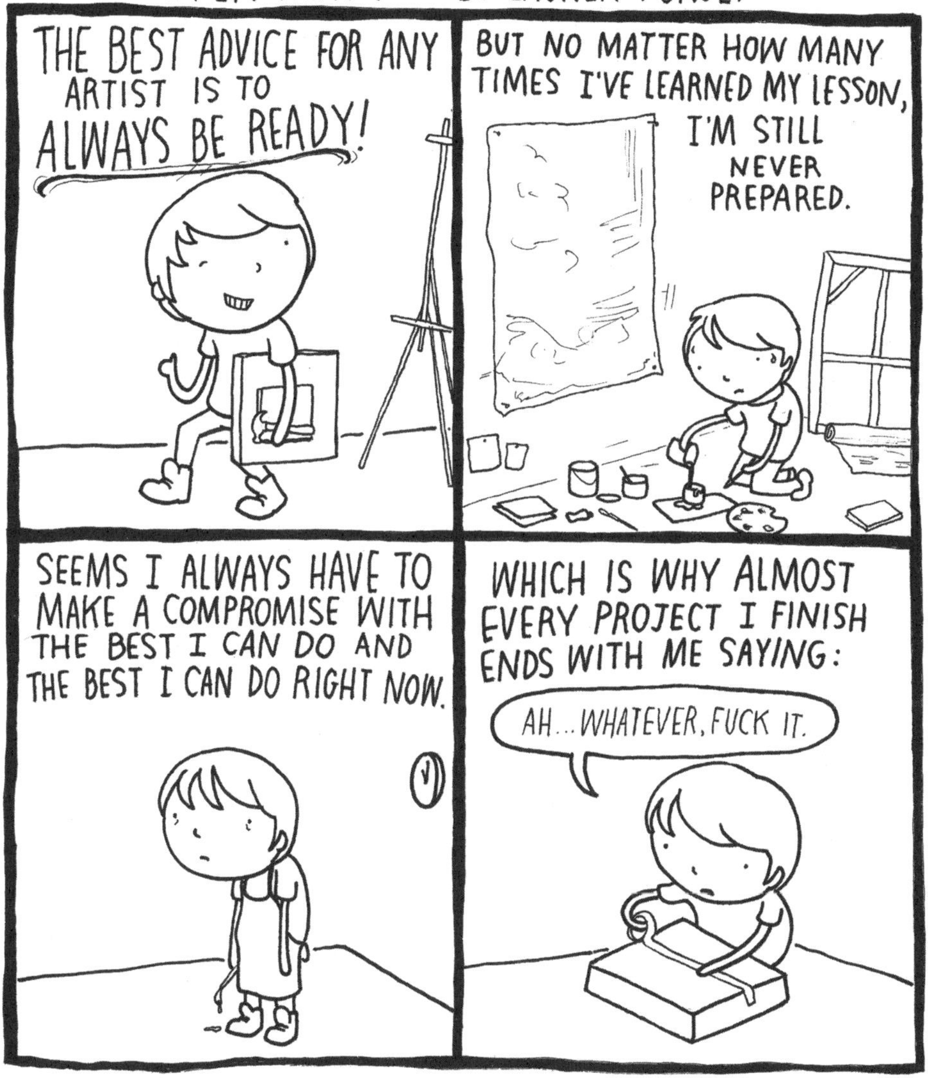
THE BEST ADVICE FOR ANY ARTIST IS TO ALWAYS BE READY!
BUT NO MATTER HOW MANY TIMES I'VE LEARNED MY LESSON,
I'M STILL NEVER PREPARED.
SEEMS I ALWAYS HAVE TO MAKE A COMPROMISE WITH THE BEST I CAN DO AND THE BEST I CAN DO RIGHT NOW.
WHICH IS WHY ALMOST EVERY PROJECT I FINISH ENDS WITH ME SAYING:
AH...WHATEVER, FUCK IT.

SINCERE THANK YOU LETTER BY LAUREN PURJE.

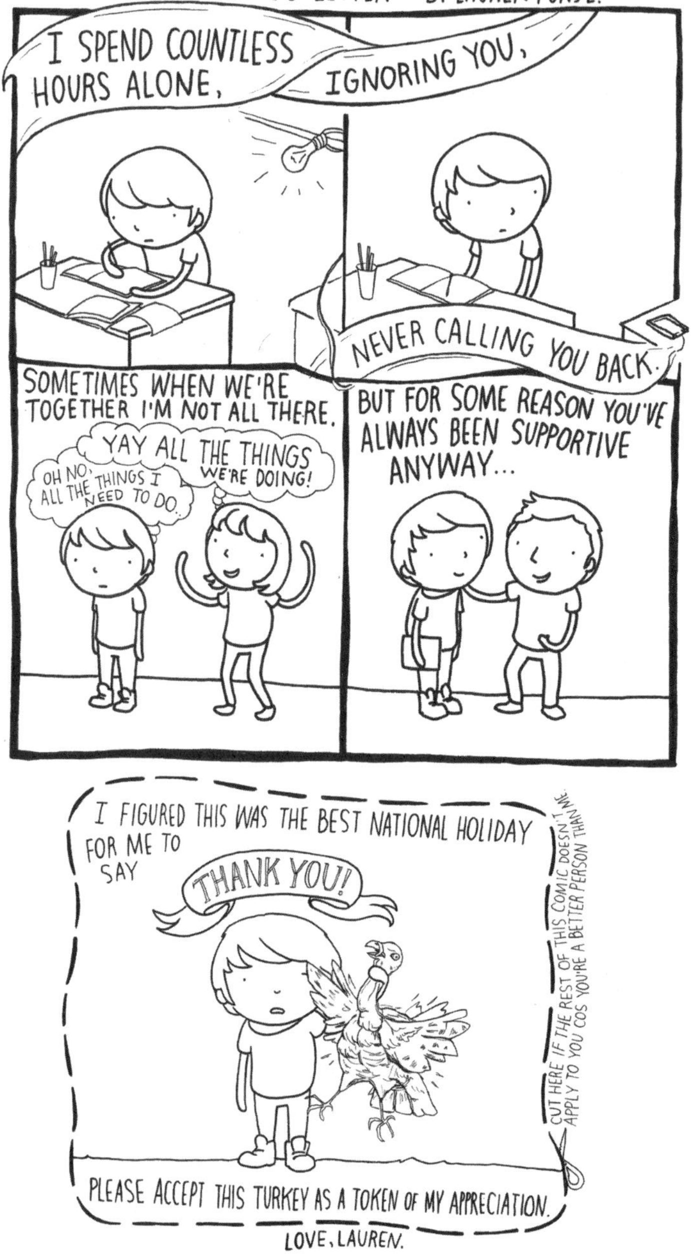

I SPEND COUNTLESS HOURS ALONE,
IGNORING YOU,
NEVER CALLING YOU BACK.
SOMETIMES WHEN WE'RE TOGETHER I'M NOT ALL THERE.
YAY ALL THE THINGS WE'RE DOING!
OH NO, ALL THE THINGS I NEED TO DO...
BUT FOR SOME REASON YOU'VE ALWAYS BEEN SUPPORTIVE ANYWAY...
I FIGURED THIS WAS THE BEST NATIONAL HOLIDAY FOR ME TO SAY
THANK YOU!
CUT HERE IF THE REST OF THIS COMIC DOESN'T APPLY TO YOU COS YOU'RE A BETTER PERSON THAN ME.
PLEASE ACCEPT THIS TURKEY AS A TOKEN OF MY APPRECIATION.
LOVE, LAUREN.

I DON'T WANNA GROW UP BY LAUREN PURJE.

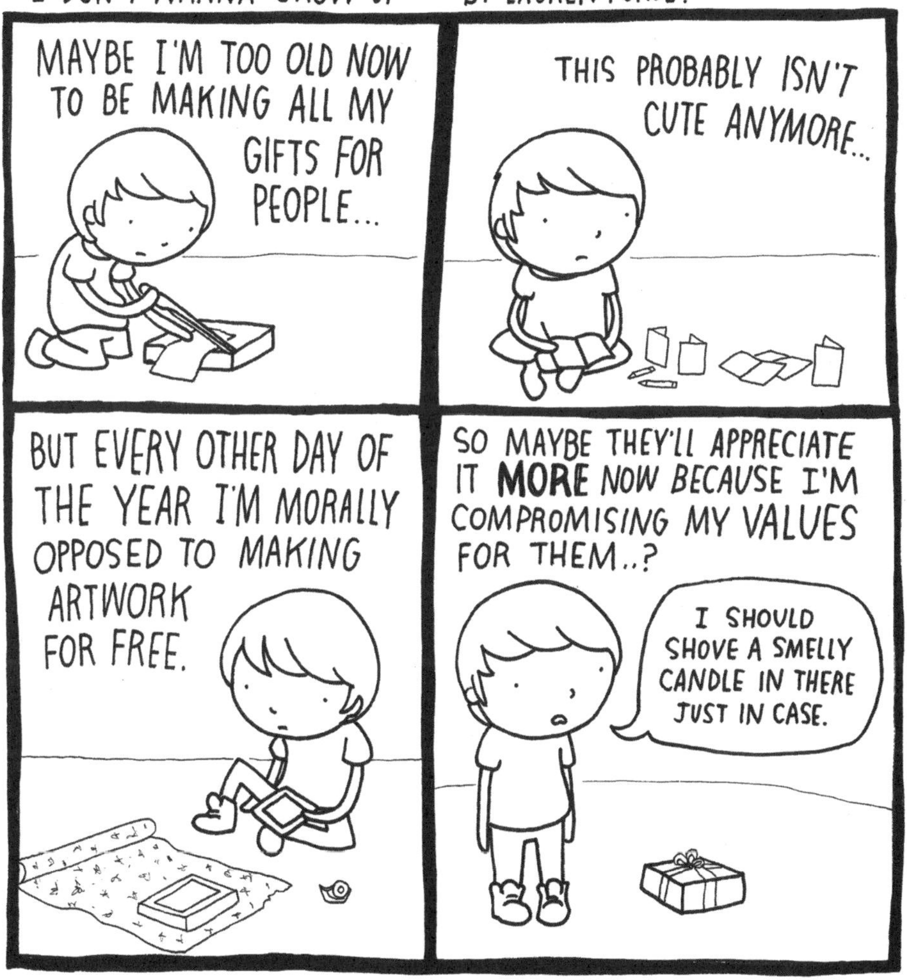
MAYBE I'M TOO OLD NOW TO BE MAKING ALL MY GIFTS FOR PEOPLE...
THIS PROBABLY ISN'T CUTE ANYMORE...
BUT EVERY OTHER DAY OF THE YEAR I'M MORALLY OPPOSED TO MAKING ARTWORK FOR FREE.
SO MAYBE THEY'LL APPRECIATE IT **MORE** NOW BECAUSE I'M COMPROMISING MY VALUES FOR THEM..?
I SHOULD SHOVE A SMELLY CANDLE IN THERE JUST IN CASE.

I'M NOT A RELIGIOUS PERSON, BUT

A GOOD DAY IN THE STUDIO FEELS LIKE...

AND A BAD DAY FEELS LIKE...

BY LAUREN PURJE.

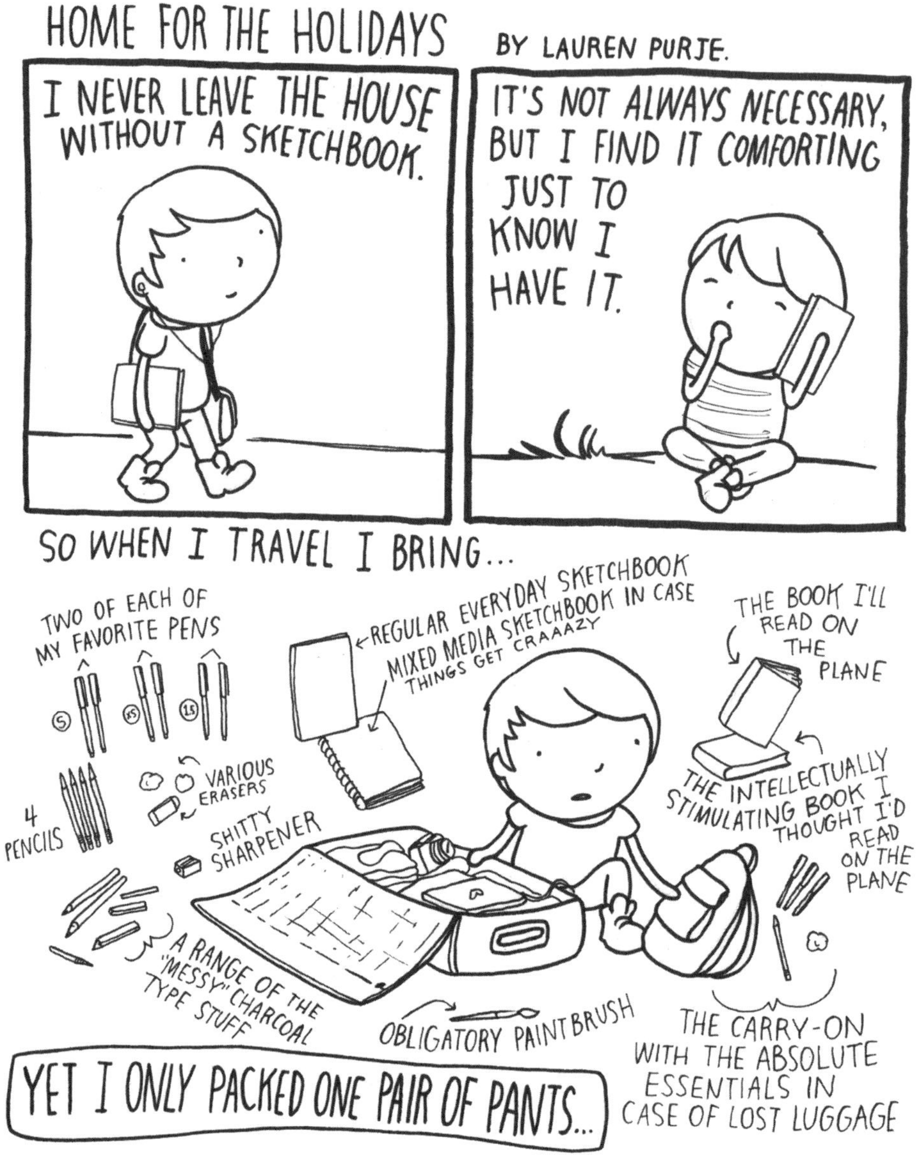
HOME FOR THE HOLIDAYS
BY LAUREN PURJE.
I NEVER LEAVE THE HOUSE WITHOUT A SKETCHBOOK.
IT'S NOT ALWAYS NECESSARY, BUT I FIND IT COMFORTING JUST TO KNOW I HAVE IT.
SO WHEN I TRAVEL I BRING...
TWO OF EACH OF MY FAVORITE PENS
4 PENCILS
VARIOUS ERASERS
SHITTY SHARPENER
A RANGE OF THE "MESSY" CHARCOAL TYPE STUFF
REGULAR EVERYDAY SKETCHBOOK
MIXED MEDIA SKETCHBOOK IN CASE THINGS GET CRAAAZY
THE BOOK I'LL READ ON THE PLANE
THE INTELLECTUALLY STIMULATING BOOK I THOUGHT I'D READ ON THE PLANE
OBLIGATORY PAINTBRUSH
THE CARRY-ON WITH THE ABSOLUTE ESSENTIALS IN CASE OF LOST LUGGAGE
YET I ONLY PACKED ONE PAIR OF PANTS...

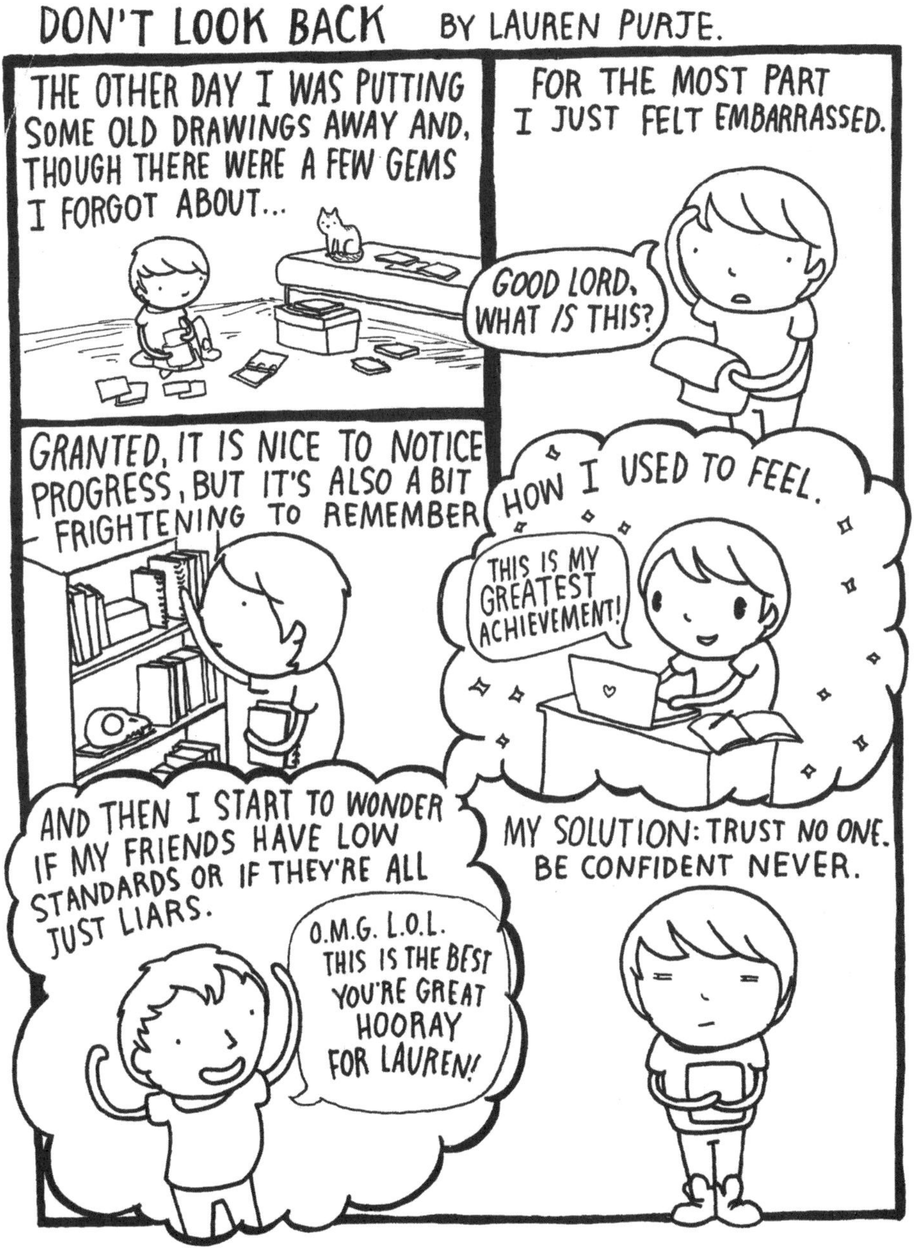
DON'T LOOK BACK BY LAUREN PURJE.
THE OTHER DAY I WAS PUTTING SOME OLD DRAWINGS AWAY AND, THOUGH THERE WERE A FEW GEMS I FORGOT ABOUT...
FOR THE MOST PART I JUST FELT EMBARRASSED.
GOOD LORD, WHAT IS THIS?
GRANTED, IT IS NICE TO NOTICE PROGRESS, BUT IT'S ALSO A BIT FRIGHTENING TO REMEMBER
HOW I USED TO FEEL.
THIS IS MY GREATEST ACHIEVEMENT!
AND THEN I START TO WONDER IF MY FRIENDS HAVE LOW STANDARDS OR IF THEY'RE ALL JUST LIARS.
O.M.G. L.O.L. THIS IS THE BEST YOU'RE GREAT HOORAY FOR LAUREN!
MY SOLUTION: TRUST NO ONE. BE CONFIDENT NEVER.

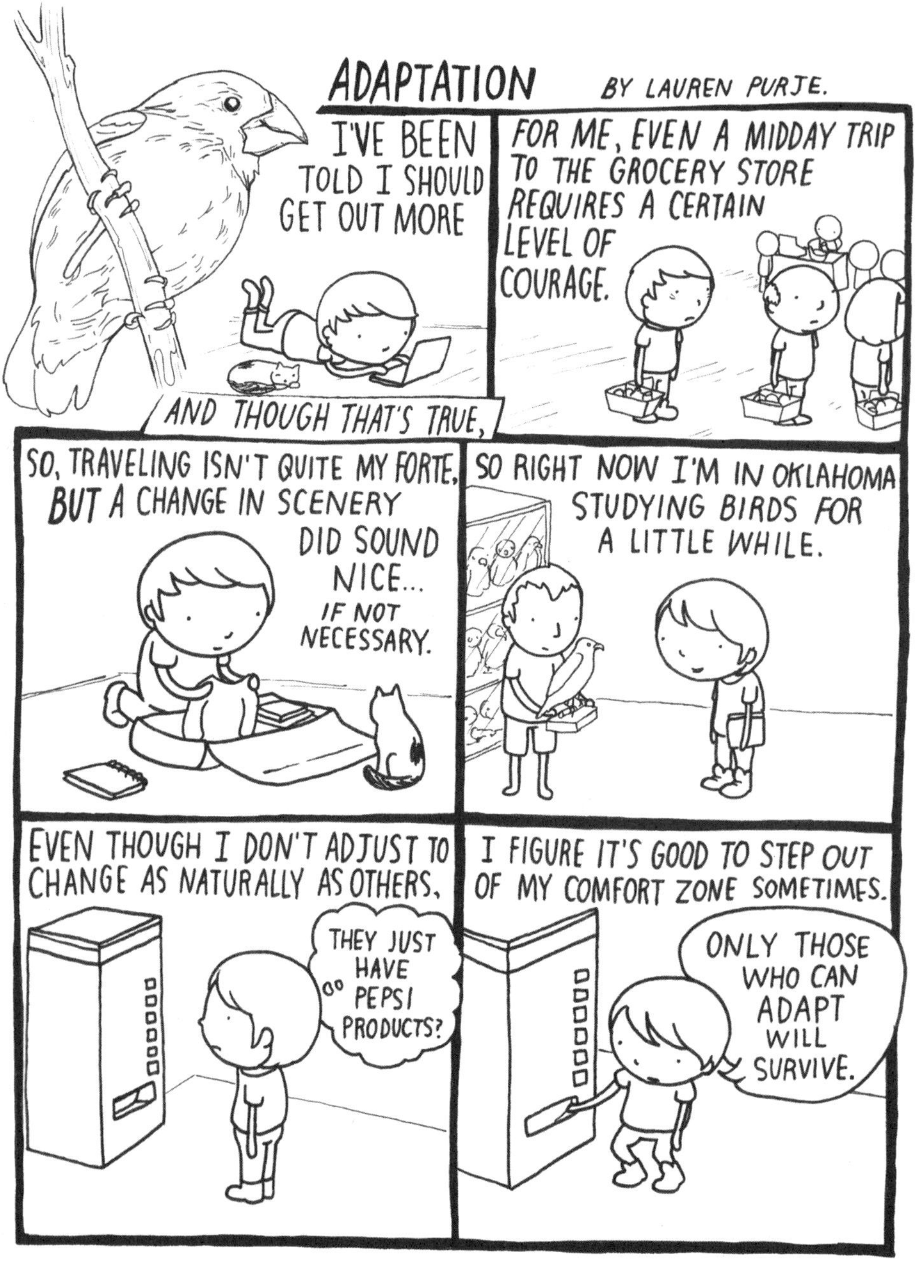
ADAPTATION
BY LAUREN PURJE.
I'VE BEEN TOLD I SHOULD GET OUT MORE
AND THOUGH THAT'S TRUE,
FOR ME, EVEN A MIDDAY TRIP TO THE GROCERY STORE REQUIRES A CERTAIN LEVEL OF COURAGE.
SO, TRAVELING ISN'T QUITE MY FORTE, BUT A CHANGE IN SCENERY DID SOUND NICE... IF NOT NECESSARY.
SO RIGHT NOW I'M IN OKLAHOMA STUDYING BIRDS FOR A LITTLE WHILE.
EVEN THOUGH I DON'T ADJUST TO CHANGE AS NATURALLY AS OTHERS,
THEY JUST HAVE PEPSI PRODUCTS?
I FIGURE IT'S GOOD TO STEP OUT OF MY COMFORT ZONE SOMETIMES.
ONLY THOSE WHO CAN ADAPT WILL SURVIVE.

THERE'S ALWAYS GOING TO BE THOSE QUESTIONS BY LAUREN PURJE.

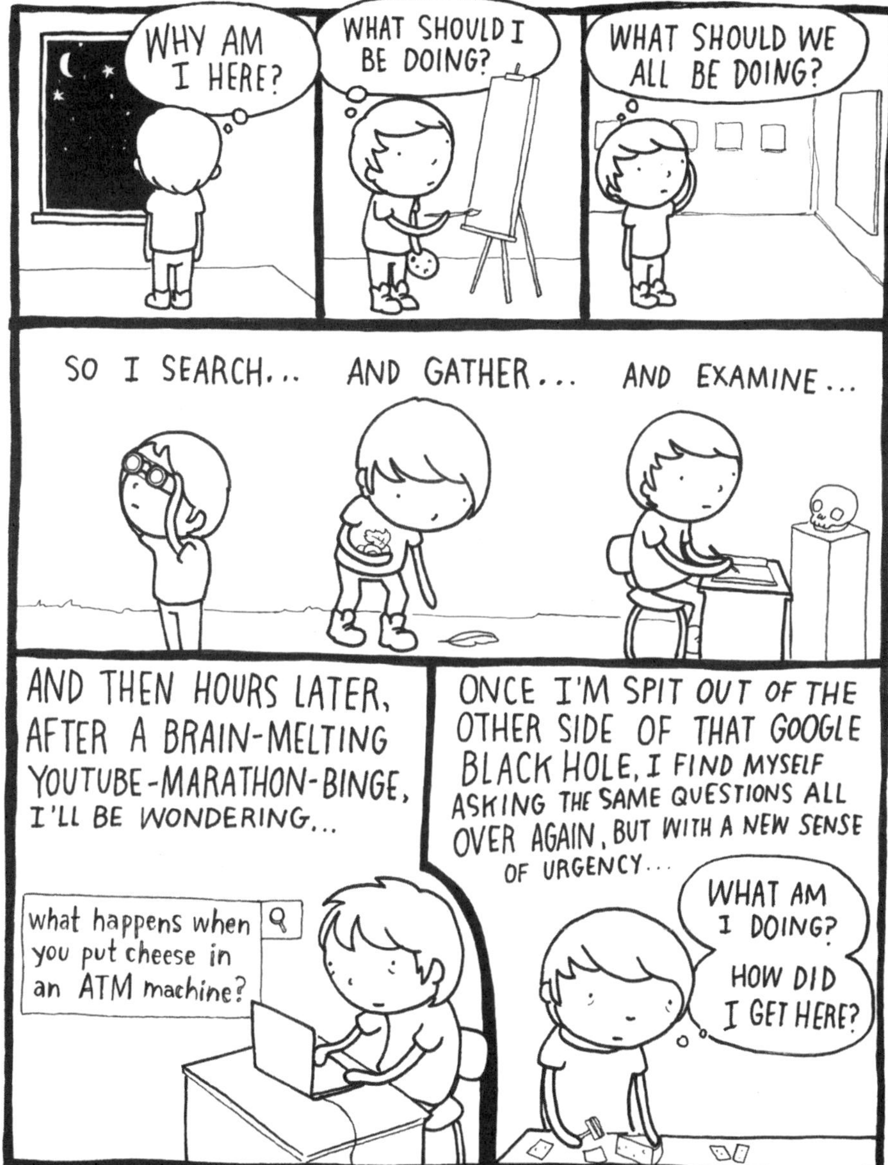
WHY AM I HERE?
WHAT SHOULD I BE DOING?
WHAT SHOULD WE ALL BE DOING?
SO I SEARCH... AND GATHER... AND EXAMINE...
AND THEN HOURS LATER, AFTER A BRAIN-MELTING YOUTUBE-MARATHON-BINGE, I'LL BE WONDERING...
what happens when you put cheese in an ATM machine?
ONCE I'M SPIT OUT OF THE OTHER SIDE OF THAT GOOGLE BLACK HOLE, I FIND MYSELF ASKING THE SAME QUESTIONS ALL OVER AGAIN, BUT WITH A NEW SENSE OF URGENCY...
WHAT AM I DOING?
HOW DID I GET HERE?

ONE TOO MANY MORNINGS

BY LAUREN PURJE.

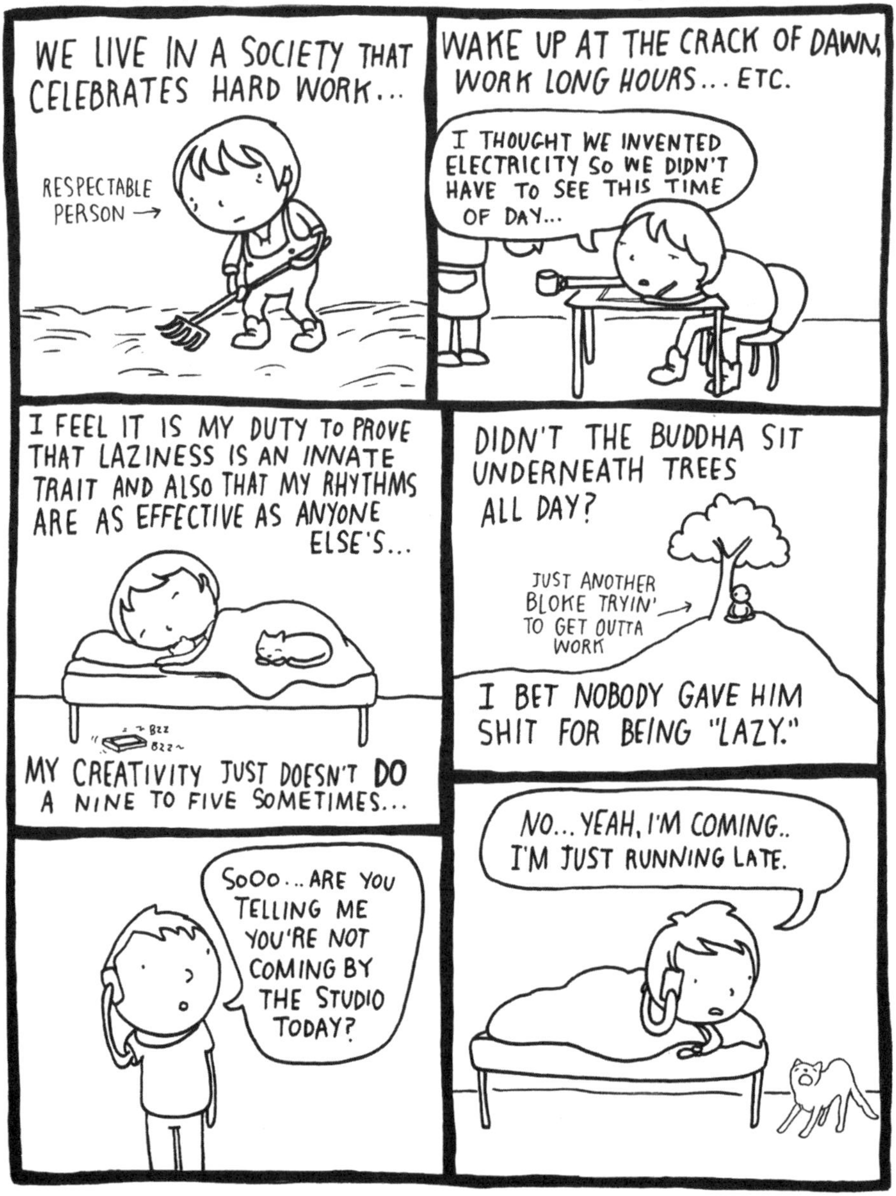
WE LIVE IN A SOCIETY THAT CELEBRATES HARD WORK...
RESPECTABLE PERSON →
WAKE UP AT THE CRACK OF DAWN, WORK LONG HOURS... ETC.
I THOUGHT WE INVENTED ELECTRICITY SO WE DIDN'T HAVE TO SEE THIS TIME OF DAY...
I FEEL IT IS MY DUTY TO PROVE THAT LAZINESS IS AN INNATE TRAIT AND ALSO THAT MY RHYTHMS ARE AS EFFECTIVE AS ANYONE ELSE'S...
MY CREATIVITY JUST DOESN'T DO A NINE TO FIVE SOMETIMES...
DIDN'T THE BUDDHA SIT UNDERNEATH TREES ALL DAY?
JUST ANOTHER BLOKE TRYIN' TO GET OUTTA WORK →
I BET NOBODY GAVE HIM SHIT FOR BEING "LAZY."
SoOo... ARE YOU TELLING ME YOU'RE NOT COMING BY THE STUDIO TODAY?
NO... YEAH, I'M COMING.. I'M JUST RUNNING LATE.

I DIDN'T HAVE INTERNET ACCESS

BY LAUREN PURJE.

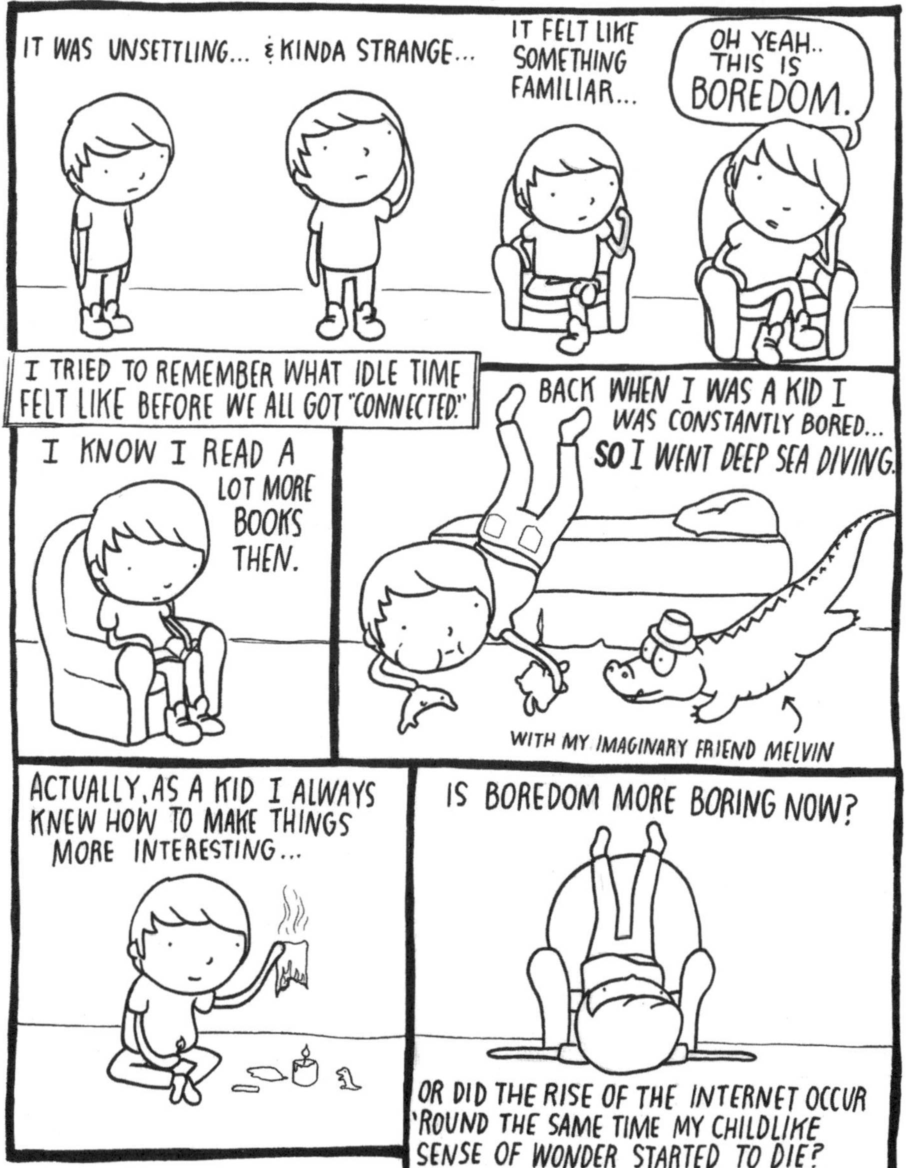
IT WAS UNSETTLING...
& KINDA STRANGE...
IT FELT LIKE SOMETHING FAMILIAR...
OH YEAH.. THIS IS BOREDOM.
I TRIED TO REMEMBER WHAT IDLE TIME FELT LIKE BEFORE WE ALL GOT "CONNECTED."
I KNOW I READ A LOT MORE BOOKS THEN.
BACK WHEN I WAS A KID I WAS CONSTANTLY BORED... SO I WENT DEEP SEA DIVING.
WITH MY IMAGINARY FRIEND MELVIN
ACTUALLY, AS A KID I ALWAYS KNEW HOW TO MAKE THINGS MORE INTERESTING...
IS BOREDOM MORE BORING NOW?
OR DID THE RISE OF THE INTERNET OCCUR 'ROUND THE SAME TIME MY CHILDLIKE SENSE OF WONDER STARTED TO DIE?

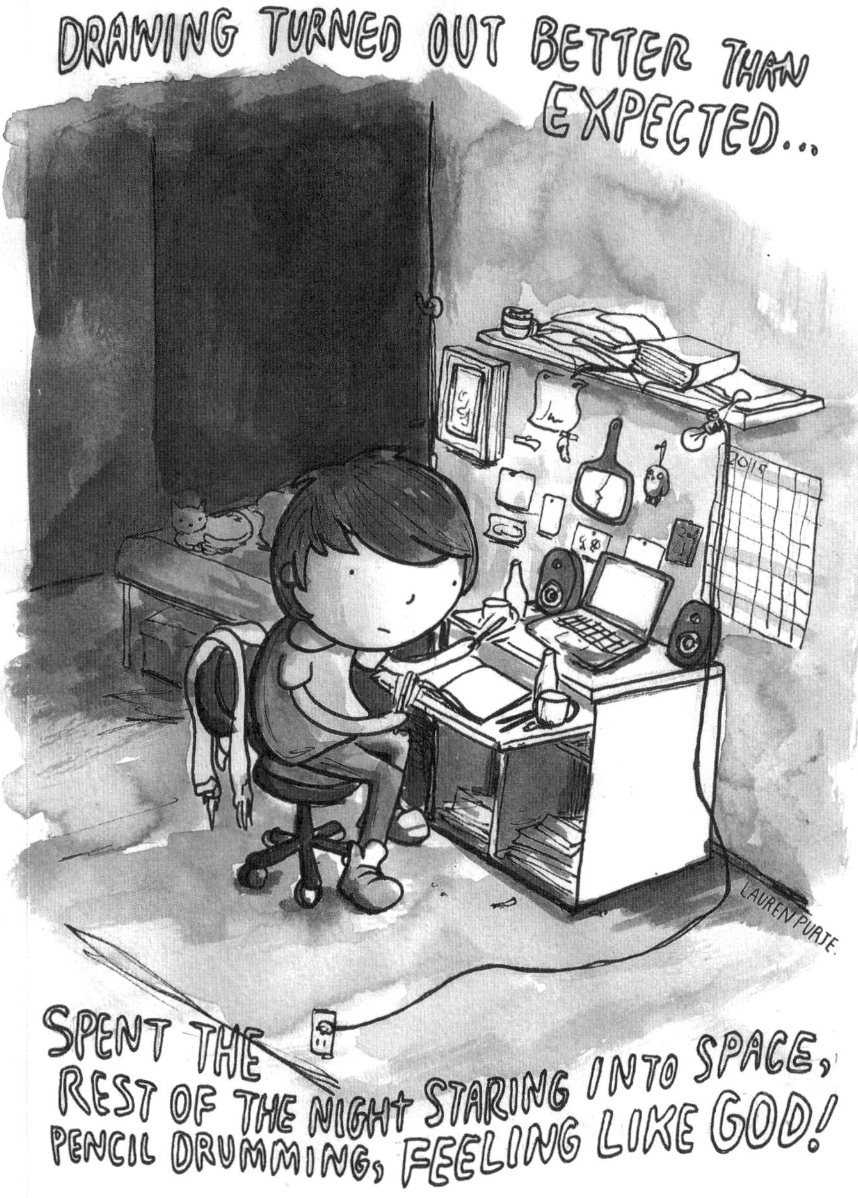
DRAWING TURNED OUT BETTER THAN EXPECTED...
2019
LAUREN PURJE.
SPENT THE REST OF THE NIGHT STARING INTO SPACE, PENCIL DRUMMING, FEELING LIKE GOD!

ABOUT A MAN MAN [WITH HONUS HONUS] BY LAUREN PURJE.

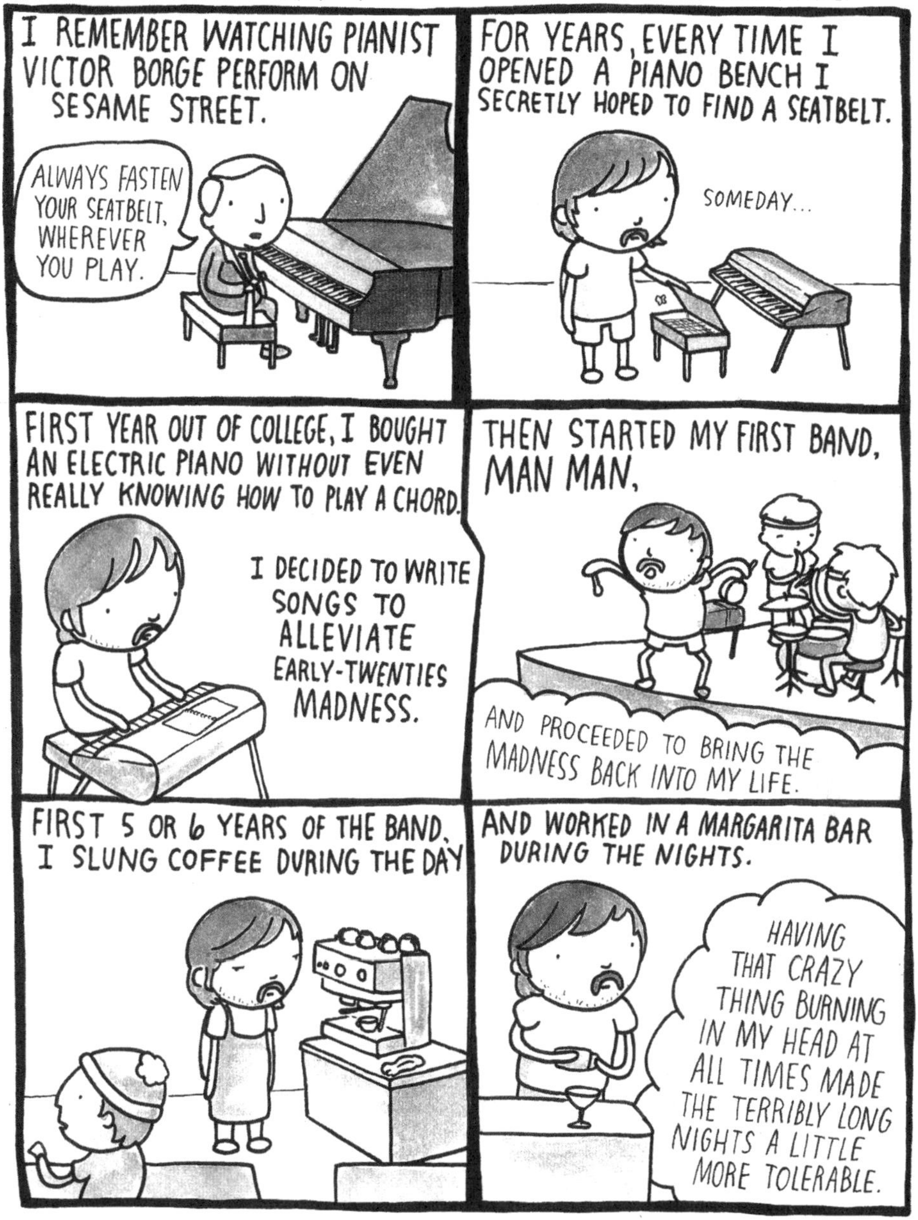
I REMEMBER WATCHING PIANIST VICTOR BORGE PERFORM ON SESAME STREET.
ALWAYS FASTEN YOUR SEATBELT, WHEREVER YOU PLAY.
FOR YEARS, EVERY TIME I OPENED A PIANO BENCH I SECRETLY HOPED TO FIND A SEATBELT.
SOMEDAY...
FIRST YEAR OUT OF COLLEGE, I BOUGHT AN ELECTRIC PIANO WITHOUT EVEN REALLY KNOWING HOW TO PLAY A CHORD.
I DECIDED TO WRITE SONGS TO ALLEVIATE EARLY-TWENTIES MADNESS.
THEN STARTED MY FIRST BAND, MAN MAN,
AND PROCEEDED TO BRING THE MADNESS BACK INTO MY LIFE.
FIRST 5 OR 6 YEARS OF THE BAND, I SLUNG COFFEE DURING THE DAY
AND WORKED IN A MARGARITA BAR DURING THE NIGHTS.
HAVING THAT CRAZY THING BURNING IN MY HEAD AT ALL TIMES MADE THE TERRIBLY LONG NIGHTS A LITTLE MORE TOLERABLE.

CONTINUED →

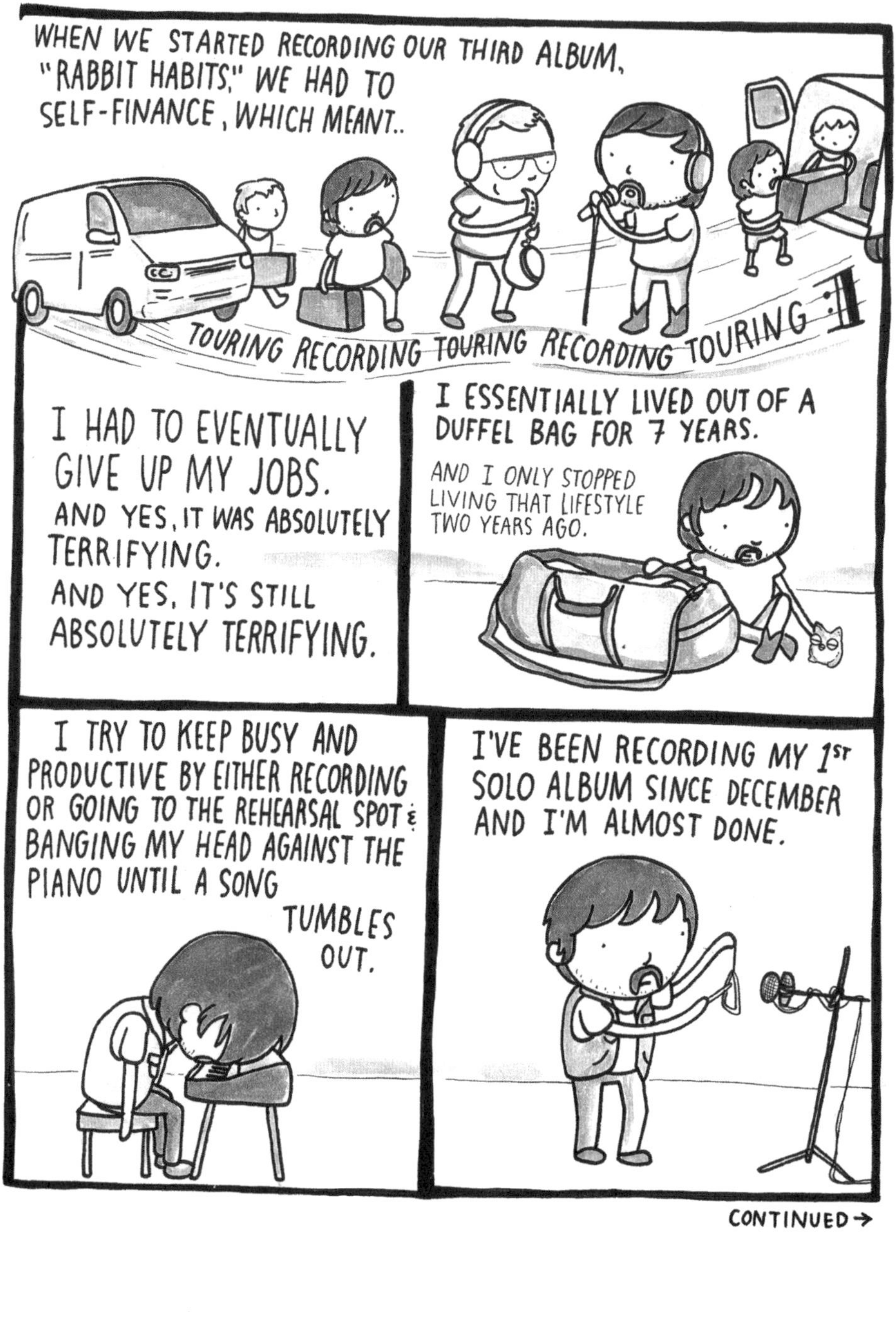
WHEN WE STARTED RECORDING OUR THIRD ALBUM, "RABBIT HABITS," WE HAD TO SELF-FINANCE, WHICH MEANT..
TOURING RECORDING TOURING RECORDING TOURING
I HAD TO EVENTUALLY GIVE UP MY JOBS.
AND YES, IT WAS ABSOLUTELY TERRIFYING.
AND YES, IT'S STILL ABSOLUTELY TERRIFYING.
I ESSENTIALLY LIVED OUT OF A DUFFEL BAG FOR 7 YEARS.
AND I ONLY STOPPED LIVING THAT LIFESTYLE TWO YEARS AGO.
I TRY TO KEEP BUSY AND PRODUCTIVE BY EITHER RECORDING OR GOING TO THE REHEARSAL SPOT & BANGING MY HEAD AGAINST THE PIANO UNTIL A SONG TUMBLES OUT.
I'VE BEEN RECORDING MY 1ST SOLO ALBUM SINCE DECEMBER AND I'M ALMOST DONE.

CONTINUED →

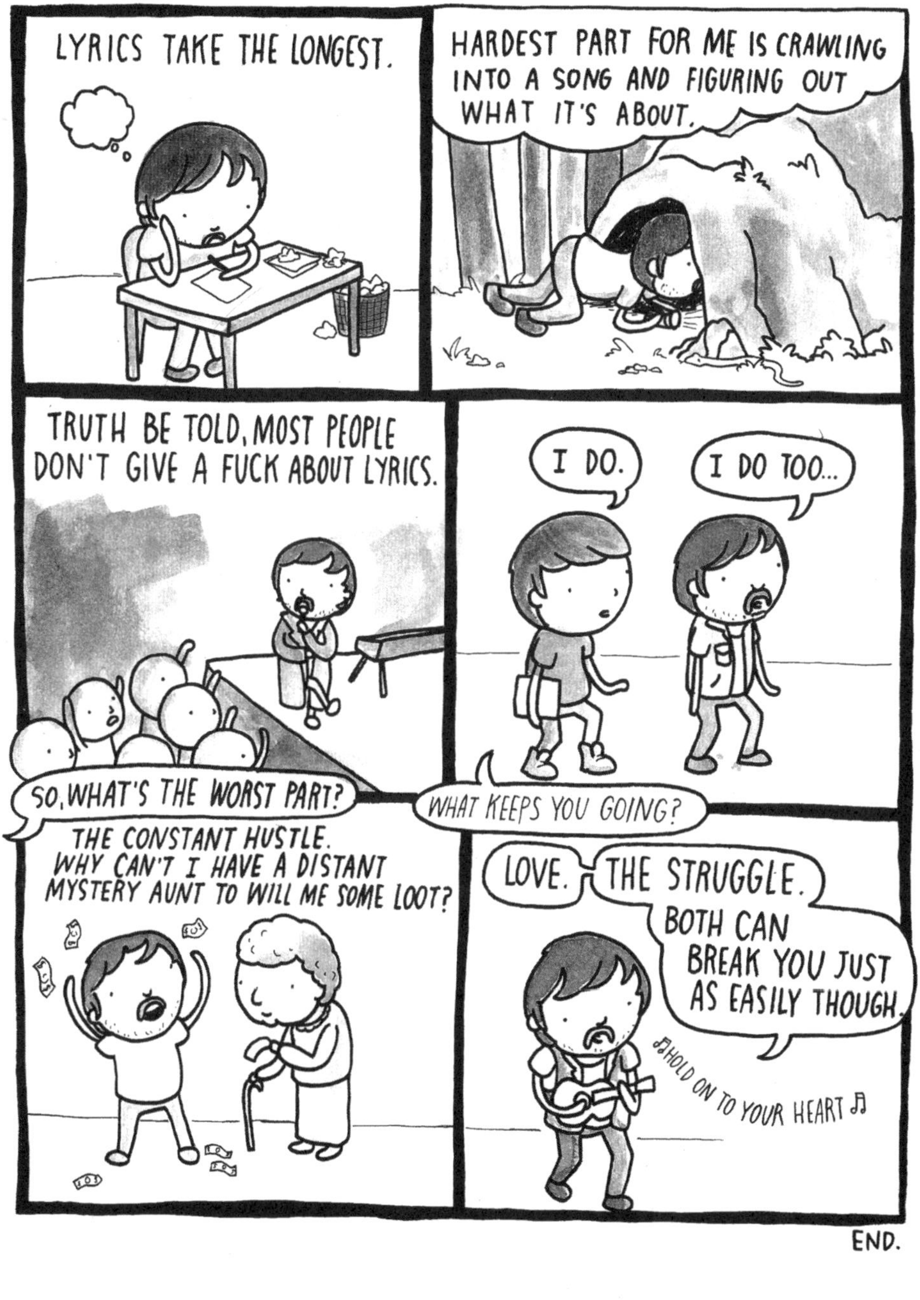
LYRICS TAKE THE LONGEST.
HARDEST PART FOR ME IS CRAWLING INTO A SONG AND FIGURING OUT WHAT IT'S ABOUT.
TRUTH BE TOLD, MOST PEOPLE DON'T GIVE A FUCK ABOUT LYRICS.
I DO.
I DO TOO...
SO, WHAT'S THE WORST PART?
THE CONSTANT HUSTLE. WHY CAN'T I HAVE A DISTANT MYSTERY AUNT TO WILL ME SOME LOOT?
WHAT KEEPS YOU GOING?
LOVE.
THE STRUGGLE.
BOTH CAN BREAK YOU JUST AS EASILY THOUGH.
♫ HOLD ON TO YOUR HEART ♫

END.

XTREME DRAWING!!

BY LAUREN PURJE.

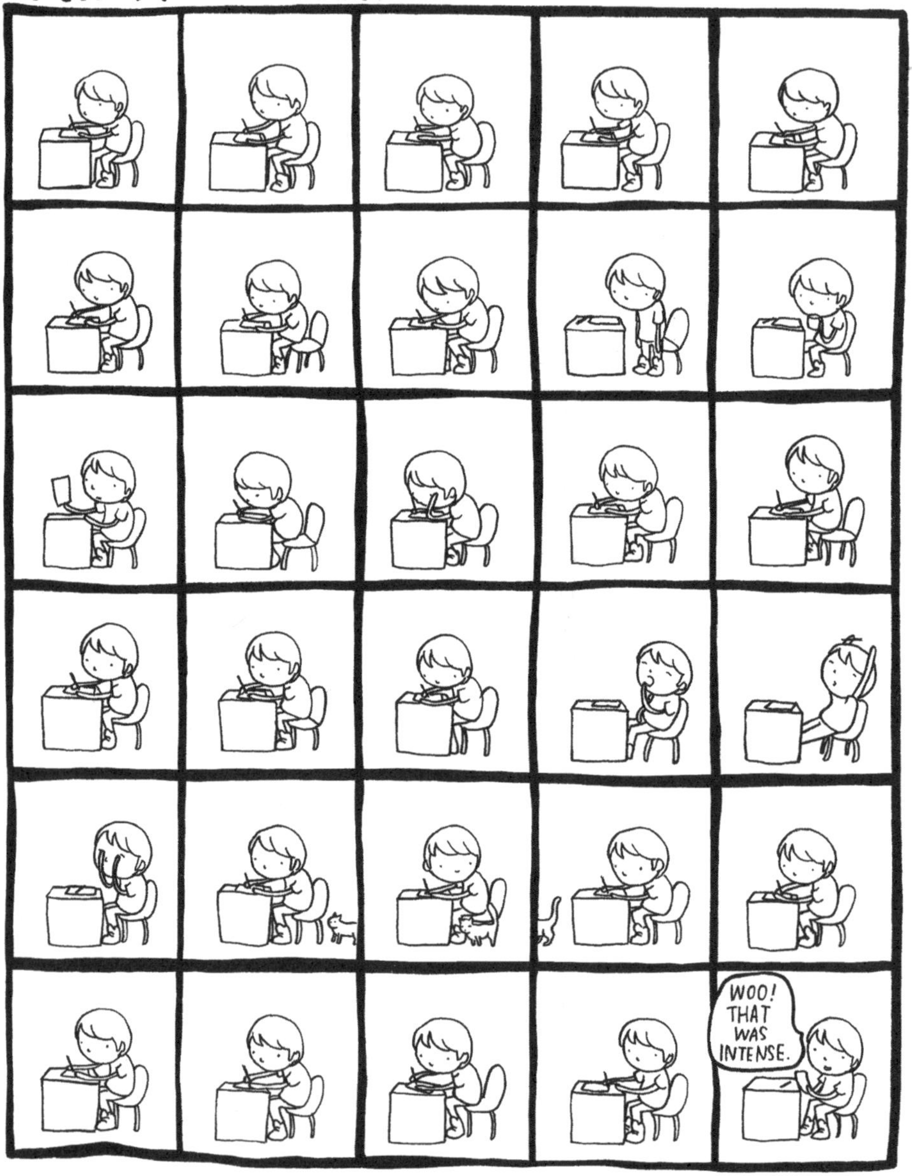
WOO! THAT WAS INTENSE.

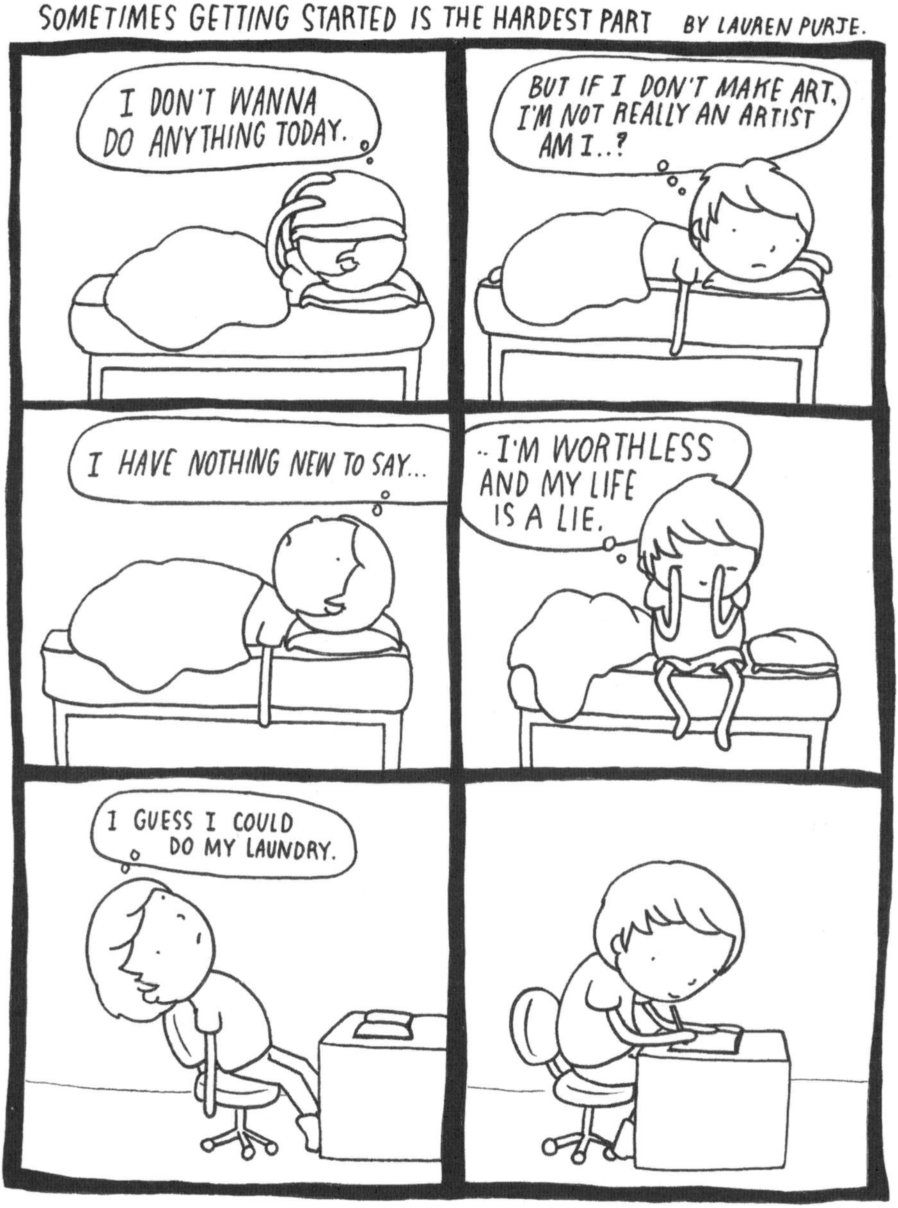
SOMETIMES GETTING STARTED IS THE HARDEST PART BY LAUREN PURJE.
I DON'T WANNA DO ANYTHING TODAY.
BUT IF I DON'T MAKE ART, I'M NOT REALLY AN ARTIST AM I..?
I HAVE NOTHING NEW TO SAY...
..I'M WORTHLESS AND MY LIFE IS A LIE.
I GUESS I COULD DO MY LAUNDRY.

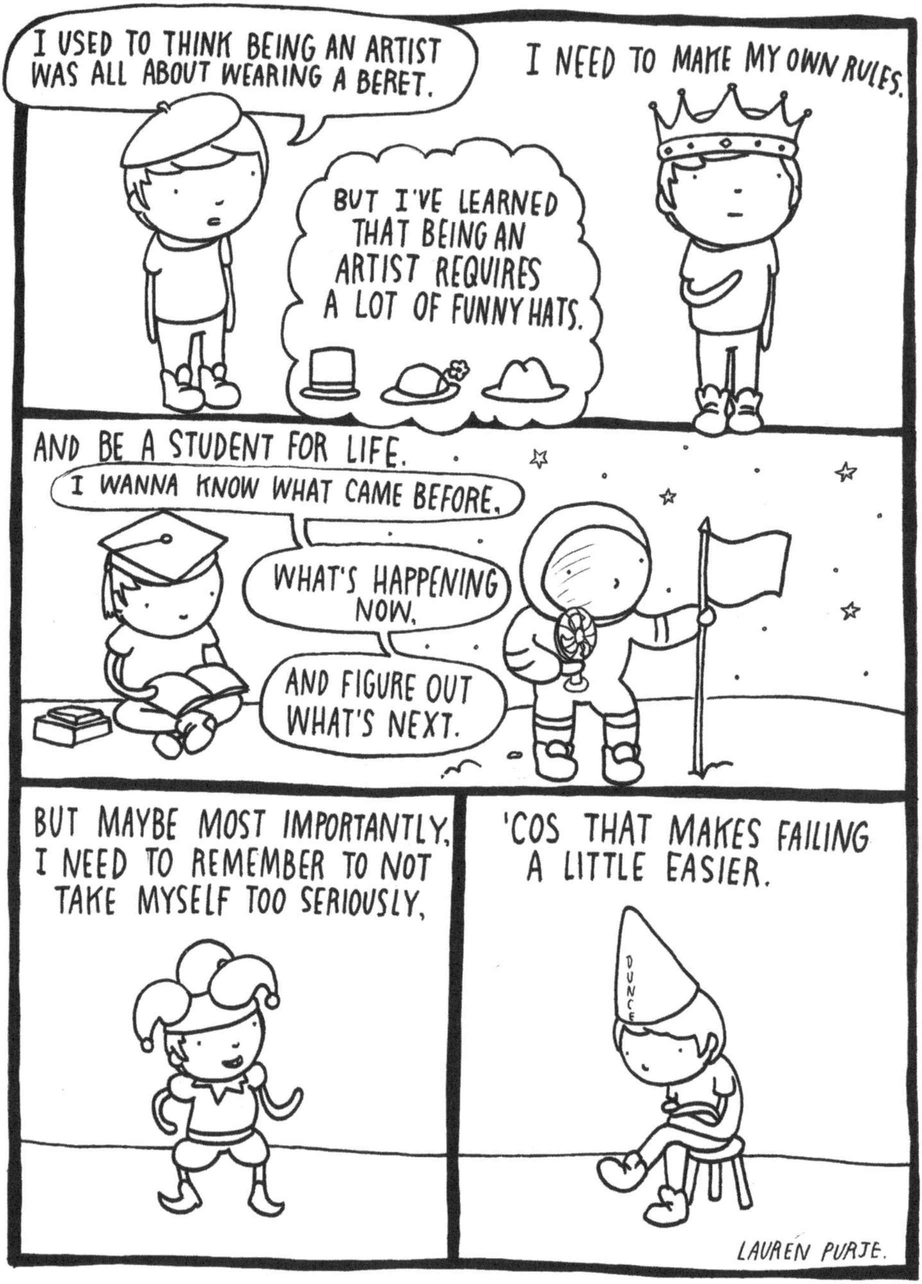
I USED TO THINK BEING AN ARTIST WAS ALL ABOUT WEARING A BERET.
BUT I'VE LEARNED THAT BEING AN ARTIST REQUIRES A LOT OF FUNNY HATS.
I NEED TO MAKE MY OWN RULES.
AND BE A STUDENT FOR LIFE.
I WANNA KNOW WHAT CAME BEFORE,
WHAT'S HAPPENING NOW,
AND FIGURE OUT WHAT'S NEXT.
BUT MAYBE MOST IMPORTANTLY, I NEED TO REMEMBER TO NOT TAKE MYSELF TOO SERIOUSLY,
'COS THAT MAKES FAILING A LITTLE EASIER.
DUNCE
LAUREN PURJE.

CALCULATING CONTENTMENT

BY LAUREN PURJE.

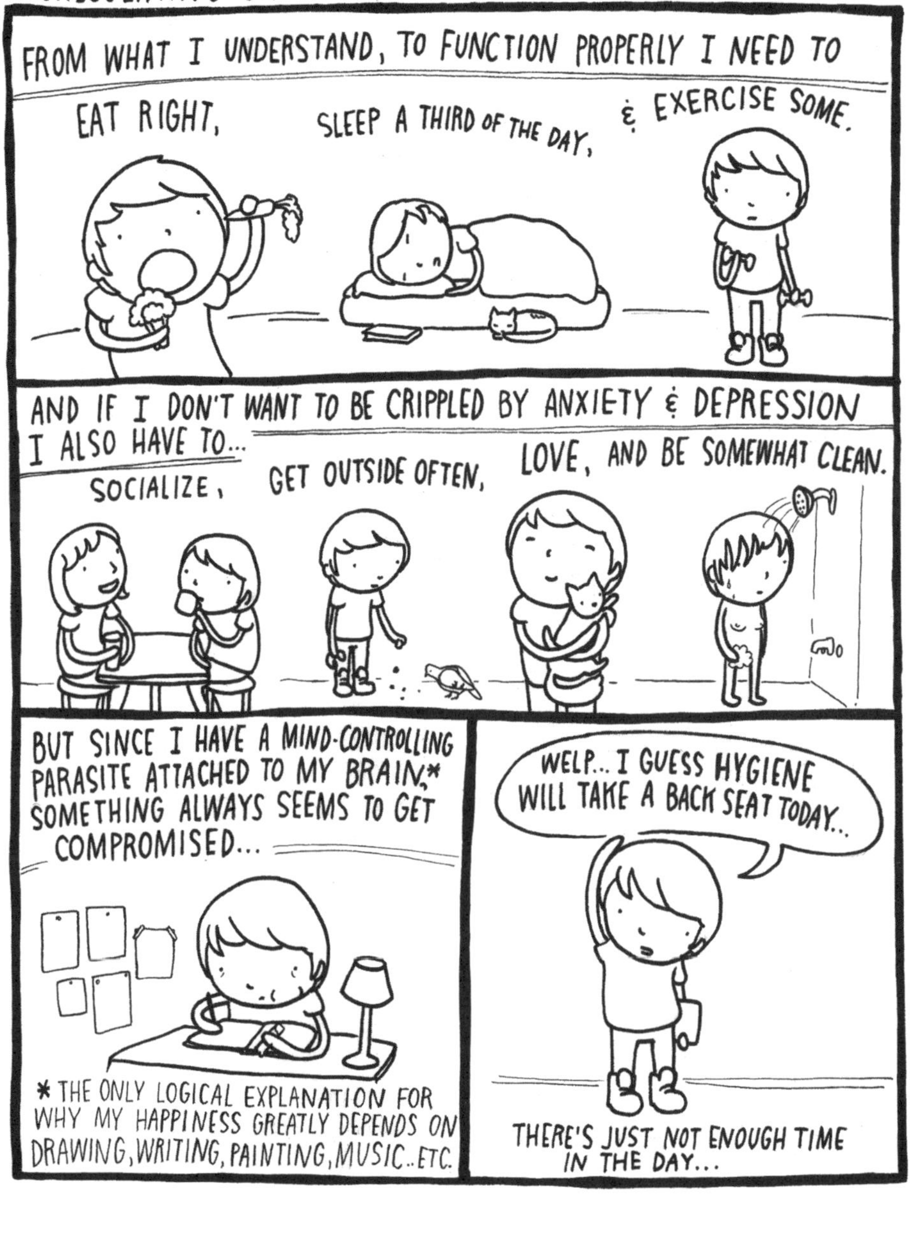
FROM WHAT I UNDERSTAND, TO FUNCTION PROPERLY I NEED TO
EAT RIGHT,
SLEEP A THIRD OF THE DAY,
& EXERCISE SOME.
AND IF I DON'T WANT TO BE CRIPPLED BY ANXIETY & DEPRESSION I ALSO HAVE TO...
SOCIALIZE,
GET OUTSIDE OFTEN,
LOVE, AND BE SOMEWHAT CLEAN.
BUT SINCE I HAVE A MIND-CONTROLLING PARASITE ATTACHED TO MY BRAIN,* SOMETHING ALWAYS SEEMS TO GET COMPROMISED...
* THE ONLY LOGICAL EXPLANATION FOR WHY MY HAPPINESS GREATLY DEPENDS ON DRAWING, WRITING, PAINTING, MUSIC.. ETC.
WELP... I GUESS HYGIENE WILL TAKE A BACK SEAT TODAY...
THERE'S JUST NOT ENOUGH TIME IN THE DAY...

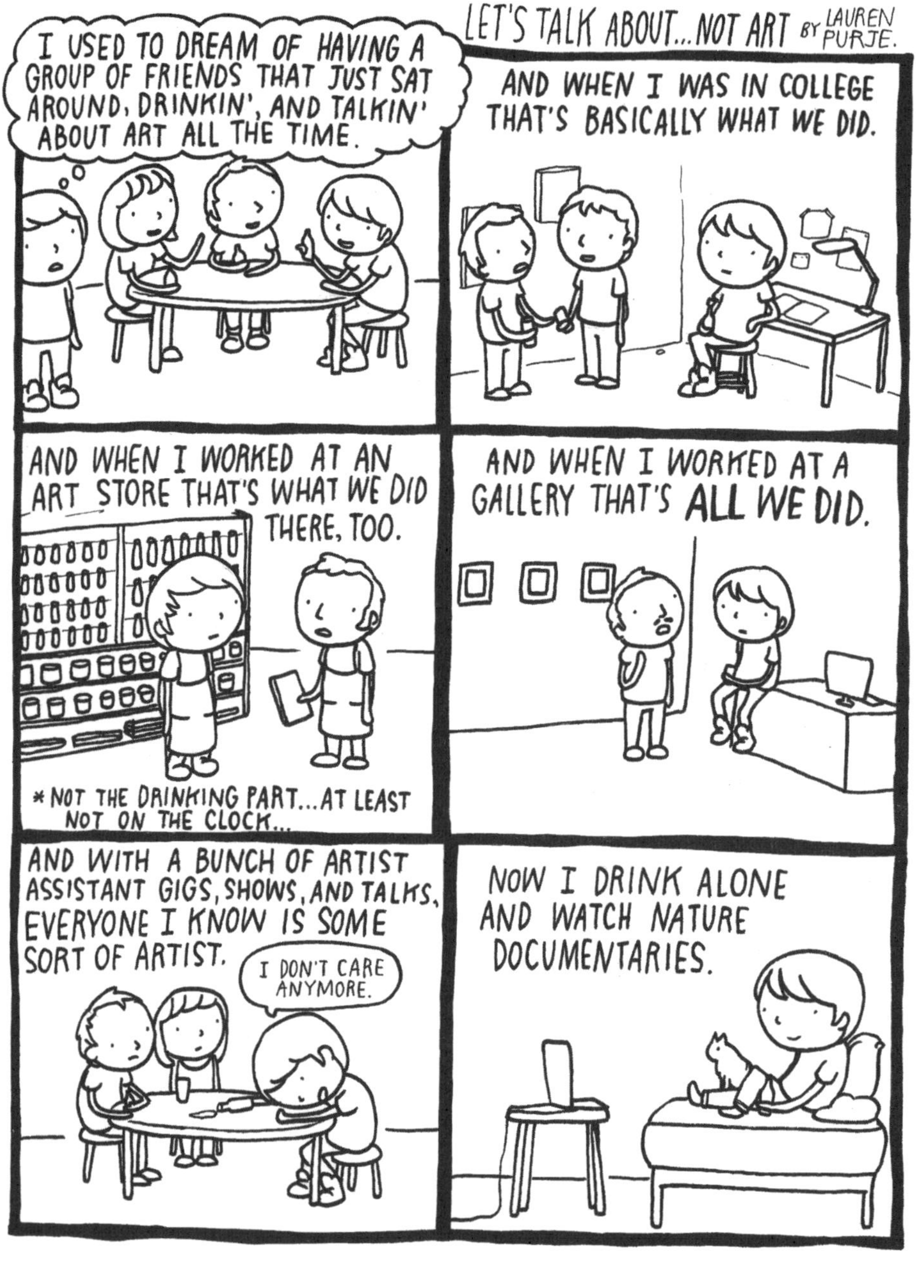
LET'S TALK ABOUT...NOT ART BY LAUREN PURJE.
I USED TO DREAM OF HAVING A GROUP OF FRIENDS THAT JUST SAT AROUND, DRINKIN', AND TALKIN' ABOUT ART ALL THE TIME.
AND WHEN I WAS IN COLLEGE THAT'S BASICALLY WHAT WE DID.
AND WHEN I WORKED AT AN ART STORE THAT'S WHAT WE DID THERE, TOO.
* NOT THE DRINKING PART...AT LEAST NOT ON THE CLOCK...
AND WHEN I WORKED AT A GALLERY THAT'S ALL WE DID.
AND WITH A BUNCH OF ARTIST ASSISTANT GIGS, SHOWS, AND TALKS, EVERYONE I KNOW IS SOME SORT OF ARTIST.
I DON'T CARE ANYMORE.
NOW I DRINK ALONE AND WATCH NATURE DOCUMENTARIES.

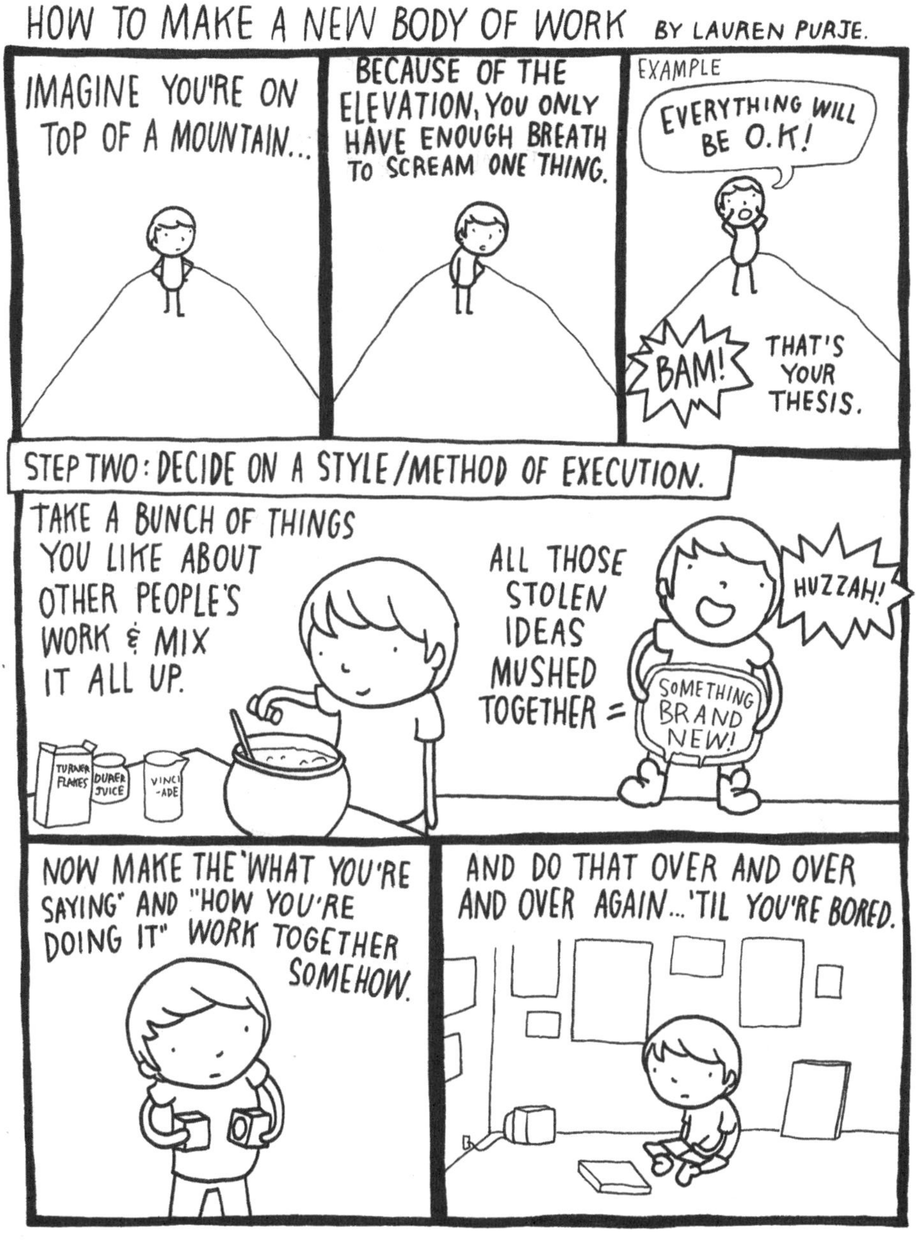
HOW TO MAKE A NEW BODY OF WORK BY LAUREN PURJE.
IMAGINE YOU'RE ON TOP OF A MOUNTAIN...
BECAUSE OF THE ELEVATION, YOU ONLY HAVE ENOUGH BREATH TO SCREAM ONE THING.
EXAMPLE
EVERYTHING WILL BE O.K!
BAM!
THAT'S YOUR THESIS.
STEP TWO: DECIDE ON A STYLE/METHOD OF EXECUTION.
TAKE A BUNCH OF THINGS YOU LIKE ABOUT OTHER PEOPLE'S WORK & MIX IT ALL UP.
TURNER FLAKES
DURER JUICE
VINCI-ADE
ALL THOSE STOLEN IDEAS MUSHED TOGETHER =
SOMETHING BRAND NEW!
HUZZAH!
NOW MAKE THE "WHAT YOU'RE SAYING" AND "HOW YOU'RE DOING IT" WORK TOGETHER SOMEHOW.
AND DO THAT OVER AND OVER AND OVER AGAIN...'TIL YOU'RE BORED.

ART SAVES BY LAUREN PURJE.

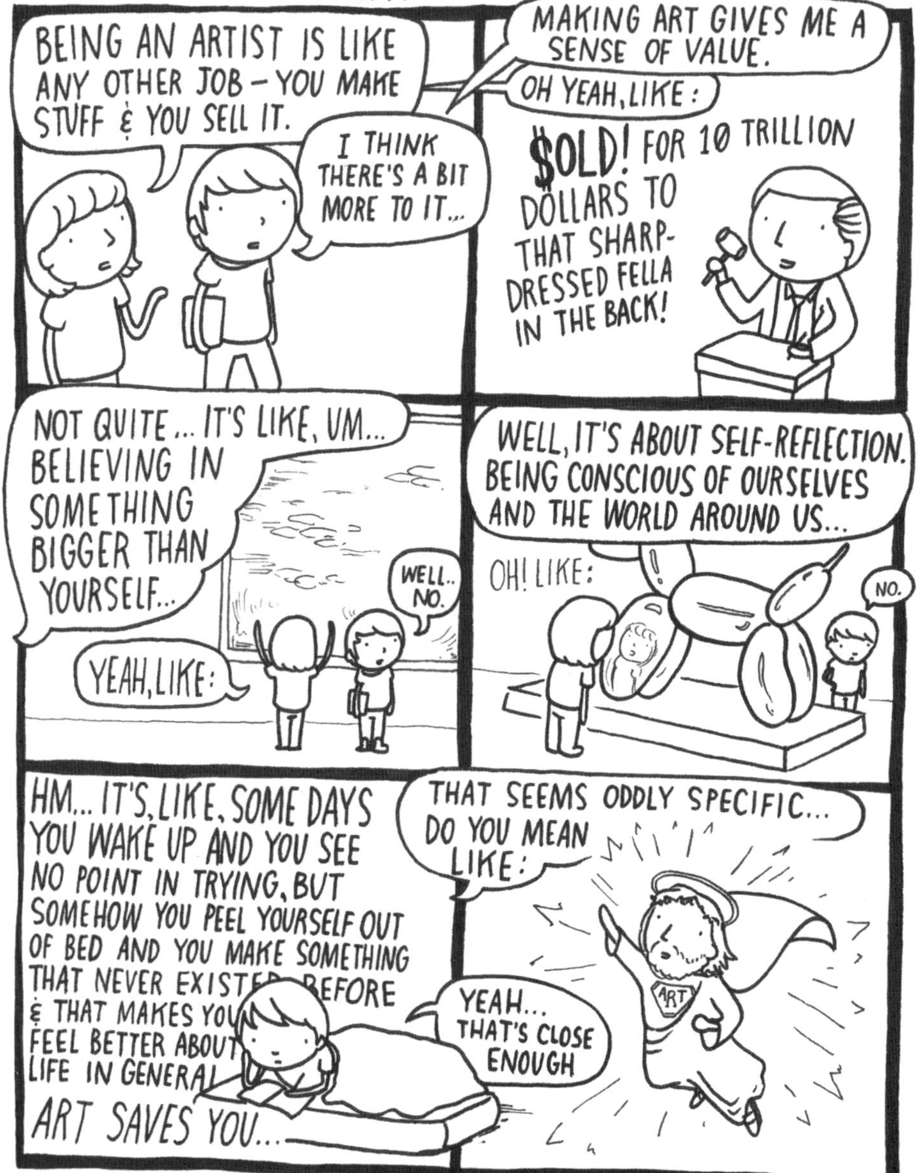
BEING AN ARTIST IS LIKE ANY OTHER JOB – YOU MAKE STUFF & YOU SELL IT.
I THINK THERE'S A BIT MORE TO IT...
MAKING ART GIVES ME A SENSE OF VALUE.
OH YEAH, LIKE:
$OLD! FOR 10 TRILLION DOLLARS TO THAT SHARP-DRESSED FELLA IN THE BACK!
NOT QUITE... IT'S LIKE, UM... BELIEVING IN SOMETHING BIGGER THAN YOURSELF...
YEAH, LIKE:
WELL.. NO.
WELL, IT'S ABOUT SELF-REFLECTION. BEING CONSCIOUS OF OURSELVES AND THE WORLD AROUND US...
OH! LIKE:
NO.
HM... IT'S, LIKE, SOME DAYS YOU WAKE UP AND YOU SEE NO POINT IN TRYING, BUT SOMEHOW YOU PEEL YOURSELF OUT OF BED AND YOU MAKE SOMETHING THAT NEVER EXISTED BEFORE & THAT MAKES YOU FEEL BETTER ABOUT LIFE IN GENERAL
ART SAVES YOU...
THAT SEEMS ODDLY SPECIFIC... DO YOU MEAN LIKE:
ART
YEAH... THAT'S CLOSE ENOUGH

SOME MISERABLE DUDES' LAST WORDS

BY LAUREN PURJE.

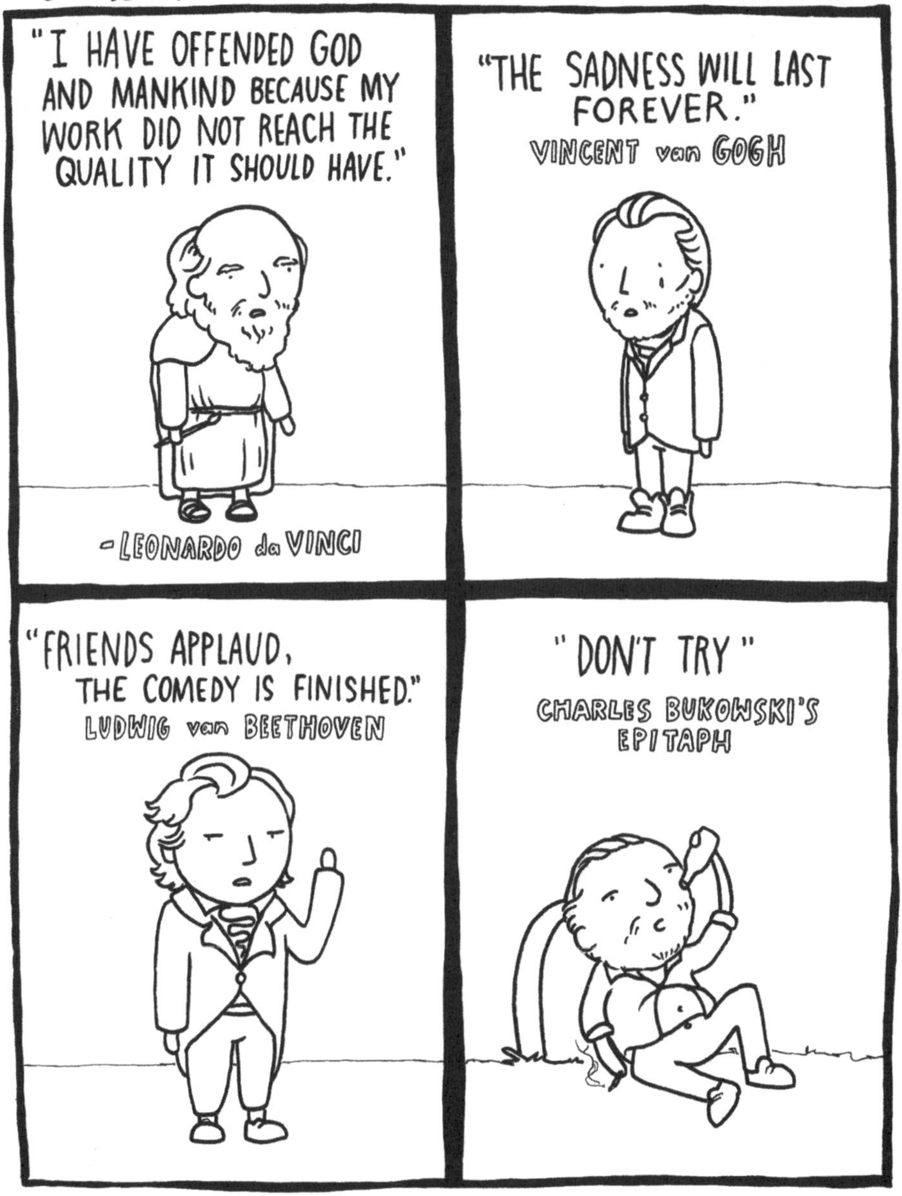
"I HAVE OFFENDED GOD AND MANKIND BECAUSE MY WORK DID NOT REACH THE QUALITY IT SHOULD HAVE."
-LEONARDO da VINCI
"THE SADNESS WILL LAST FOREVER."
VINCENT van GOGH
"FRIENDS APPLAUD, THE COMEDY IS FINISHED."
LUDWIG van BEETHOVEN
"DON'T TRY"
CHARLES BUKOWSKI'S EPITAPH

NOT ALONE

BY LAUREN PURJE.

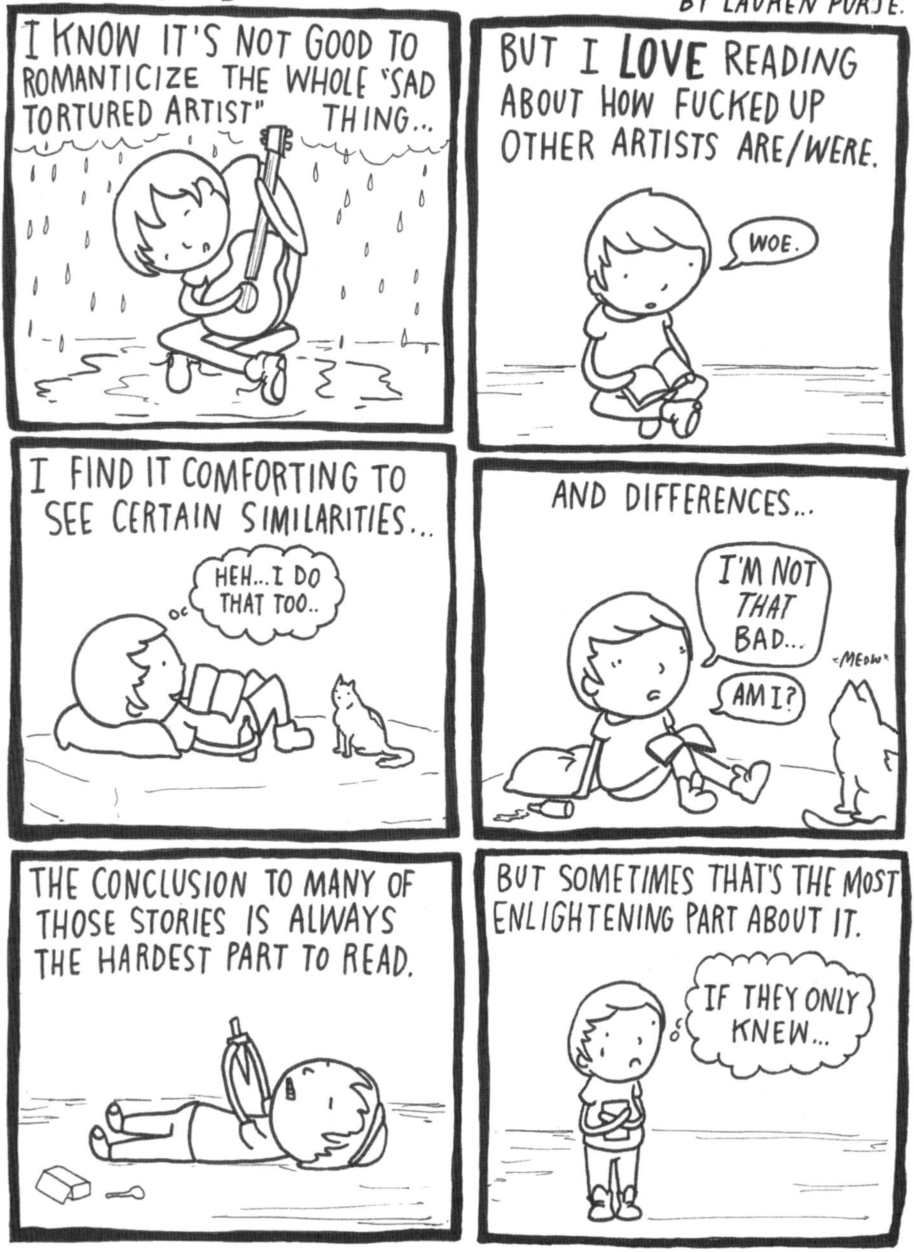
I KNOW IT'S NOT GOOD TO ROMANTICIZE THE WHOLE "SAD TORTURED ARTIST" THING...
BUT I **LOVE** READING ABOUT HOW FUCKED UP OTHER ARTISTS ARE/WERE.
WOE.
I FIND IT COMFORTING TO SEE CERTAIN SIMILARITIES...
HEH...I DO THAT TOO..
AND DIFFERENCES...
I'M NOT *THAT* BAD...
AM I?
MEOW
THE CONCLUSION TO MANY OF THOSE STORIES IS ALWAYS THE HARDEST PART TO READ.
BUT SOMETIMES THAT'S THE MOST ENLIGHTENING PART ABOUT IT.
IF THEY ONLY KNEW...

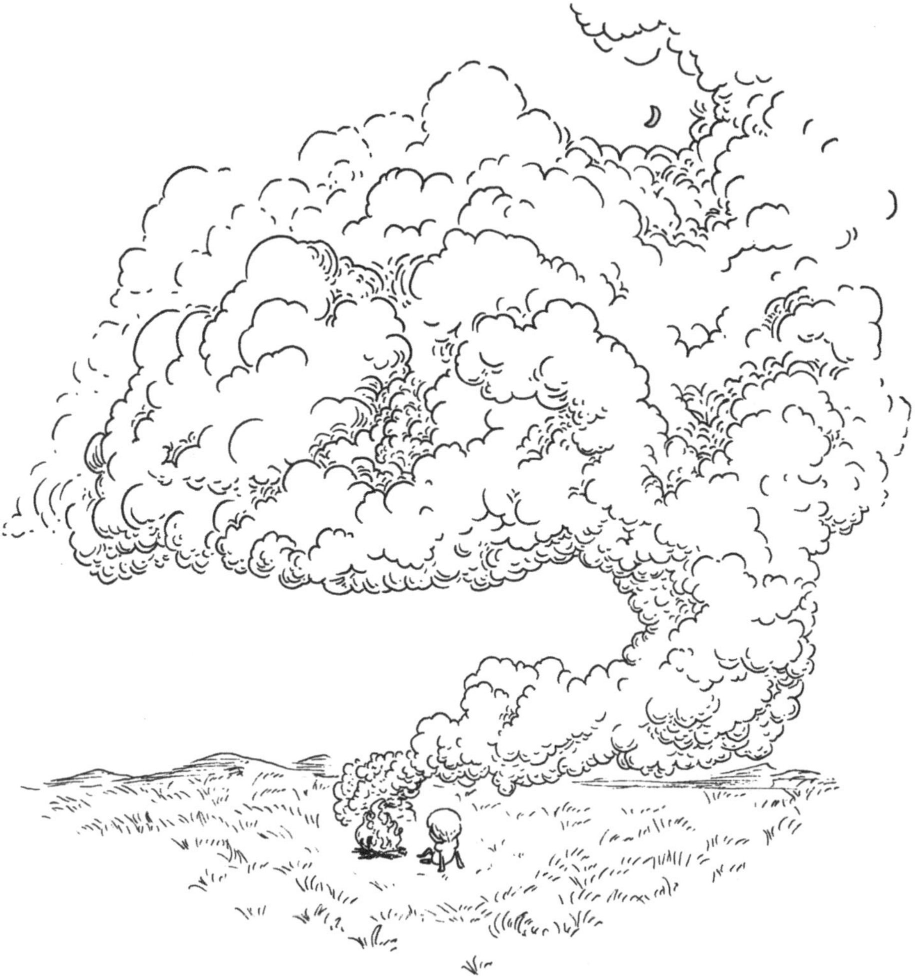

YOU HAVE NO IDEA HOW IMPORTANT YOU ARE.
[KEEP THAT FIRE BURNING.]

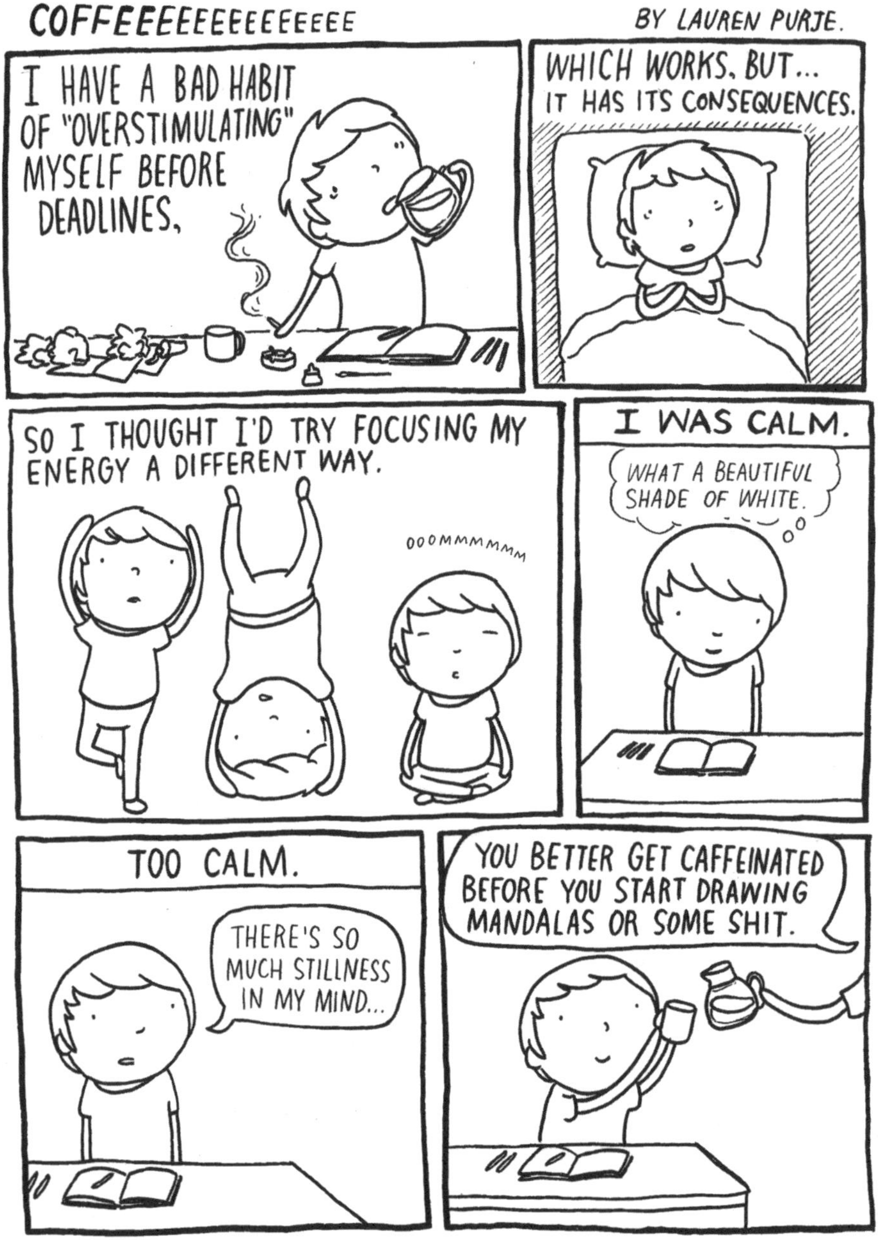
COFFEEEEEEEEEEEEEE
BY LAUREN PURJE.
I HAVE A BAD HABIT OF "OVERSTIMULATING" MYSELF BEFORE DEADLINES,
WHICH WORKS, BUT... IT HAS ITS CONSEQUENCES.
SO I THOUGHT I'D TRY FOCUSING MY ENERGY A DIFFERENT WAY.
OOOMMMMMMM
I WAS CALM.
WHAT A BEAUTIFUL SHADE OF WHITE.
TOO CALM.
THERE'S SO MUCH STILLNESS IN MY MIND...
YOU BETTER GET CAFFEINATED BEFORE YOU START DRAWING MANDALAS OR SOME SHIT.

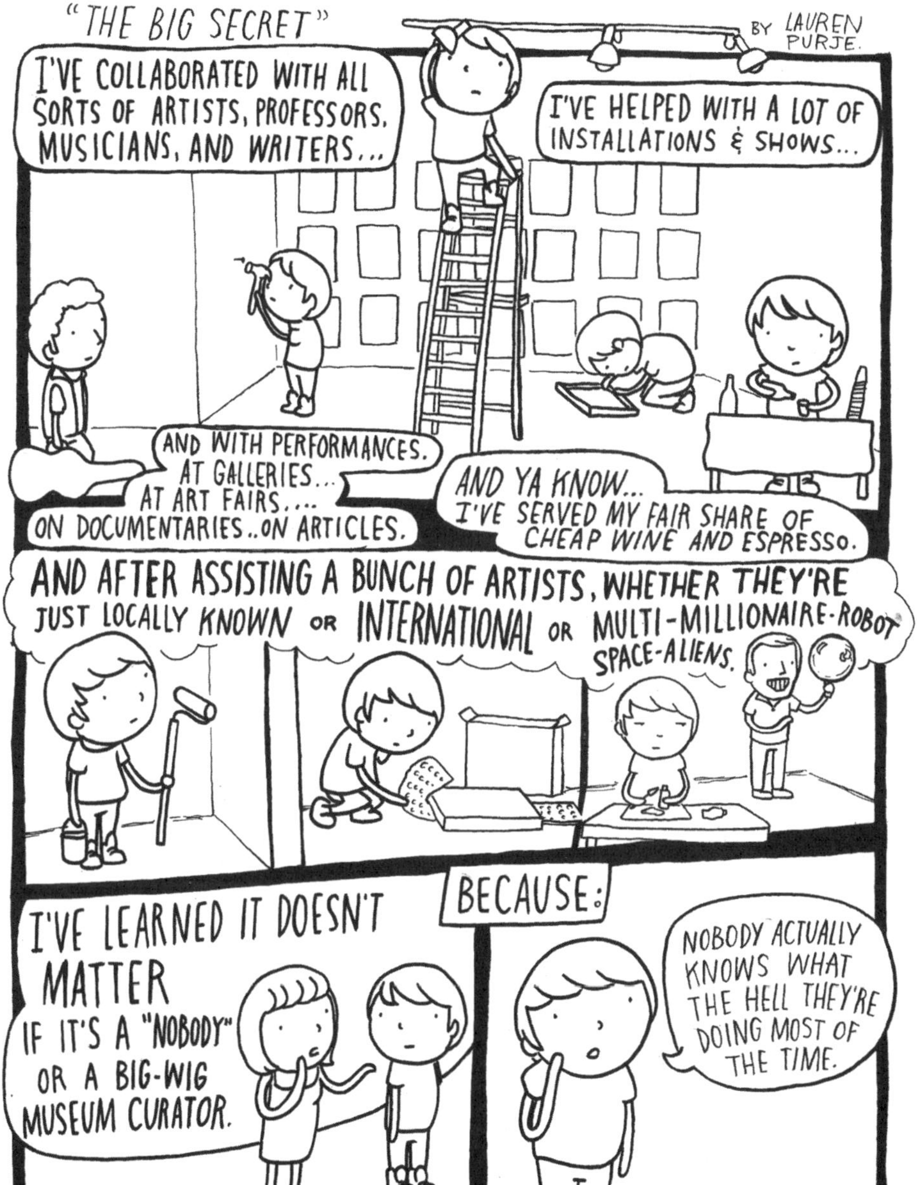
"THE BIG SECRET"
BY LAUREN PURJE.
I'VE COLLABORATED WITH ALL SORTS OF ARTISTS, PROFESSORS, MUSICIANS, AND WRITERS...
I'VE HELPED WITH A LOT OF INSTALLATIONS & SHOWS...
AND WITH PERFORMANCES. AT GALLERIES... AT ART FAIRS,... ON DOCUMENTARIES..ON ARTICLES.
AND YA KNOW... I'VE SERVED MY FAIR SHARE OF CHEAP WINE AND ESPRESSO.
AND AFTER ASSISTING A BUNCH OF ARTISTS, WHETHER THEY'RE JUST LOCALLY KNOWN OR INTERNATIONAL OR MULTI-MILLIONAIRE-ROBOT SPACE-ALIENS.
BECAUSE:
I'VE LEARNED IT DOESN'T MATTER IF IT'S A "NOBODY" OR A BIG-WIG MUSEUM CURATOR.
NOBODY ACTUALLY KNOWS WHAT THE HELL THEY'RE DOING MOST OF THE TIME.

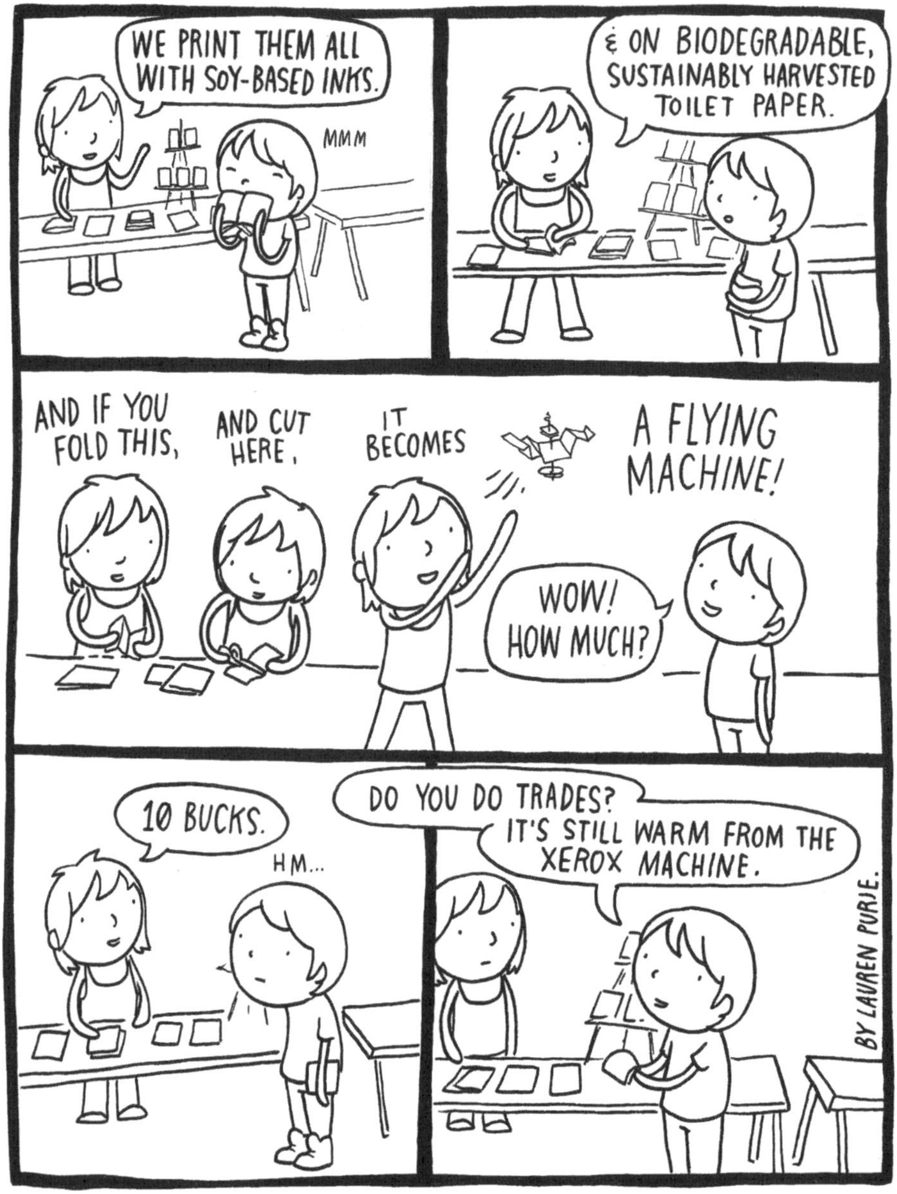
WE PRINT THEM ALL WITH SOY-BASED INKS.
MMM
& ON BIODEGRADABLE, SUSTAINABLY HARVESTED TOILET PAPER.
AND IF YOU FOLD THIS,
AND CUT HERE,
IT BECOMES
A FLYING MACHINE!
WOW! HOW MUCH?
10 BUCKS.
HM...
DO YOU DO TRADES?
IT'S STILL WARM FROM THE XEROX MACHINE.
BY LAUREN PURJE.

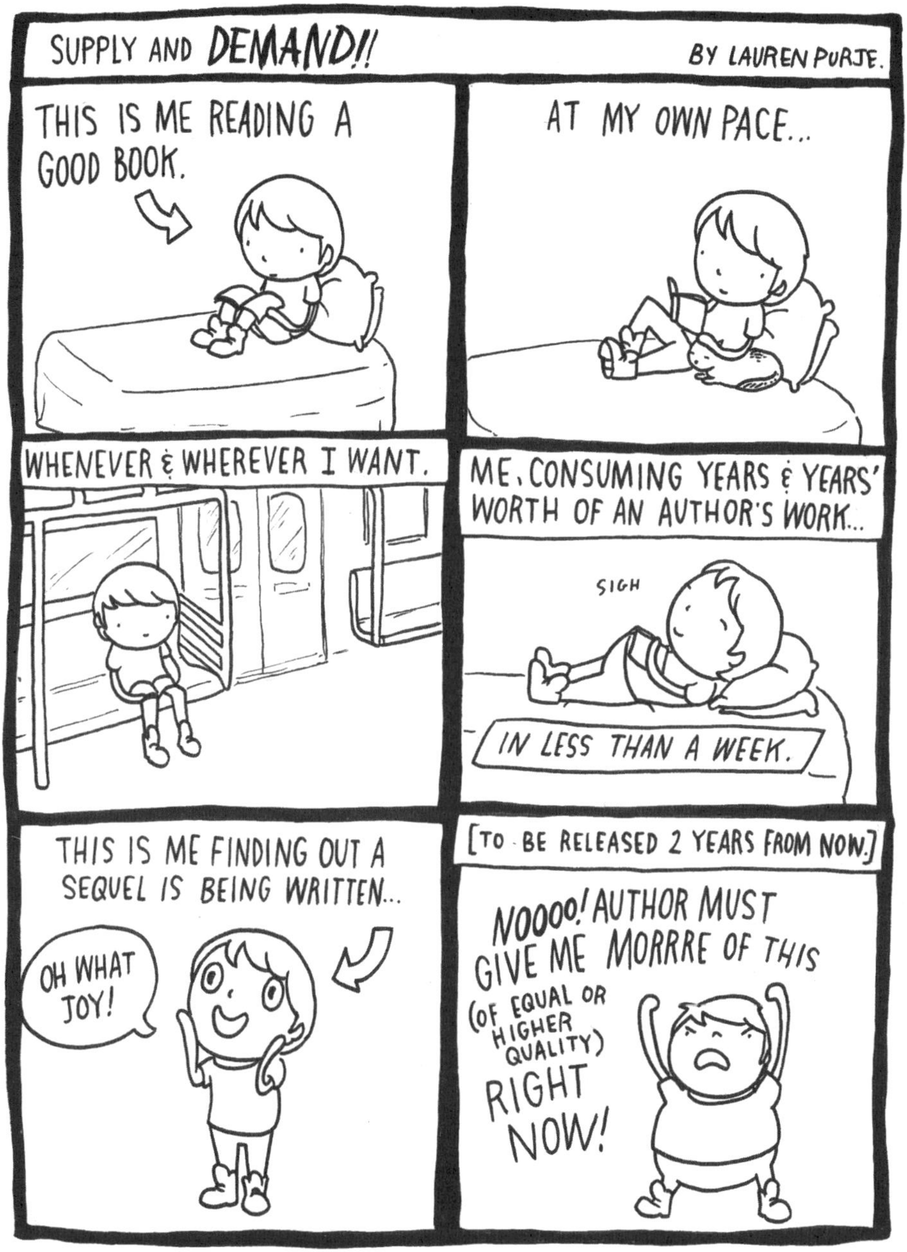

SUPPLY AND DEMAND!!
BY LAUREN PURJE.
THIS IS ME READING A GOOD BOOK.
AT MY OWN PACE...
WHENEVER & WHEREVER I WANT.
ME, CONSUMING YEARS & YEARS' WORTH OF AN AUTHOR'S WORK...
SIGH
IN LESS THAN A WEEK.
THIS IS ME FINDING OUT A SEQUEL IS BEING WRITTEN...
OH WHAT JOY!
[TO BE RELEASED 2 YEARS FROM NOW.]
NOOOO! AUTHOR MUST GIVE ME MORRRE OF THIS
(OF EQUAL OR HIGHER QUALITY)
RIGHT NOW!

OLD MAN & THE MAGNIFYING GLASS

BY LAUREN PURJE.

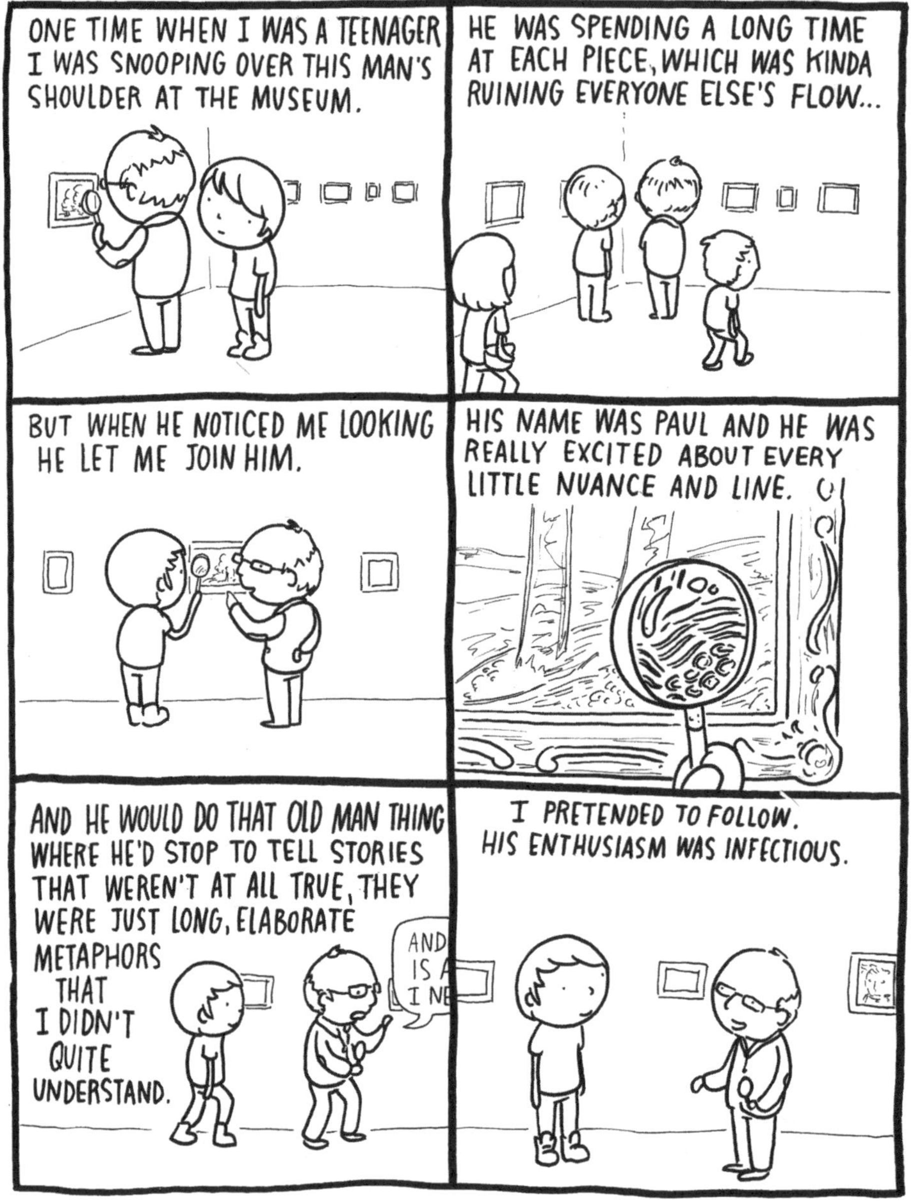
ONE TIME WHEN I WAS A TEENAGER I WAS SNOOPING OVER THIS MAN'S SHOULDER AT THE MUSEUM.
HE WAS SPENDING A LONG TIME AT EACH PIECE, WHICH WAS KINDA RUINING EVERYONE ELSE'S FLOW...
BUT WHEN HE NOTICED ME LOOKING HE LET ME JOIN HIM.
HIS NAME WAS PAUL AND HE WAS REALLY EXCITED ABOUT EVERY LITTLE NUANCE AND LINE.
AND HE WOULD DO THAT OLD MAN THING WHERE HE'D STOP TO TELL STORIES THAT WEREN'T AT ALL TRUE, THEY WERE JUST LONG, ELABORATE METAPHORS THAT I DIDN'T QUITE UNDERSTAND.
AND
IS
I N
I PRETENDED TO FOLLOW. HIS ENTHUSIASM WAS INFECTIOUS.

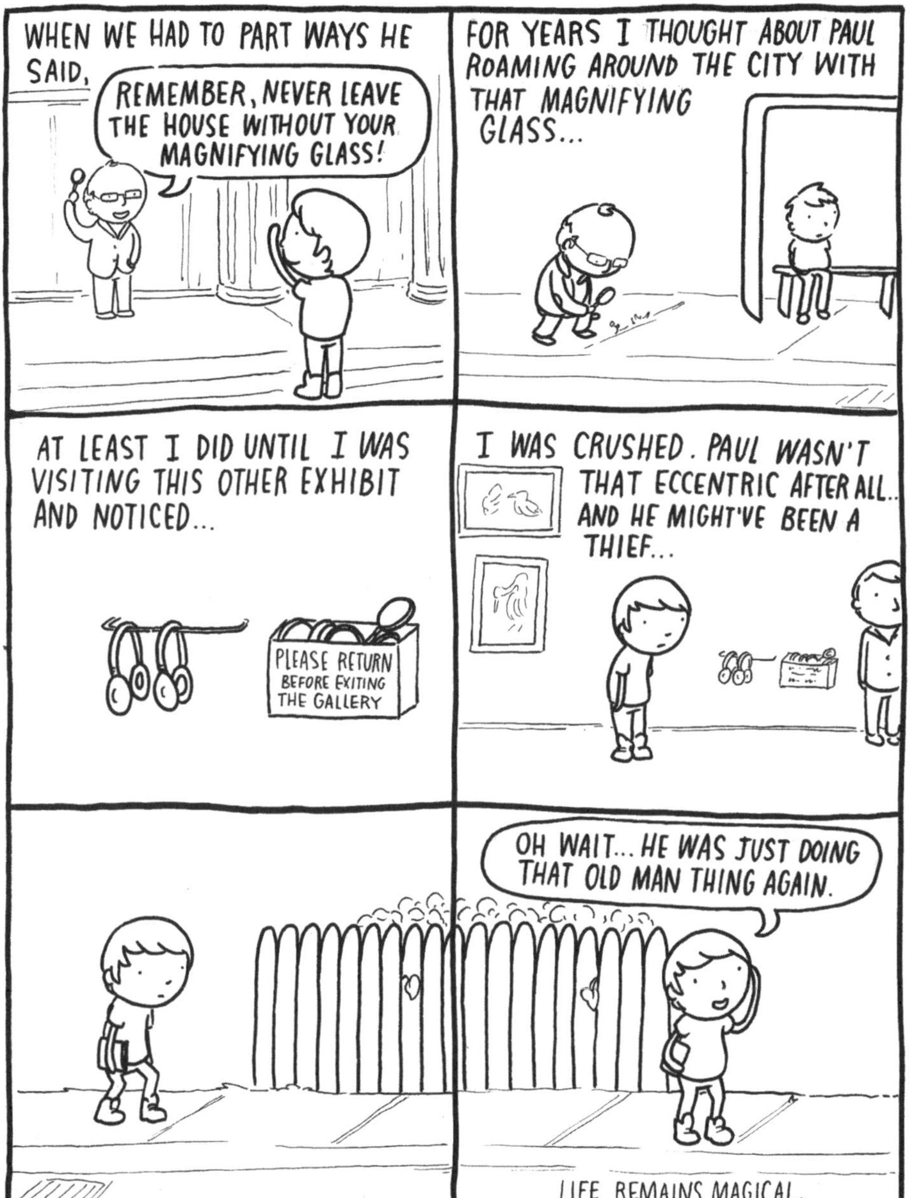
WHEN WE HAD TO PART WAYS HE SAID,
REMEMBER, NEVER LEAVE THE HOUSE WITHOUT YOUR MAGNIFYING GLASS!
FOR YEARS I THOUGHT ABOUT PAUL ROAMING AROUND THE CITY WITH THAT MAGNIFYING GLASS...
AT LEAST I DID UNTIL I WAS VISITING THIS OTHER EXHIBIT AND NOTICED...
PLEASE RETURN BEFORE EXITING THE GALLERY
I WAS CRUSHED. PAUL WASN'T THAT ECCENTRIC AFTER ALL... AND HE MIGHT'VE BEEN A THIEF...
OH WAIT... HE WAS JUST DOING THAT OLD MAN THING AGAIN.
LIFE REMAINS MAGICAL.

MY PROCESS

BY LAUREN PURJE.

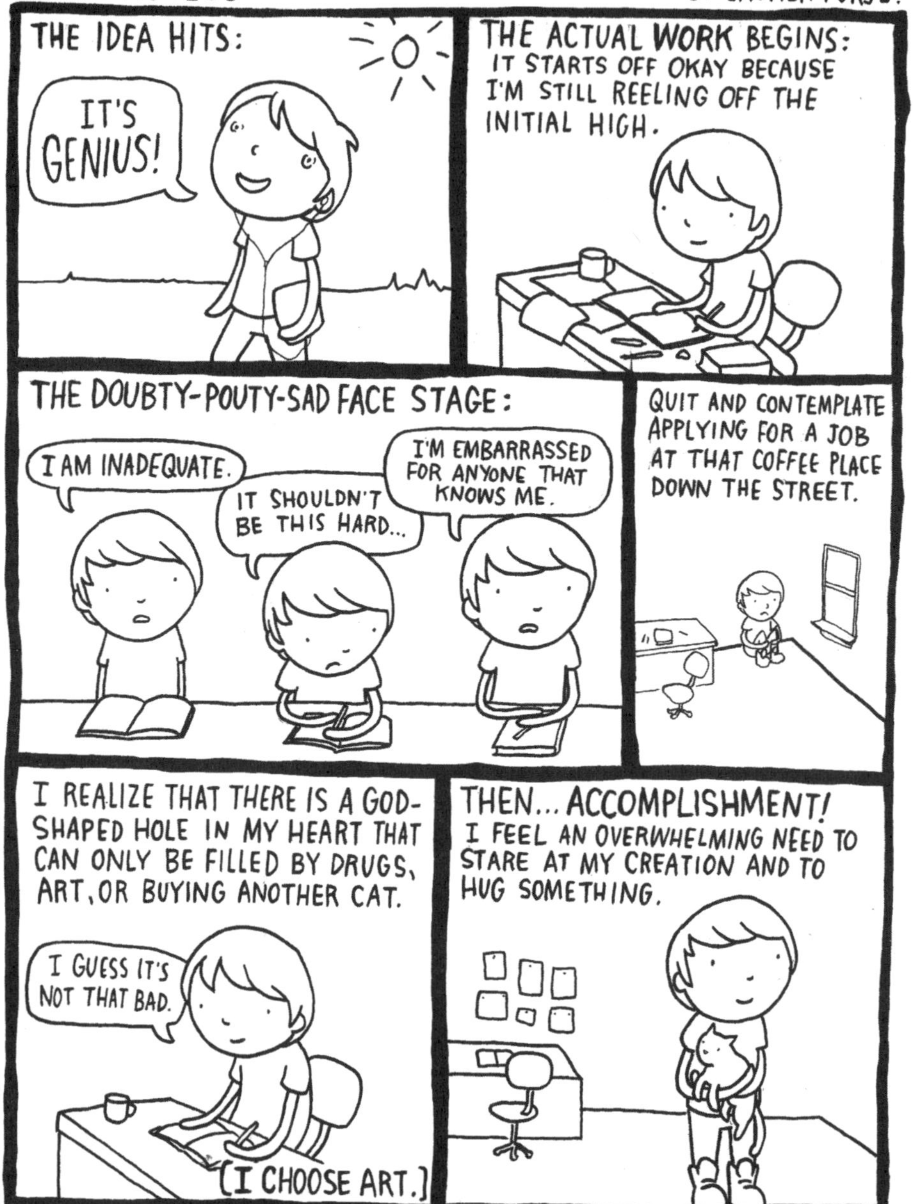
THE IDEA HITS:
IT'S GENIUS!
THE ACTUAL WORK BEGINS: IT STARTS OFF OKAY BECAUSE I'M STILL REELING OFF THE INITIAL HIGH.
THE DOUBTY-POUTY-SAD FACE STAGE:
I AM INADEQUATE.
IT SHOULDN'T BE THIS HARD...
I'M EMBARRASSED FOR ANYONE THAT KNOWS ME.
QUIT AND CONTEMPLATE APPLYING FOR A JOB AT THAT COFFEE PLACE DOWN THE STREET.
I REALIZE THAT THERE IS A GOD-SHAPED HOLE IN MY HEART THAT CAN ONLY BE FILLED BY DRUGS, ART, OR BUYING ANOTHER CAT.
I GUESS IT'S NOT THAT BAD.
[I CHOOSE ART.]
THEN... ACCOMPLISHMENT! I FEEL AN OVERWHELMING NEED TO STARE AT MY CREATION AND TO HUG SOMETHING.

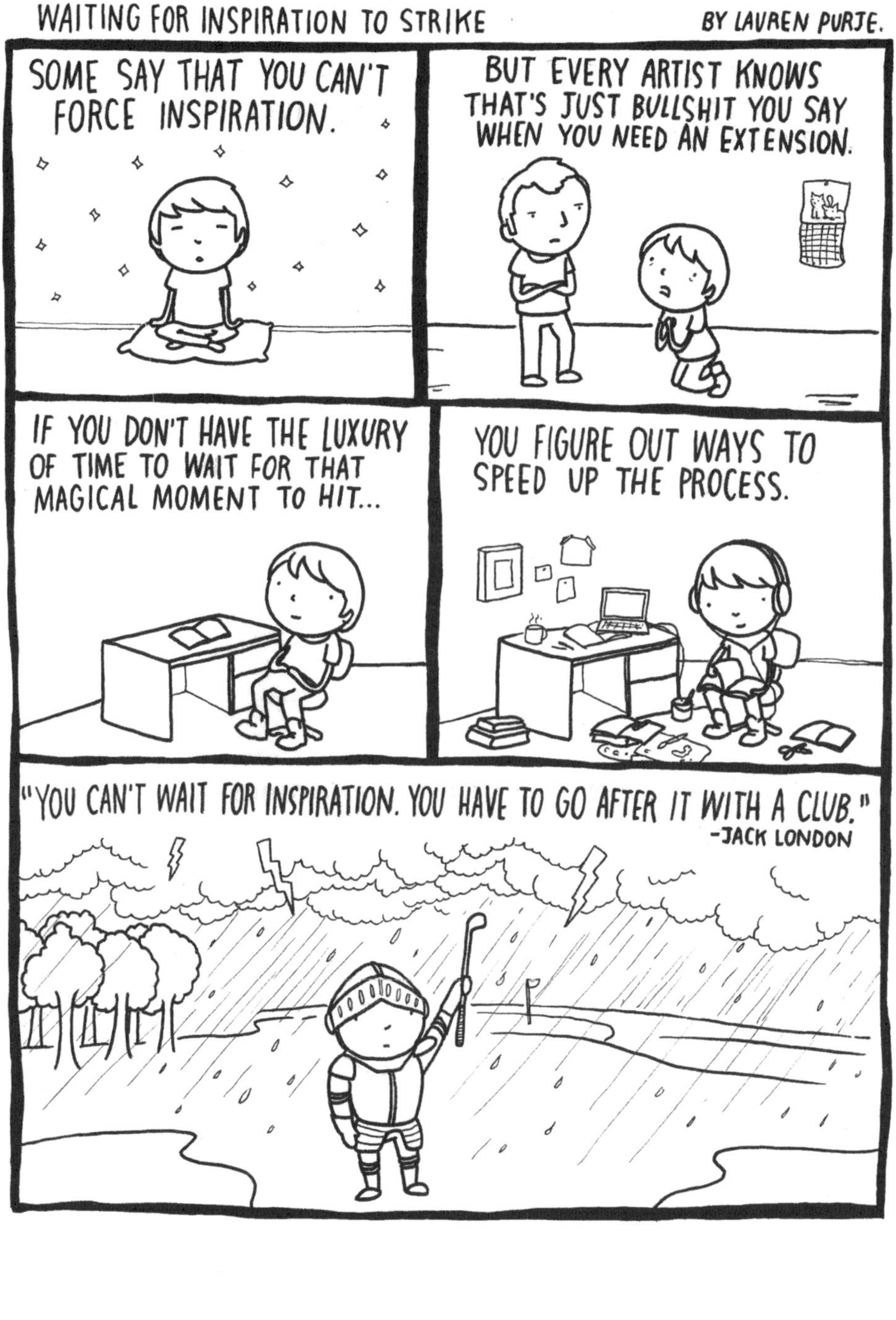
WAITING FOR INSPIRATION TO STRIKE
BY LAUREN PURJE.
SOME SAY THAT YOU CAN'T FORCE INSPIRATION.
BUT EVERY ARTIST KNOWS THAT'S JUST BULLSHIT YOU SAY WHEN YOU NEED AN EXTENSION.
IF YOU DON'T HAVE THE LUXURY OF TIME TO WAIT FOR THAT MAGICAL MOMENT TO HIT...
YOU FIGURE OUT WAYS TO SPEED UP THE PROCESS.
"YOU CAN'T WAIT FOR INSPIRATION. YOU HAVE TO GO AFTER IT WITH A CLUB."
-JACK LONDON

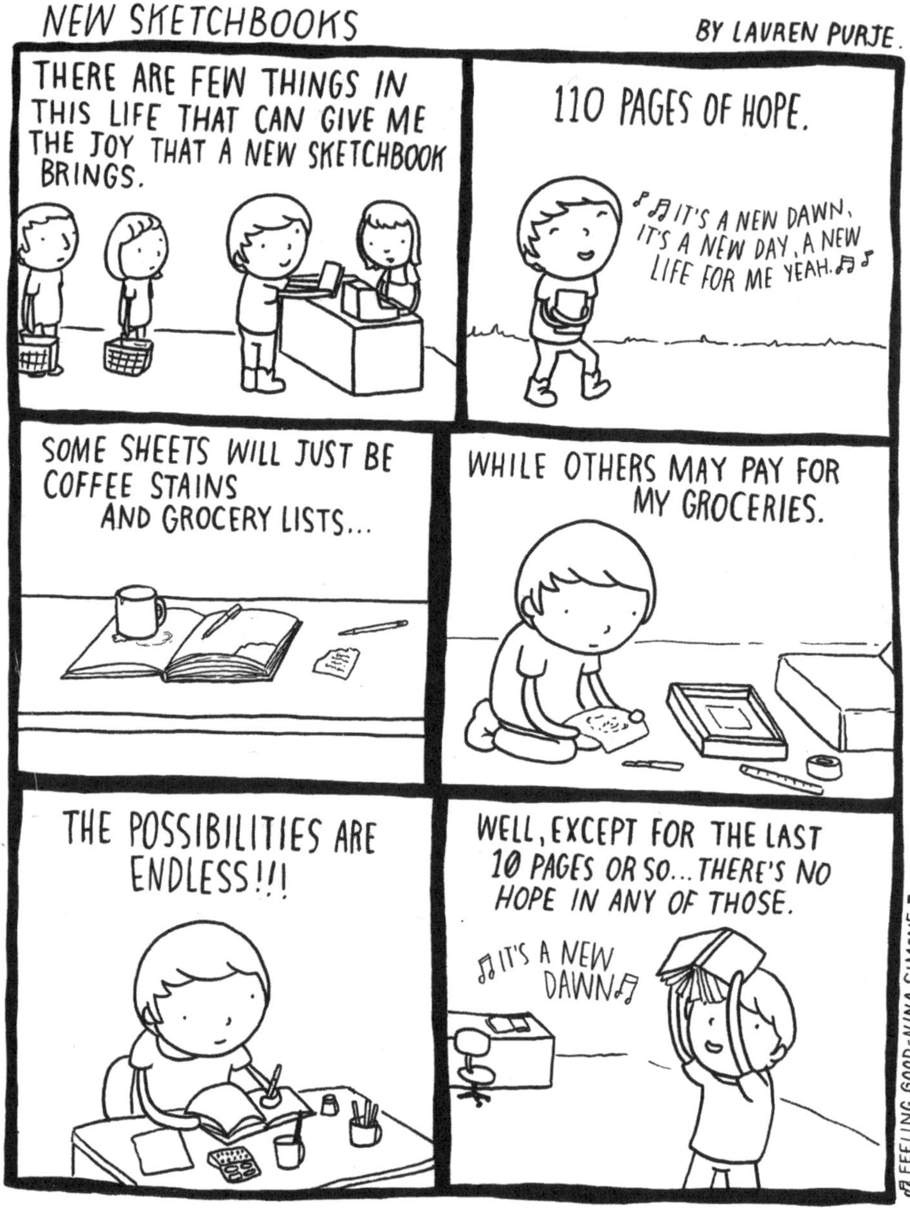
NEW SKETCHBOOKS
BY LAUREN PURJE.
THERE ARE FEW THINGS IN THIS LIFE THAT CAN GIVE ME THE JOY THAT A NEW SKETCHBOOK BRINGS.
110 PAGES OF HOPE.
IT'S A NEW DAWN, IT'S A NEW DAY, A NEW LIFE FOR ME YEAH.
SOME SHEETS WILL JUST BE COFFEE STAINS AND GROCERY LISTS...
WHILE OTHERS MAY PAY FOR MY GROCERIES.
THE POSSIBILITIES ARE ENDLESS!!!
WELL, EXCEPT FOR THE LAST 10 PAGES OR SO... THERE'S NO HOPE IN ANY OF THOSE.
IT'S A NEW DAWN
FEELING GOOD-NINA SIMONE

A SUPER-SCIENTIFIC ANALYSIS OF MIMETIC BEHAVIOR IN ARTISTS

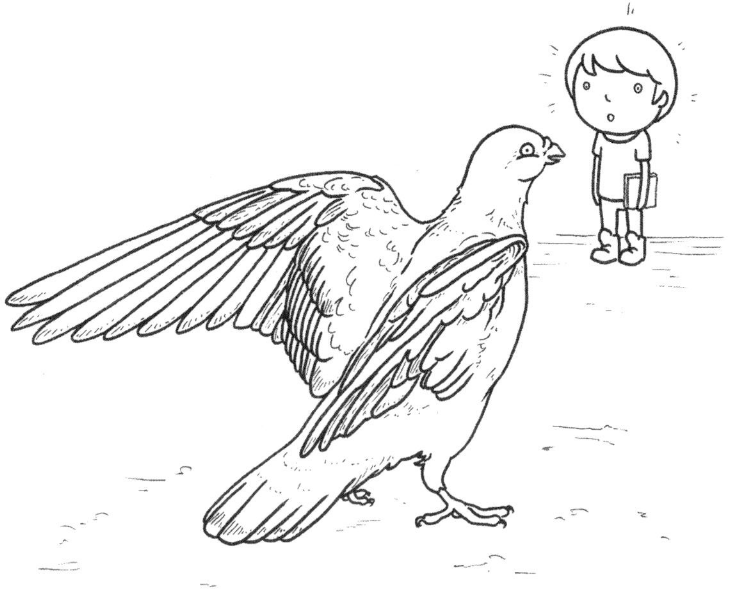

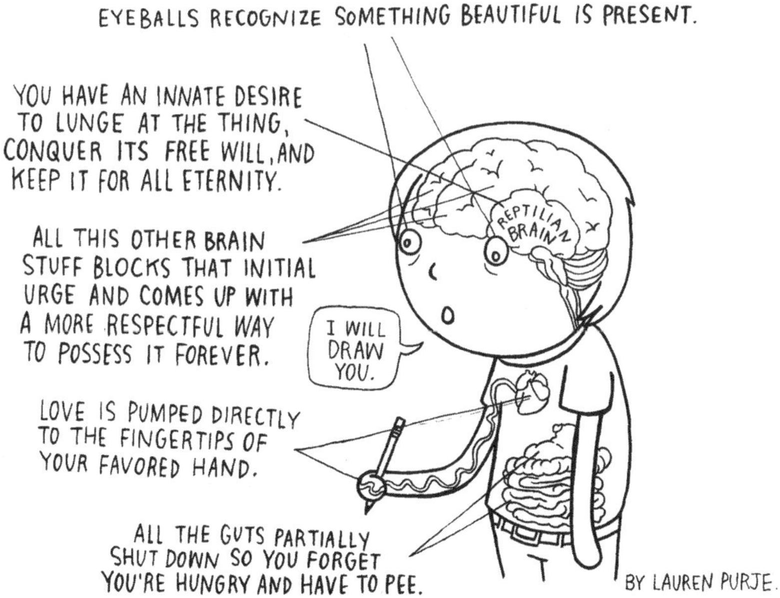
EYEBALLS RECOGNIZE SOMETHING BEAUTIFUL IS PRESENT.
YOU HAVE AN INNATE DESIRE TO LUNGE AT THE THING, CONQUER ITS FREE WILL, AND KEEP IT FOR ALL ETERNITY.
REPTILIAN BRAIN
ALL THIS OTHER BRAIN STUFF BLOCKS THAT INITIAL URGE AND COMES UP WITH A MORE RESPECTFUL WAY TO POSSESS IT FOREVER.
I WILL DRAW YOU.
LOVE IS PUMPED DIRECTLY TO THE FINGERTIPS OF YOUR FAVORED HAND.
ALL THE GUTS PARTIALLY SHUT DOWN SO YOU FORGET YOU'RE HUNGRY AND HAVE TO PEE.

BY LAUREN PURJE.

WHEN WERE MY "FORMATIVE YEARS" AS AN ARTIST?

BY LAUREN PURJE.

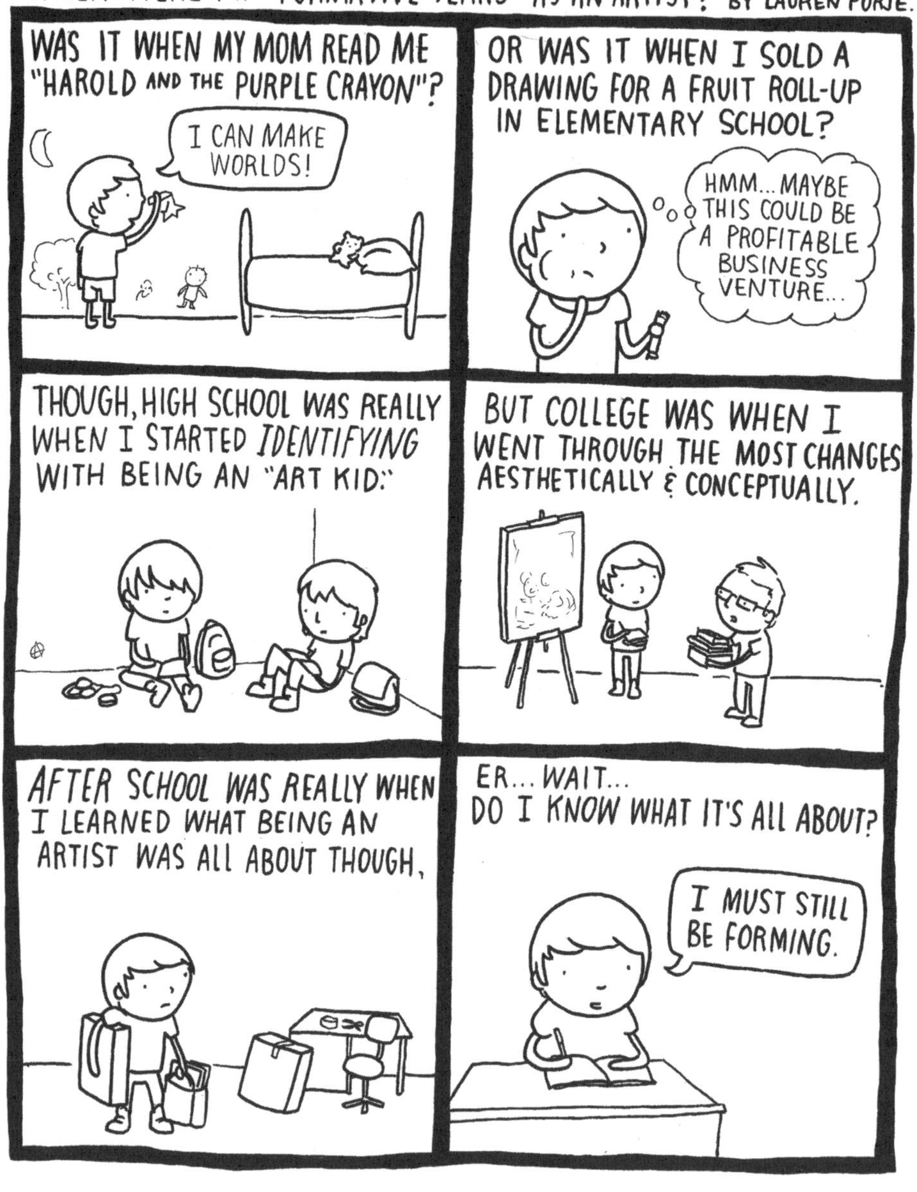
WAS IT WHEN MY MOM READ ME "HAROLD AND THE PURPLE CRAYON"?
I CAN MAKE WORLDS!
OR WAS IT WHEN I SOLD A DRAWING FOR A FRUIT ROLL-UP IN ELEMENTARY SCHOOL?
HMM... MAYBE THIS COULD BE A PROFITABLE BUSINESS VENTURE...
THOUGH, HIGH SCHOOL WAS REALLY WHEN I STARTED IDENTIFYING WITH BEING AN "ART KID."
BUT COLLEGE WAS WHEN I WENT THROUGH THE MOST CHANGES AESTHETICALLY & CONCEPTUALLY.
AFTER SCHOOL WAS REALLY WHEN I LEARNED WHAT BEING AN ARTIST WAS ALL ABOUT THOUGH,
ER... WAIT... DO I KNOW WHAT IT'S ALL ABOUT?
I MUST STILL BE FORMING.

HELL IS OTHER SHARPENERS

BY LAUREN PURJE.

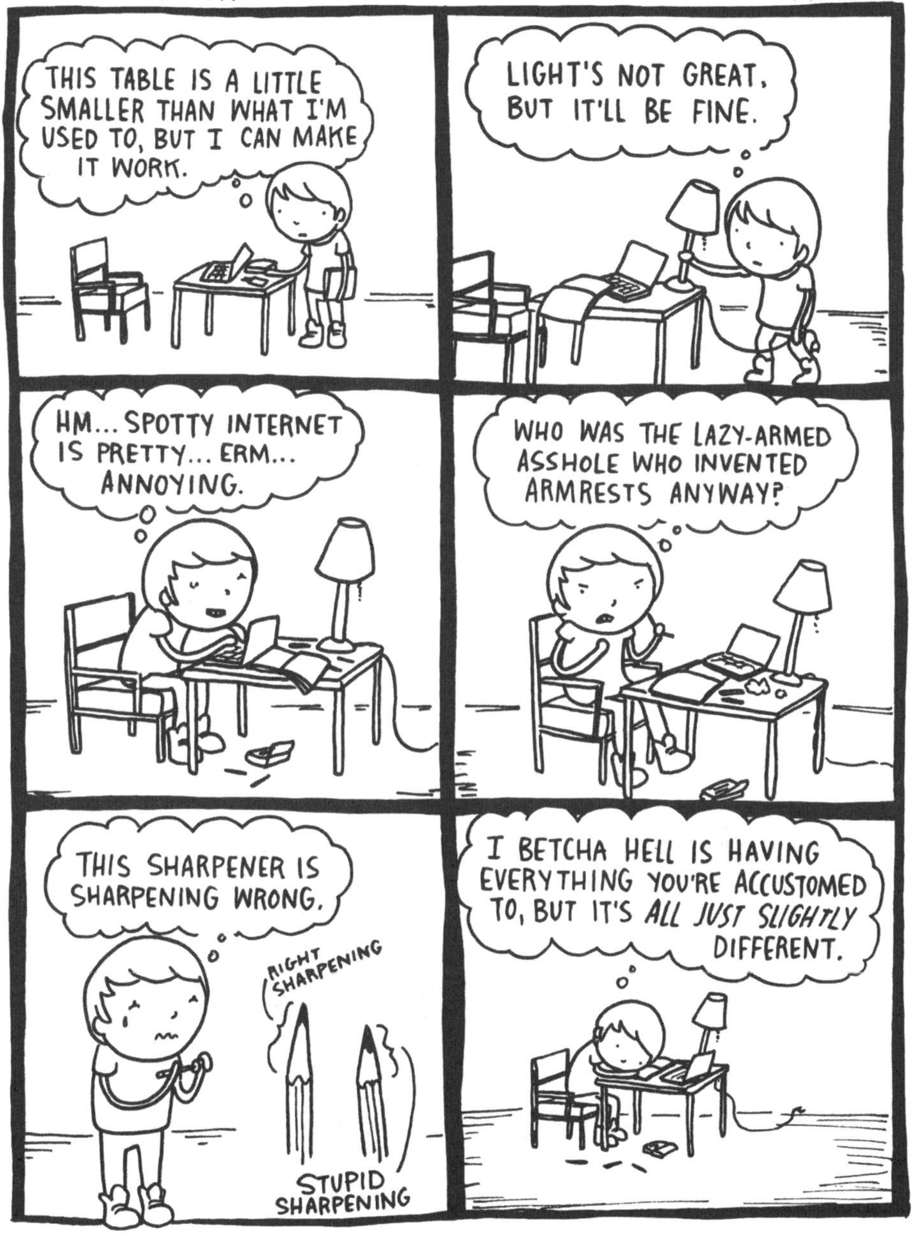
THIS TABLE IS A LITTLE SMALLER THAN WHAT I'M USED TO, BUT I CAN MAKE IT WORK.
LIGHT'S NOT GREAT, BUT IT'LL BE FINE.
HM... SPOTTY INTERNET IS PRETTY... ERM... ANNOYING.
WHO WAS THE LAZY-ARMED ASSHOLE WHO INVENTED ARMRESTS ANYWAY?
THIS SHARPENER IS SHARPENING WRONG.
RIGHT SHARPENING
STUPID SHARPENING
I BETCHA HELL IS HAVING EVERYTHING YOU'RE ACCUSTOMED TO, BUT IT'S *ALL JUST SLIGHTLY* DIFFERENT.

JINXED BY LAUREN PURJE.

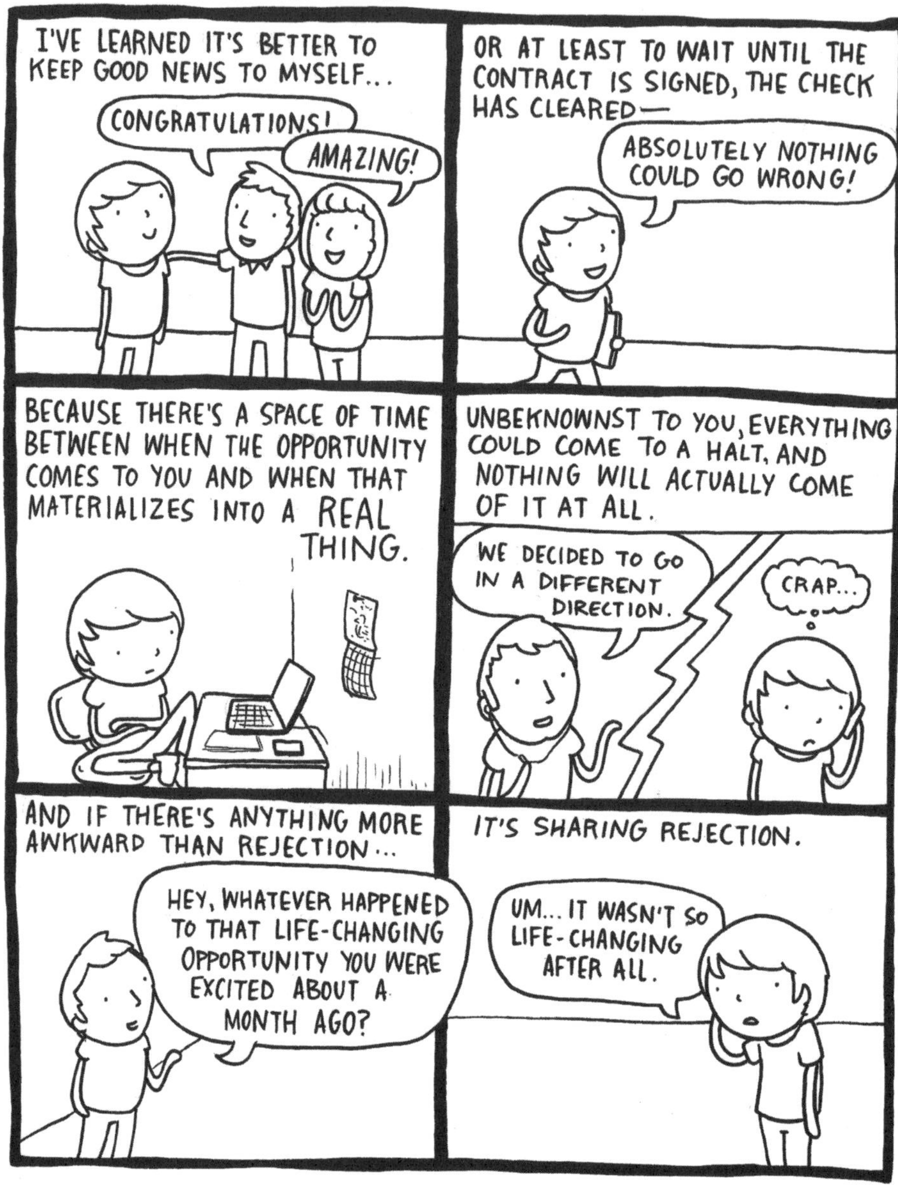
I'VE LEARNED IT'S BETTER TO KEEP GOOD NEWS TO MYSELF...
CONGRATULATIONS!
AMAZING!
OR AT LEAST TO WAIT UNTIL THE CONTRACT IS SIGNED, THE CHECK HAS CLEARED—
ABSOLUTELY NOTHING COULD GO WRONG!
BECAUSE THERE'S A SPACE OF TIME BETWEEN WHEN THE OPPORTUNITY COMES TO YOU AND WHEN THAT MATERIALIZES INTO A REAL THING.
UNBEKNOWNST TO YOU, EVERYTHING COULD COME TO A HALT, AND NOTHING WILL ACTUALLY COME OF IT AT ALL.
WE DECIDED TO GO IN A DIFFERENT DIRECTION.
CRAP...
AND IF THERE'S ANYTHING MORE AWKWARD THAN REJECTION...
HEY, WHATEVER HAPPENED TO THAT LIFE-CHANGING OPPORTUNITY YOU WERE EXCITED ABOUT A MONTH AGO?
IT'S SHARING REJECTION.
UM... IT WASN'T SO LIFE-CHANGING AFTER ALL.

LETTER OF ACCEPTANCE BY LAUREN PURJE.

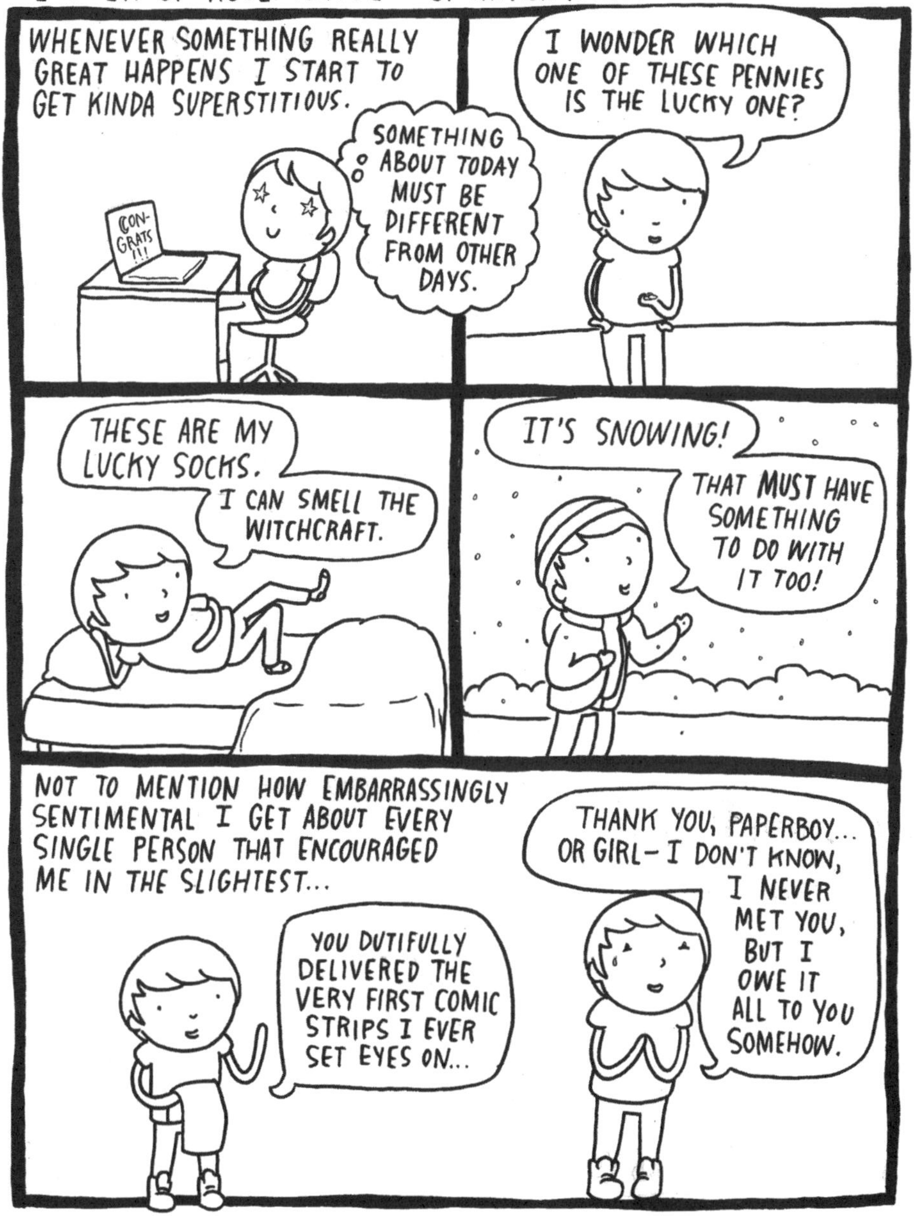
WHENEVER SOMETHING REALLY GREAT HAPPENS I START TO GET KINDA SUPERSTITIOUS.
CON-GRATS !!!
SOMETHING ABOUT TODAY MUST BE DIFFERENT FROM OTHER DAYS.
I WONDER WHICH ONE OF THESE PENNIES IS THE LUCKY ONE?
THESE ARE MY LUCKY SOCKS.
I CAN SMELL THE WITCHCRAFT.
IT'S SNOWING!
THAT MUST HAVE SOMETHING TO DO WITH IT TOO!
NOT TO MENTION HOW EMBARRASSINGLY SENTIMENTAL I GET ABOUT EVERY SINGLE PERSON THAT ENCOURAGED ME IN THE SLIGHTEST...
YOU DUTIFULLY DELIVERED THE VERY FIRST COMIC STRIPS I EVER SET EYES ON...
THANK YOU, PAPERBOY... OR GIRL— I DON'T KNOW, I NEVER MET YOU, BUT I OWE IT ALL TO YOU SOMEHOW.

ART AND ILLUSTRATION BY LAUREN PURJE.

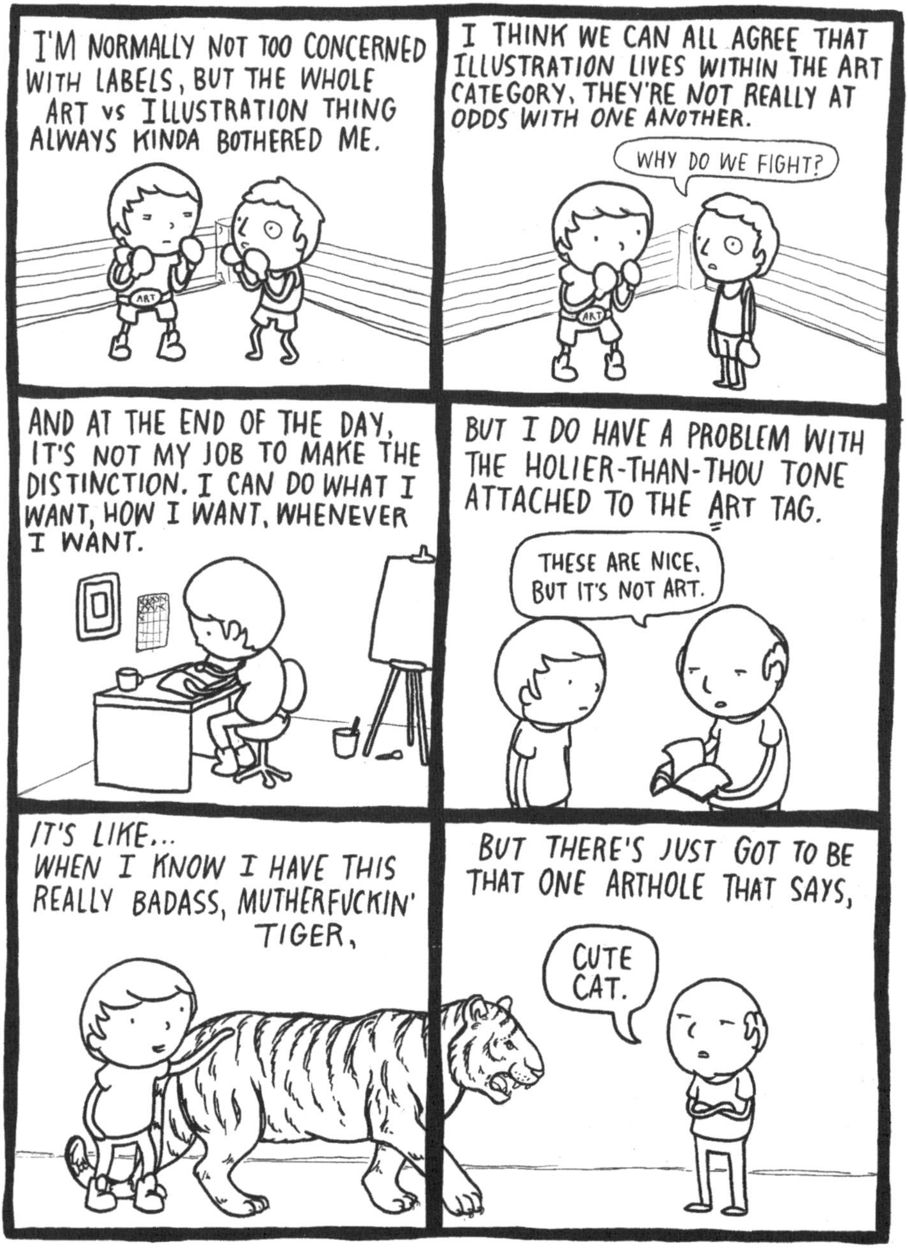
I'M NORMALLY NOT TOO CONCERNED WITH LABELS, BUT THE WHOLE ART vs ILLUSTRATION THING ALWAYS KINDA BOTHERED ME.
ART
I THINK WE CAN ALL AGREE THAT ILLUSTRATION LIVES WITHIN THE ART CATEGORY, THEY'RE NOT REALLY AT ODDS WITH ONE ANOTHER.
WHY DO WE FIGHT?
ART
AND AT THE END OF THE DAY, IT'S NOT MY JOB TO MAKE THE DISTINCTION. I CAN DO WHAT I WANT, HOW I WANT, WHENEVER I WANT.
BUT I DO HAVE A PROBLEM WITH THE HOLIER-THAN-THOU TONE ATTACHED TO THE ART TAG.
THESE ARE NICE, BUT IT'S NOT ART.
IT'S LIKE... WHEN I KNOW I HAVE THIS REALLY BADASS, MUTHERFUCKIN' TIGER,
BUT THERE'S JUST GOT TO BE THAT ONE ARTHOLE THAT SAYS,
CUTE CAT.

AN ARTIST CHECKING HER VITALS

BY LAUREN PURJE.

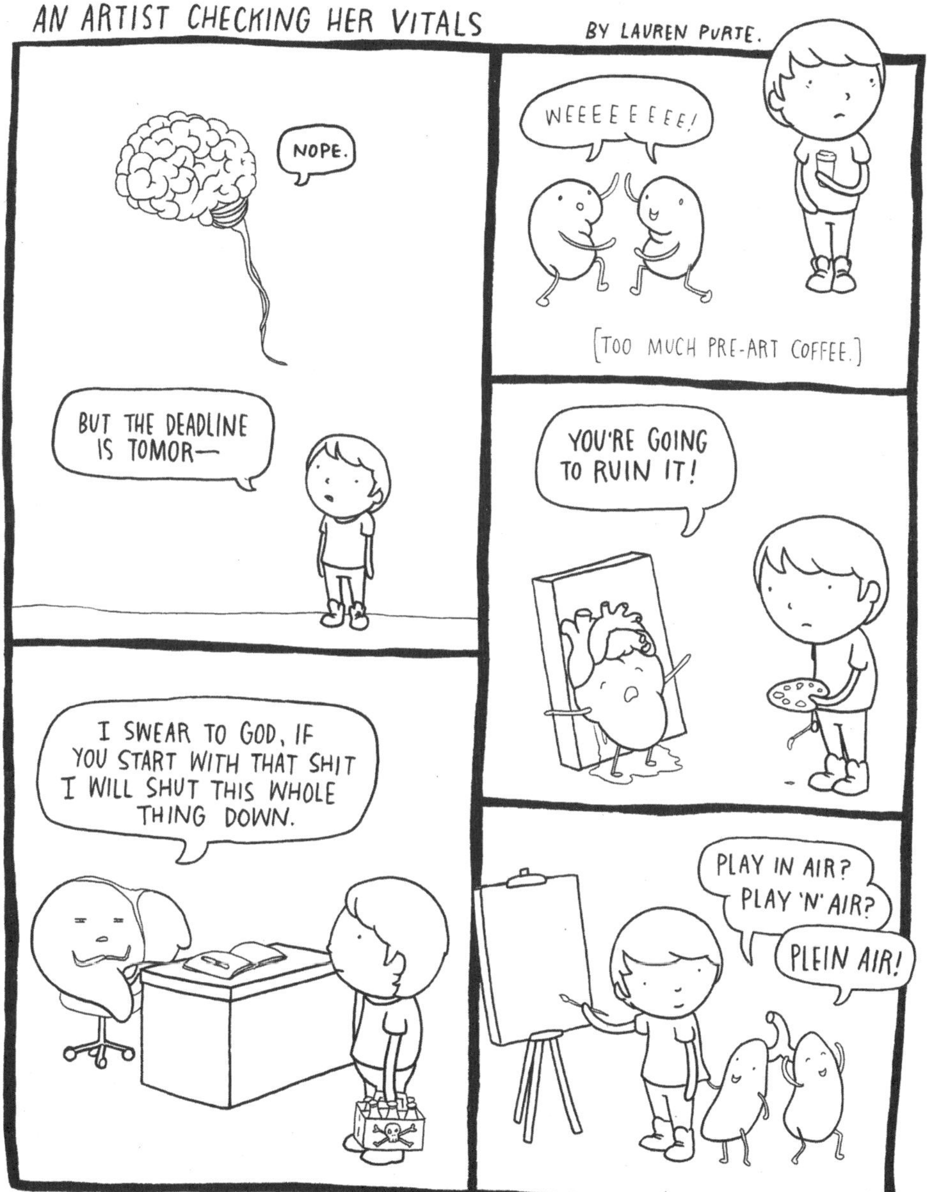
NOPE.
BUT THE DEADLINE IS TOMOR—
WEEEEEEEE!
[TOO MUCH PRE-ART COFFEE.]
YOU'RE GOING TO RUIN IT!
I SWEAR TO GOD, IF YOU START WITH THAT SHIT I WILL SHUT THIS WHOLE THING DOWN.
PLAY IN AIR?
PLAY 'N' AIR?
PLEIN AIR!

TOO EXCITED TO WORK

BY LAUREN PURJE.

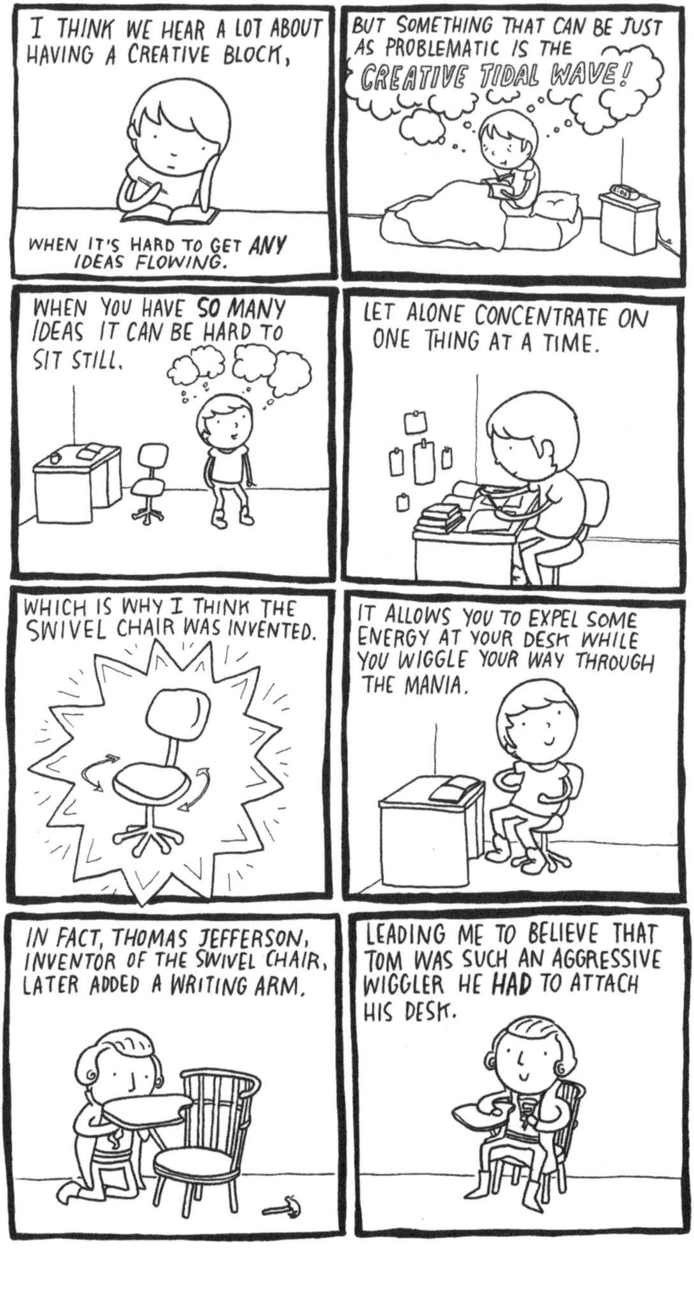
I THINK WE HEAR A LOT ABOUT HAVING A CREATIVE BLOCK,
WHEN IT'S HARD TO GET ANY IDEAS FLOWING.
BUT SOMETHING THAT CAN BE JUST AS PROBLEMATIC IS THE
CREATIVE TIDAL WAVE!
WHEN YOU HAVE SO MANY IDEAS IT CAN BE HARD TO SIT STILL,
LET ALONE CONCENTRATE ON ONE THING AT A TIME.
WHICH IS WHY I THINK THE SWIVEL CHAIR WAS INVENTED.
IT ALLOWS YOU TO EXPEL SOME ENERGY AT YOUR DESK WHILE YOU WIGGLE YOUR WAY THROUGH THE MANIA.
IN FACT, THOMAS JEFFERSON, INVENTOR OF THE SWIVEL CHAIR, LATER ADDED A WRITING ARM.
LEADING ME TO BELIEVE THAT TOM WAS SUCH AN AGGRESSIVE WIGGLER HE HAD TO ATTACH HIS DESK.

CHARACTER FLAWS

BY LAUREN PURJE.

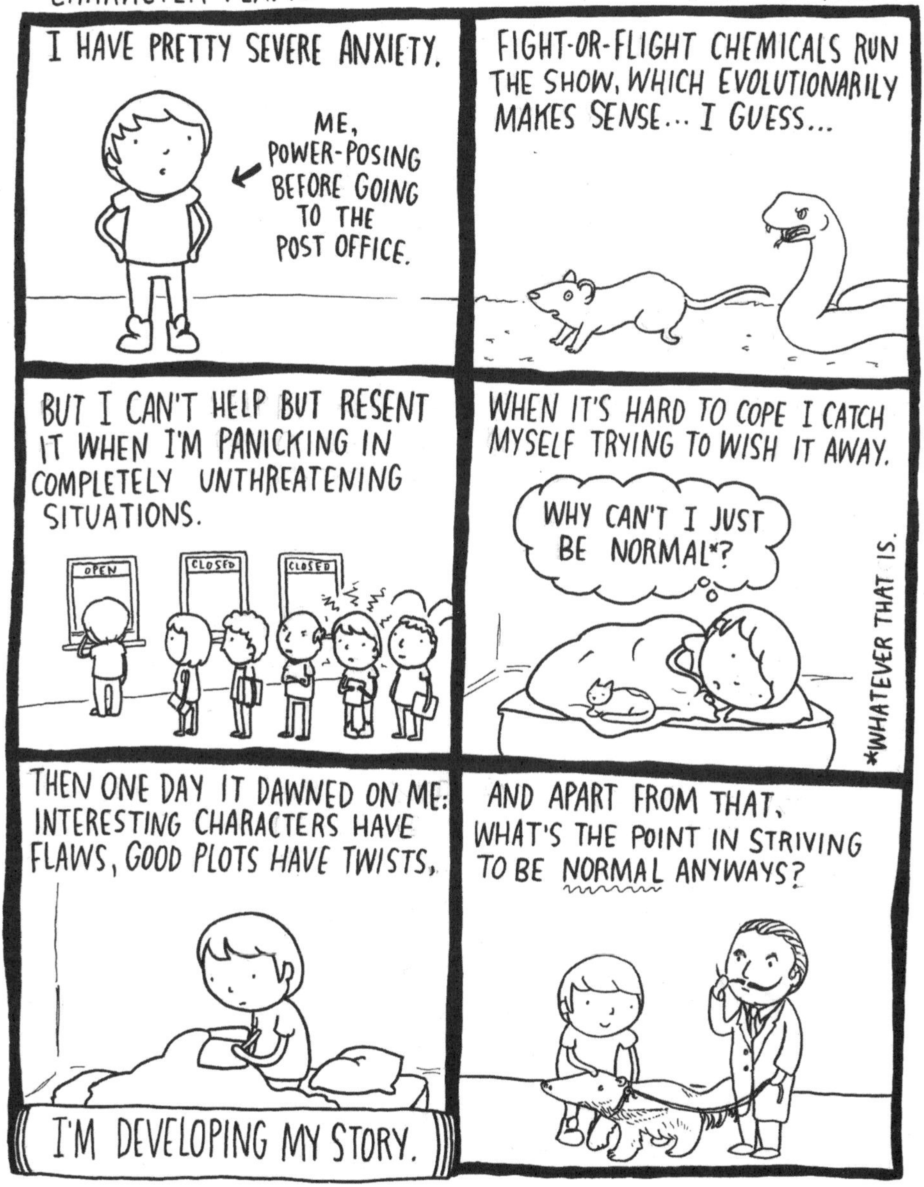
I HAVE PRETTY SEVERE ANXIETY.
ME, POWER-POSING BEFORE GOING TO THE POST OFFICE.
FIGHT-OR-FLIGHT CHEMICALS RUN THE SHOW, WHICH EVOLUTIONARILY MAKES SENSE... I GUESS...
BUT I CAN'T HELP BUT RESENT IT WHEN I'M PANICKING IN COMPLETELY UNTHREATENING SITUATIONS.
OPEN
CLOSED
CLOSED
WHEN IT'S HARD TO COPE I CATCH MYSELF TRYING TO WISH IT AWAY.
WHY CAN'T I JUST BE NORMAL*?
*WHATEVER THAT IS.
THEN ONE DAY IT DAWNED ON ME: INTERESTING CHARACTERS HAVE FLAWS, GOOD PLOTS HAVE TWISTS,
I'M DEVELOPING MY STORY.
AND APART FROM THAT, WHAT'S THE POINT IN STRIVING TO BE NORMAL ANYWAYS?

AIN'T THAT THE TRUTHS

BY LAUREN PURJE.

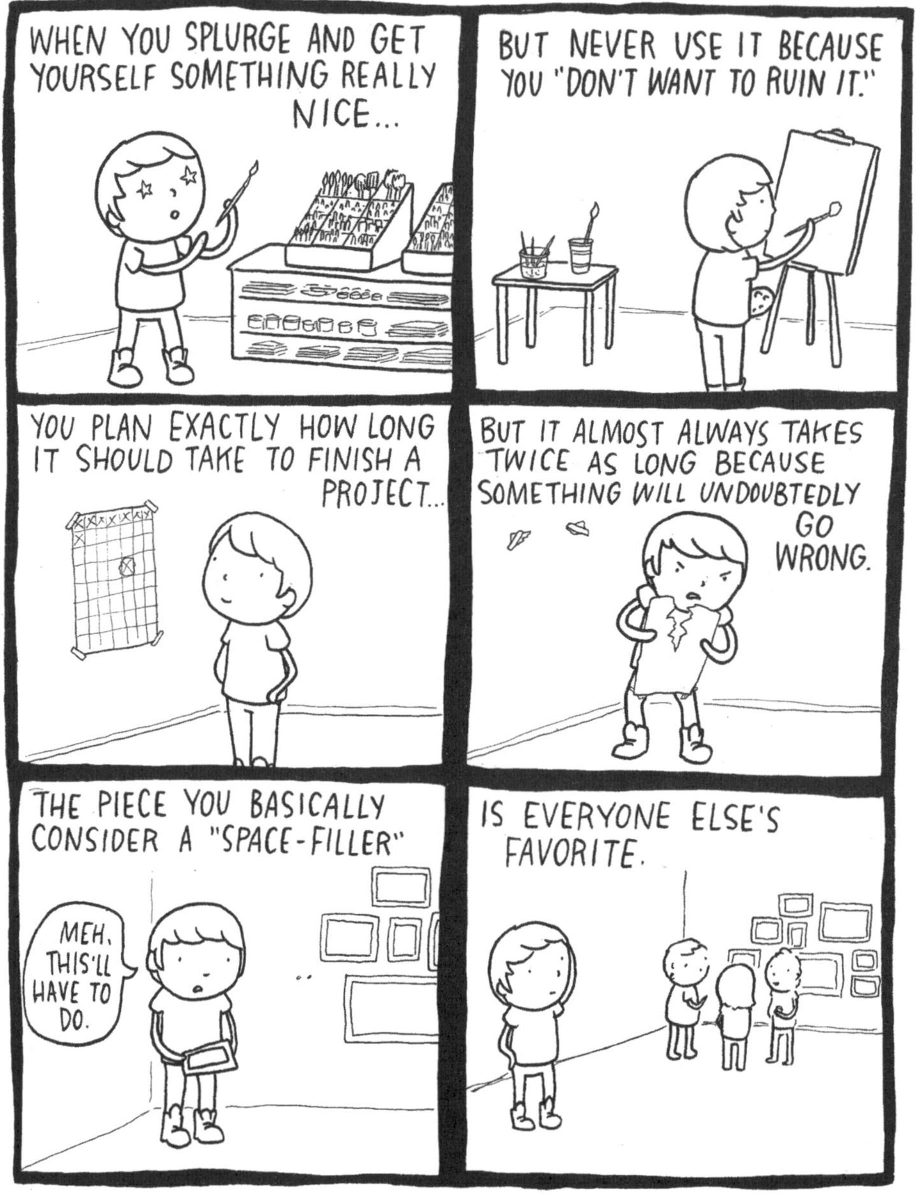
WHEN YOU SPLURGE AND GET YOURSELF SOMETHING REALLY NICE...
BUT NEVER USE IT BECAUSE YOU "DON'T WANT TO RUIN IT."
YOU PLAN EXACTLY HOW LONG IT SHOULD TAKE TO FINISH A PROJECT...
BUT IT ALMOST ALWAYS TAKES TWICE AS LONG BECAUSE SOMETHING WILL UNDOUBTEDLY GO WRONG.
THE PIECE YOU BASICALLY CONSIDER A "SPACE-FILLER"
MEH. THIS'LL HAVE TO DO.
IS EVERYONE ELSE'S FAVORITE.

UP TO INTERPRETATION

BY LAUREN PURJE.

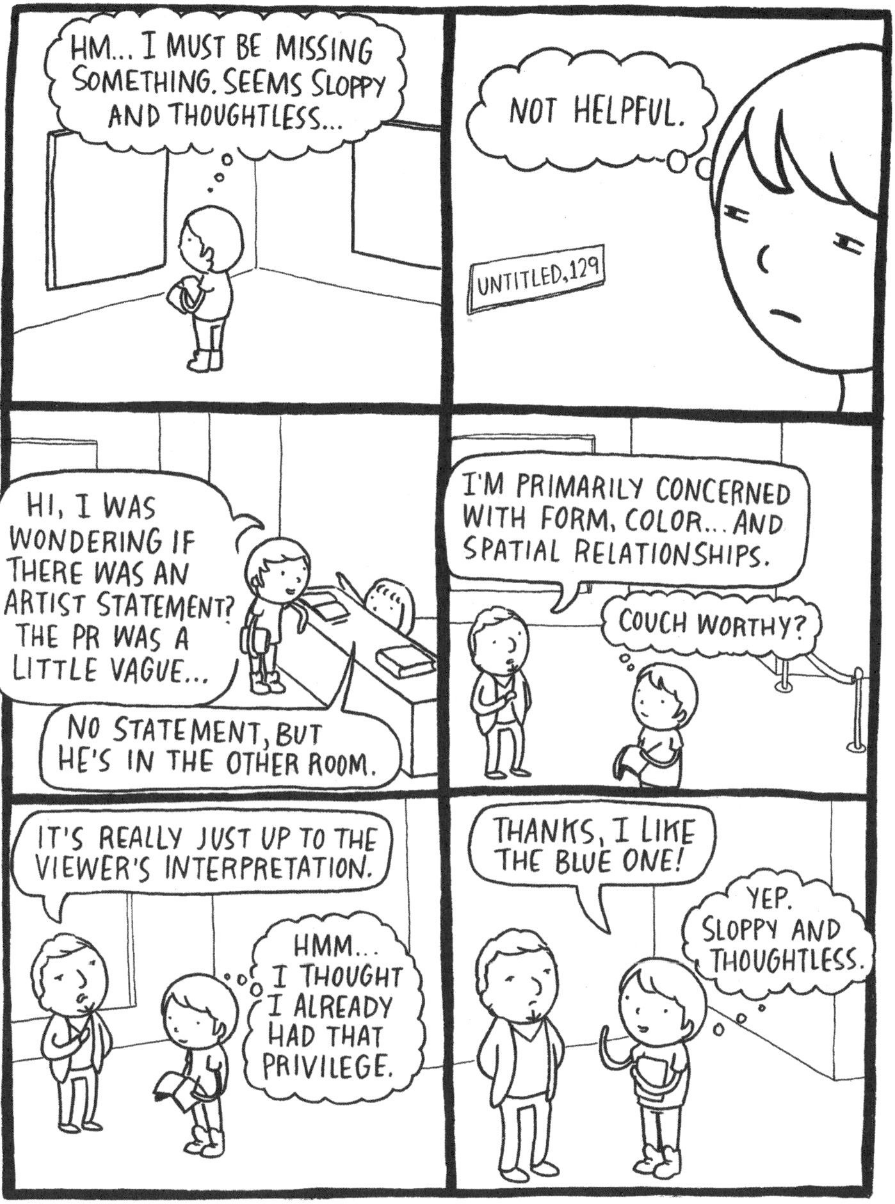
HM... I MUST BE MISSING SOMETHING. SEEMS SLOPPY AND THOUGHTLESS...
NOT HELPFUL.
UNTITLED, 129
HI, I WAS WONDERING IF THERE WAS AN ARTIST STATEMENT? THE PR WAS A LITTLE VAGUE...
NO STATEMENT, BUT HE'S IN THE OTHER ROOM.
I'M PRIMARILY CONCERNED WITH FORM, COLOR... AND SPATIAL RELATIONSHIPS.
COUCH WORTHY?
IT'S REALLY JUST UP TO THE VIEWER'S INTERPRETATION.
HMM... I THOUGHT I ALREADY HAD THAT PRIVILEGE.
THANKS, I LIKE THE BLUE ONE!
YEP. SLOPPY AND THOUGHTLESS.

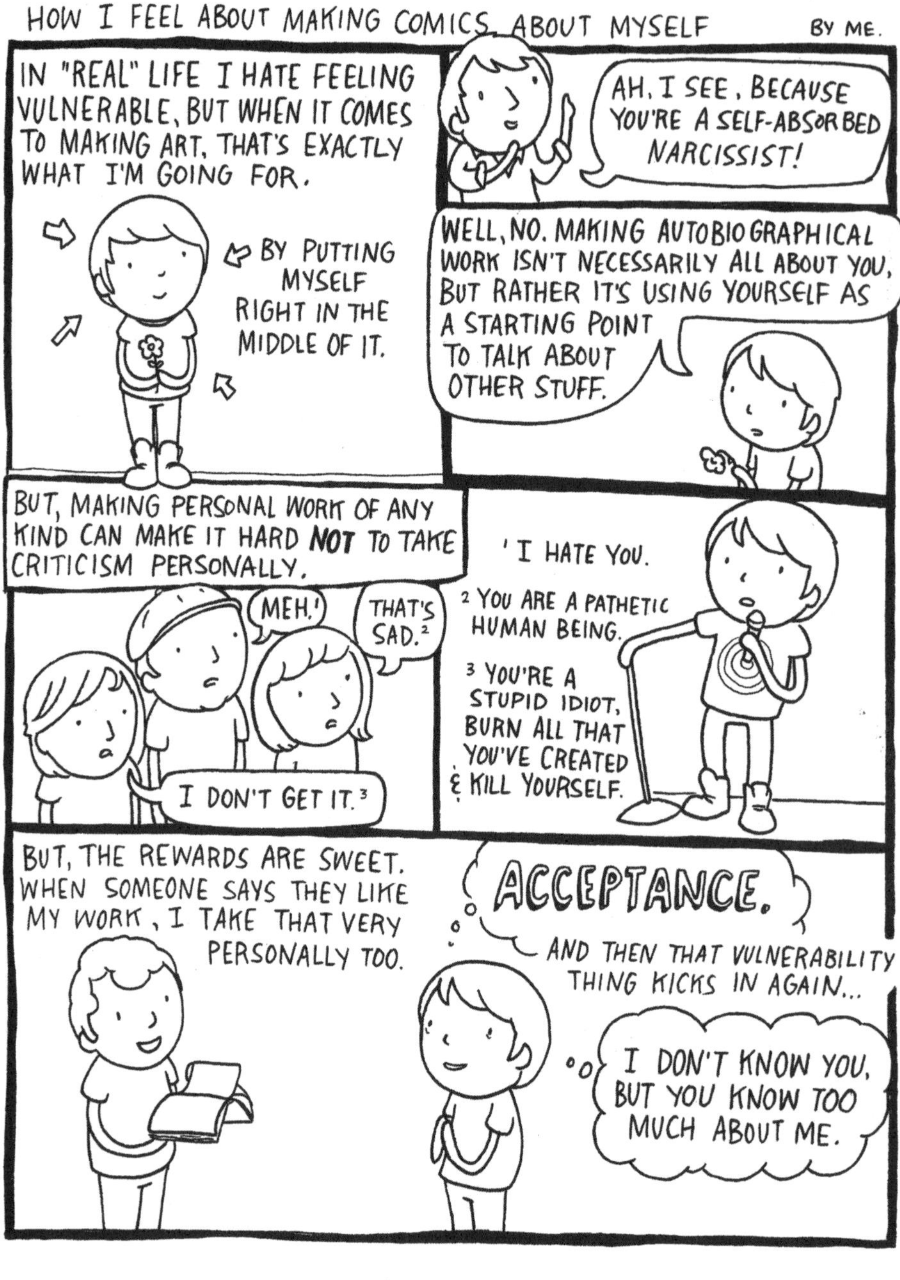
HOW I FEEL ABOUT MAKING COMICS ABOUT MYSELF
BY ME.
IN "REAL" LIFE I HATE FEELING VULNERABLE, BUT WHEN IT COMES TO MAKING ART, THAT'S EXACTLY WHAT I'M GOING FOR.
BY PUTTING MYSELF RIGHT IN THE MIDDLE OF IT.
AH, I SEE, BECAUSE YOU'RE A SELF-ABSORBED NARCISSIST!
WELL, NO. MAKING AUTOBIOGRAPHICAL WORK ISN'T NECESSARILY ALL ABOUT YOU, BUT RATHER IT'S USING YOURSELF AS A STARTING POINT TO TALK ABOUT OTHER STUFF.
BUT, MAKING PERSONAL WORK OF ANY KIND CAN MAKE IT HARD NOT TO TAKE CRITICISM PERSONALLY.
MEH.1
THAT'S SAD.2
I DON'T GET IT.3
1 I HATE YOU.
2 YOU ARE A PATHETIC HUMAN BEING.
3 YOU'RE A STUPID IDIOT, BURN ALL THAT YOU'VE CREATED & KILL YOURSELF.
BUT, THE REWARDS ARE SWEET. WHEN SOMEONE SAYS THEY LIKE MY WORK, I TAKE THAT VERY PERSONALLY TOO.
ACCEPTANCE.
AND THEN THAT VULNERABILITY THING KICKS IN AGAIN...
I DON'T KNOW YOU, BUT YOU KNOW TOO MUCH ABOUT ME.

THANKS TO MY MOM & BROTHER,
AND DAD (WISH YOU WERE HERE).
HRAG VARTANIAN (FOR SEEING
SOMETHING IN ME),
JOHN SABRAW (FOR THE ENDLESS
MORAL SUPPORT), CHRIS STAROS
(FOR GIVING ME A CHANCE),
AND CHARLES PHILLIPS (I'LL LOVE
YOU TILL THE END OF THE WORLD).

AND TO COUNTLESS OTHERS WHO HAVE
SUPPORTED ME THROUGH THE YEARS.